JavaScript
& NETSCAPE
WIZARDRY

Dan Shafer

 CORIOLIS GROUP BOOKS

PUBLISHER   KEITH WEISKAMP
EDITOR   DIANE GREEN COOK
COVER DESIGN   ANTHONY STOCK
INTERIOR DESIGN   MICHELLE STROUP
PRODUCTION   KIM EOFF
PROOFREADER   CHARLOTTE ZUCCARINI
INDEXER   KIRSTEN DEWEY

The Coriolis Group
7339 E. Acoma Drive, Suite 7
Scottsdale, AZ 85260
Phone: (602) 483-0192
Fax: (602) 483-0193
Web address: www.coriolis.com

ISBN 1-883577-86-1 : $34.99

Printed in the United States of America

10 9 8 7 6 5 4 3 2 1

CONTENTS

chapter 3   FRAMES   25

chapter 4   CLIENT-SIDE
IMAGE MAPS   53

CHAPTER 7   THE JAVASCRIPT OBJECT MODEL   103

chapter 9   javascript in action   177

chapter 10   using java applets   211

chapter 11   Calling CGIS and External Applications   233

chapter 12   JavaScript on the Web   239

PREFACE

Netscape is cool. You probably already believe that or this book wouldn't even have found its way into your hands. But I just want to reassure you that Netscape really *is* cool. As one who has been described as a "rotund gray-hair of the software industry," I've been around the block a few times. I've seen a huge amount of technology in my day.

I remember quite clearly the first day I saw a World Wide Web browser. I was visiting the offices of the now-all-but-defunct Taligent Corp. researching a book that never got published. One of the senior technical people invited me into his office to see NCSA Mosaic. I was awestruck. I said then that it was the coolest piece of software I'd seen in 10 years.

I was wrong.

It was the coolest piece of software I'd *ever* seen.

And now there is Netscape, the younger but far more precocious brother of Mosaic, designed and created by some of the same amazing programmers who designed and created Mosaic. Now in a reasonably mature release, Netscape has established itself—at least for the foreseeable future—as *the* standard World Wide Web browser.

And it is still cool.

This book describes this coolness. If you have half as much fun exploring the new release of Netscape with this book as I had writing it, you're in for a real treat.

Who Should Read This Book?

This book is intended for people who have had some experience surfing the Web with earlier versions of Netscape (prior to 2.x) and who have at least a nodding acquaintence with HTML (Hypertext Markup Language). You don't need to be an HTML guru capable of whipping out hundreds of pages a week of scintillating animations and whizzy graphics. Nor do you need to have any prior experience in programming or scripting.

You must, however, be curious. Curious about the deeper things that you can do with Netscape that other books and the user documentation either ignore or gloss over lightly. Because I take you into the depths of the wonder of Netscape in this book and to linger there long enough to benefit from it, you can't be someone who is just interested in how to load your favorite URL.

What's in This Book?

The first two chapters of this book look at the new release of Netscape to define what the coolest of the newest features are. In the process, I'll let you know where in the book those features are covered.

So rather than provide you with the obligatory chapter-by-chapter preview of what the book covers here, I'm going to try to give you some of the flavor of the book's contents.

This book is a little schizophrenic. I hate writing books that are like that, but I didn't feel I had much choice in this case. Because Netscape, when it released Version 2 and subsequent upgrades, really created a kind of split-personality product.

On the one hand, there are a number of new features that will appeal to the curious end user. (I refuse to use the word "power user." It is too imprecise and it leaves everyone who doesn't think they are a power user feeling powerless. There's enough powerlessness in the world already.) Such things as frames, the built-in ability to deal with mail and Internet news groups, and the use of the new and exciting plug-in architecture are there for the taking.

But the other side of the coin—and in many ways the more exciting—is JavaScript. I've been a fan and advocate of end-user scripting and programming languages and tools for longer than almost anybody in the industry by now. It's my *raison d'etre*, if you will. From the time I wrote my first best-selling book about Apple Computer's HyperTalk scripting language until today, some 40 books later, I remain excited by the prospects of scripting languages and tools. Moving the power center nearer and nearer to the user is my idea of what computing should be about.

JavaScript, even in its first release, is an exciting tool. It can do some perfectly awesome stuff. That's why something more than half of this book is devoted to JavaScript, including a fairly significant number of examples of the use of the language. I scoured the world of JavaScript online for Chapter 12 and found some gems that do stuff in JavaScript that even the folks who wrote JavaScript are probably surprised about. (It's a fundamental principle of this industry that the people who write the tools almost never predict with any accuracy what people will actually *do* with them.)

So the book deals with both end-user and scripting-level enhancements to the first releases of Netscape. It focuses on what's new, what's cool, why you should learn about it, and what it can do.

A Word About 'Netscapisms'

Given that this book is about Netscape, it is inevitable that there are some features of World Wide Web browsers included here that are not, at this writing, supported by any other browsers. These features have come to be known as "Netscapisms." There is a lot of consternation in the Webmaster community, of which I am an entrenched member, over the issue of whether it is wise or fair or appropriate to include such features on a Web page.

The Web began life as a serious attempt to achieve cross-platform and browser-independent access to the trillions of bytes of data that live on the Internet or are accessible directly from it. In the early days of World Wide Web design, Webmasters agreed that we should keep things very simple, minimize the use of graphics, accommodate text-only browsers, and stay within the HTML 1.0 specification.

All that has long since changed, due in large part to the success of the Web, which in turn is due in large part to the success of Netscape. At this writing, estimates are that Netscape controls between 60 percent and 75 percent of the total market for desktop Web browsers. It appears that Microsoft's challenge with its own excellent Internet Explorer has already begun to make some inroads into that base, but even the most optimistic Microsoft supporters doubt that Netscape's share of this market will fall below 50 percent before mid-1997.

The situation is so out of control that the governing bodies of the Web have all but given up trying to create a single, monolithic standard for HTML. The planned HTML 2.0 specification, in draft at this writing, may in fact never see the light of day as a single document released at one time. Instead, we may well see standards for various aspects of the World Wide Web and HTML emerge as the market drives the decisions.

All of this means that there is only a relatively little danger in designing your Web sites for Netscape. There are, as I'll point out, ways to accommodate non-Netscape browsers in such a way that your pages don't "break" when viewed with them.

My advice—which we follow at SALON Internet, Inc. (http://www.salon1999.com) where I am Senior Webmaster and Director of Technology—is to use the Netscapisms but be sure not to lock out any other graphical browser. Try to accommodate the textual browsers as much as possible, but don't compromise design and quality to do so.

That's not a view that everyone will find acceptable, but that's what makes a circus.

Contacting the Author

I love hearing from my readers. Email is definitely the best way to contact me. Now that I have a permanent address with my own Internet domain, you can be sure that even if I switch Internet Service Providers, this address will be good as long as I'm online. So send me email "valentines and vituperations" (to borrow a phrase from the magazine where I work) at: dan@gui.com.

I'll look forward to hearing from you!

acknowledgments

I appreciate the help and support of the following people, without whom this book would have been more difficult or even impossible:

- **Keith Weiskamp**, publisher at The Coriolis Group and a long-time and valued friend, for suggesting the idea, seeing it through to completion, working with me personally, and putting up with my delays.

- **Tony Potts** of The Coriolis Group who worked with me on technical issues, searched out the stuff for the CD-ROM and constructed it.

- **The Coriolis Group Production and Editorial Staff** consisting of Michelle Stroup, Kim Eoff, Anthony Stock, Gary Smith, Ron Pronk, Denise Constantine, and Brad Grannis, who performed heroic service in shepherding this book so quickly through the editorial and production maze.

- **Brendan Eich** of Netscape, Inc., who answered technical questions, pointed out errors in samples, and generally provided support at a hectic time in his life and Netscape's growth.

- **JavaScript experts and authors** from all over the world whose work appears on the Web and from whom I have learned and even borrowed (hopefully with appropriate attribution). I'm particularly grateful to those JavaScripters whose work appears in this book through their generosity and kindness: Jason Bloomberg, Thomas van der Heijden, Kouichirou Eto, Jim Tipton, Steven Weinberger, Stephen Heise, and Cameron Gregory.

- **David Zweig and David Talbot**, publisher and editor, respectively, of SALON, the online magazine of books, the arts, and ideas where I earn my daily bread these days, for understanding my need to keep writing these books and listening to me enthuse about this one over lunch and around the old water cooler.

- **My wife, Carolyn,** who was busy building a business of her own while I was writing this book and who showed her usual calm support and enthusiasm even on those days when I was railing against my computer and the universe.

what's new in netscape?

When Netscape, Inc., introduced Version 2 of its wildly popular Netscape Navigator product for home computers, it did more than provide an upgrade with a few new features and some cool enhancements. It added a host of features to its flagship product and in the process, raised the entry barrier for other companies, notably Microsoft, wishing to enter the browser arena.

In this chapter, we'll take a quick look at the primary additions and enhancements in the new Netscape Navigator. Many of these new features are the topics of much longer discussions later in the book; where that's the case, I'll mention it, but several of the new features are not within the focus of this book's attention. They are either entirely oriented to the end user with only incidental impact on Webmasters and developers or they are so simple that they don't require amplification.

I'll divide the list of new features into two broad categories: those primarily of interest to end users who simply browse the Web using the Navigator, and those of interest to Webmasters and other developers who maintain Web pages and sites. (Recall from the Preface that when I talk about Webmasters, I include people who maintain a personal Web site as well as those who get paid for maintaining large, multi-page sites for organizations.)

End-User Features

The features in the new Netscape Navigator that make it more useful and accessible to end users include the following:

- integrated electronic mail
- integrated newsgroup management and interaction
- greatly improved and extended multimedia performance and capability
- file upload capability
- ease of use and more powerful bookmarks

Integrated Email

Earlier versions of the Netscape Navigator permitted users to mail messages to people who had included "mailto:" tags in the HTML of their Web pages. That feature was the extent of email support.

In the new Netscape Navigator, email is completely integrated, permitting the user to manage all email activities without leaving the Navigator application. To make use of this capability you must have:

@ a PPP or SLIP Internet account at your mail provider (America OnLine, CompuServe, and Prodigy users cannot take advantage of this feature for all of their mail activities)

@ enough knowledge about your mail configuration to set up your mail account information in Netscape

Once you set up your mail account information in the Navigator, you can access your email by choosing "Netscape Mail" from the Window menu. When you do, a three-paned window appears. The upper left pane shows you all of your mail folders; initially, there will only be one but you can easily create as many as you need. The upper right pane shows you all the messages contained in the selected folder. When you select a message, its content appears in the bottom large pane.

While Netscape mail is not a full-featured mail program like Eudora, it does have two primary advantages over stand-alone applications:

@ It is integrated with the Netscape Navigator environment so that you don't need to learn and use an entirely different user interface just to handle your email.

@ It permits you to include URLs and other browser content in your email without needing to remember such information as you switch between the browser and your mail program.

Chapter 2 describes integrated electronic mail in greater detail.

Integrated Newsgroup Management

Internet newsgroups offer a staggering array of groups where you can interact with other people who have similar interests. There are tens of thousands of groups to which you can subscribe. When you join a newsgroup, your emailbox might become instantly inundated with messages from other members. In a newsgroup, everything you write is sent to everyone in the group.

As with Netscape Mail, Netscape News requires you to provide some setup information. Once you set it up, you can open it by choosing "Netscape News" from the "Window" menu. You will see a three-pane window that bears a strong resemblance to the Netscape Mail window I described earlier.

In the upper left corner of the window is a pane that lists all of the newsgroups to which you are subscribed. Each group shows you how many messages are available in the group and how many of them you have not yet read. When you click on a group, the upper right pane displays all the messages—read and unread—in that group. Clicking on a message results in its contents being displayed in the large pane at the bottom of the window.

Subscribing to newsgroups can be a fairly cumbersome process. If you know the exact name of the group you want to join, it is fairly straightforward. However, if you want to browse the groups to look for things that might interest you, you should plan to spend a few hours the first time you check out newsgroups.

When you read a message in a newsgroup to which you wish to reply, you can decide whether to mail the reply to the whole group, to the individual who wrote the message to which you are replying (using email), or both.

Like its counterpart mail facility, Netscape News is not as powerful or flexible as dedicated newsgroup programs such as NN. But, again, its tight integration into Netscape gives it similar advantages to those enjoyed by Netscape Mail.

I'll have more to say about integrated news groups in Chapter 2.

Multimedia Enhancements

Since the release of Netscape Navigator 2.x, you'll find three types of multimedia improvements. These types are:

- speed improvements
- a new type of animation
- multiple streams of simultaneous multimedia data types

SPEED IMPROVEMENTS

In addition to general overall speed improvement, Netscape made two larger changes that have an impact on the speed (or the perception of speed) in the Navigator.

First, Netscape provided a way to handle user clicks on mapped images (pictures intended to be used for navigation rather than simply for their aesthetic value) completely within the browser. Earlier versions of the Navigator relied completely on the Web server to deal with these user actions. The user would click the mouse on a graphic and the browser would send the server information about where the click took place. The server would then use a Common Gateway Interface (CGI) application to decode the coordinates and translate them into a URL or other action the server should take in response.

With Navigator 2, Netscape introduced the concept of client-side image maps. The decoding of the user's clicks into URLs and other actions takes place in HTML coded directly in the Web page. The Navigator itself determines what action needs to take place, without the user having to interact with the Navigator, at least until the next action has been determined.

I will explain client-side image maps and how to use them in Chapter 4.

The second speed-related enhancement implemented in versions since Netscape Navigator 2 is really only an apparent speed improvement. By implementing the concept of "progressive JPEG" display, the Navigator gives you the impression that graphic images compressed using the JPEG algorithm are displaying more quickly than those displayed by the older "baseline" JPEG image format. I'll cover this topic more thoroughly in Chapter 2.

New Type of Animation

Everyone who has used the Netscape Navigator is familiar with the constantly animating "N" in the upper right corner of the browser window. The technique used to create that animation is now supported within the entire browser.

From the beginning of the World Wide Web, there have been two Graphic Image File (GIF) format standards, dubbed GIF87a and GIF89a. The GIF89a standard supports the concept of a multi-image GIF in which more than one graphic occupies a single document or object. Web browsers didn't support this concept until Navigator 2 emerged. When older browsers encountered a multi-image GIF file, they simply displayed the first image in the file and stopped.

Now, GIF89a animation has arrived with Netscape Navigator's new release. This form of iconic animation is much more efficient and effective than the older-style animation. The older-style animation relied on either "server-push" or "client-pull" techniques, which required constant communication between the browser and the server as files kept transferring between them. This approach has a number of obvious disadvantages, all of which GIF animation overcomes.

Multiple Streams of Multimedia Data

The earlier version of Netscape Navigator relied on "helper applications" to enable users to view movies and complex animations, to hear sound, and to deal with other types of data. This approach had some disadvantages:

@ Helper applications had to run separately from the browser, opening new windows independent of the browser and losing the physical connection between the browser and the data shown in the new application window. This approach destroyed the seamless feeling of the Web experience.

@ The user had to wait until the entire file had downloaded before it could be viewed or heard.

@ Only one type of data at a time could be handled.

Since Navigator 2, Netscape has drastically altered the rules in this respect by creating the concept of plug-ins. These plug-ins are smaller than helper applications and are tightly integrated into the browser. More importantly, they deal with data in a streaming fashion, which means:

@ data begins to be displayed or played moments after the download starts and throughout the download process

@ more than one plug-in can be downloading and playing data at a time

The effect, of course, is a significant increase in user satisfaction dealing with multimedia-enriched Web sites. I'll have more to say about the details of this process in Chapters 2 and 5.

File Upload Capability

Using the standard File Transfer Protocol (FTP), you can now upload files as well as download them. This change is a major step toward improved interaction between browsers and the data sources to which they are connected, particularly in corporate intranets.

We'll learn more about how FTP uploading works in the new Netscape Navigator in Chapter 2.

Enhanced Bookmarks

You use bookmarks to keep track of World Wide Web sites to which you wish to return. Managing bookmarks was sufficiently difficult in Netscape Navigator 1.x that a small but thriving third-party industry grew up creating better programs to deal with them.

Since Navigator 2.x, Netscape has greatly enhanced the utility and manageability of bookmarks. I'll say more on this subject in Chapter 2.

Webmaster-Oriented Features

All of the features that are added to Netscape Navigator 2.x for the benefit primarily of Webmasters and developers are the subject of detailed discussions later in the book. Some of these features are shown in Figure 1.1. In this section, I'll provide brief overviews of each of these enhancements to give you an idea of the scope of the changes.

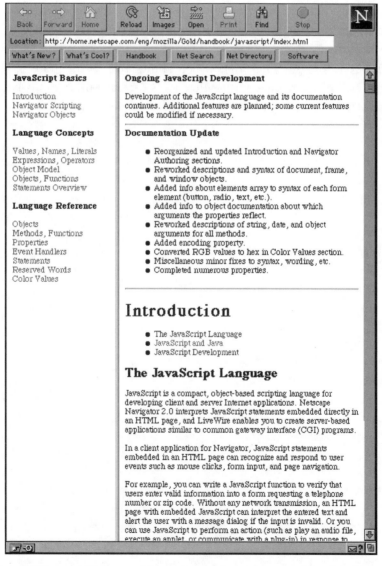

Figure 1.1   The new Netscape Navigator with its support of flexible frames.

The following key changes are described in the indicated chapters:

- frames (Chapter 3), which provide sub-windows, or panes, within browser windows that you can manage through HTML; you use these frames to provide information and navigation to users more flexibly than with a single-window model

- inline plug-ins (Chapter 5), which support more integrated use of various kinds of data, including multimedia data types

- JavaScript (Chapters 6-9), a built-in scripting language that gives you powerful new tools for controlling and enhancing the user's experience on your Web site

- OLE support (Chapter 11), which allows you to integrate objects constructed in compliance with Microsoft's Object Linking and Embedding architecture into your Windows-based users' browsers

THE NEW NETSCAPE: A BETTER BROWSER

11

Netscape 2 is a major upgrade to the most popular World Wide Web browser on the planet. It includes several significant enhancements to earlier versions of the browser; these changes affect both users and developers.

The primary focus of the other chapters in this book is on those improvements that affect Webmasters and others who develop and maintain Web sites. In this chapter, I'll concentrate on describing the changes in Netscape 2 that are of most interest to people who use it as a browser.

While there were hundreds of changes between Netscape Navigator 1.1 and Netscape Navigator 2.0, we can divide the primary changes into three major categories:

- integration of Internet functionality previously accessible only outside your Web browser
- enhanced bookmark maintenance and usage
- support for many new multimedia elements

Some of these enhancements affect users but have implications for developers as well. Where that's the case, I'll note it and refer you to the place in this book that describes the Webmaster issues.

Internet Functionality

The World Wide Web is a part of, and grew out of, the global Internet. While most of the people who have come to the Internet in the past two years have done so using the Web, the Internet itself is much larger and richer than the Web.

More specifically, users of the Internet who venture outside Web browsers—or who shun the Web altogether—engage in several activities that until now were available only as separate, stand-alone applications outside Web browsers. These activities include:

- electronic mail, including mailing lists
- newsgroup subscription and interaction
- Internet Relay Chat (IRC), a CB-radio-like real-time conversation
- file upload and download

The new Netscape Navigator integrates the first two of these activities—email and newsgroups—directly into the browser itself. This integration makes these activities more directly accessible and somewhat more understandable to the Web user.

File download has always been part of the Navigator. Since Version 2.0, Netscape incorporates file upload capability as well, so that a browser user can transfer files to storage locations from which other users may retrieve them.

Only IRC, among the major non-Web uses of the Internet, remains outside the purview of the Navigator browser, and that omission will undoubtedly be cured by a plug-in (see Chapter 5) before too long.

I'll take a look now at each of the three new integrated Internet functions in the new Netscape Navigator.

Electronic Mail and Mailing Lists

Surveys consistently show that email is far and away the number one reason that people use the Internet or any other electronic online service, such as America OnLine or CompuServe. Email is much like the postal service: You can send and receive mail to and from other individuals, or arbitrarily chosen groups of individuals, using an electronic mailbox.

Most people on the Internet probably use programs such as Eudora from QualComm as their mail program. These programs (see Figure 2.1) allow you to retrieve your email more or less automatically, sort it chronologically or by subject or sender, assist in replying, file the mail you wish to keep, and provide other support for your email activities.

Figure 2.1   The Eudora email application is popular among Internet users.

The Navigator interface for electronic mail is similar to the capabilities of Eudora, although it does not include all of the functionality of Eudora or other dedicated, commercial email programs. Figure 2.2 shows an open Netscape Mail window. The message displayed is what you receive initially after you set up mail in Netscape and then check your mailbox.

In the upper left corner of the Netscape Mail window you'll find your incoming mailbox, a trash folder (if you've deleted any mail yet), and any individual folders you create to save email after reading it. When you select a folder in the upper left pane, the upper right pane shows you each message stored in that folder. Selecting an individual message causes its content to appear in the large editing pane at the bottom of the window.

Figure 2.2 This message displays the first time you check your mail in the Netscape Mail window.

Setting up Netscape Mail is relatively straightforward. A look at Figure 2.3 and the following brief description are probably all you need to handle basic setup. (More detail is beyond the scope of this book. Check out *Netscape and HTML Explorer, 2nd Edition,* Coriolis Group Books, for more information on using Nescape to send email.)

As you can see, you'll need basic account information about your mail provider. You can obtain this from your Internet Service Provider or internal Internet or network administrator, if you don't already have it. You can also control aspects such as the appearance of mail (including separate formatting for quoted material) using other tabs in the tabbed dialog (see Figure 2.4).

With Netscape Mail, you can perform the following mail management functions:

- Check and retrieve mail from your mail server.
- Compose and send mail to other Internet users.
- Enclose attachments with your email.
- Automatically or semi-automatically quote material from mail messages to which you are replying.
- Forward mail to others, showing the forwarded material normally or as quoted material that is formatted differently from normal mail text.

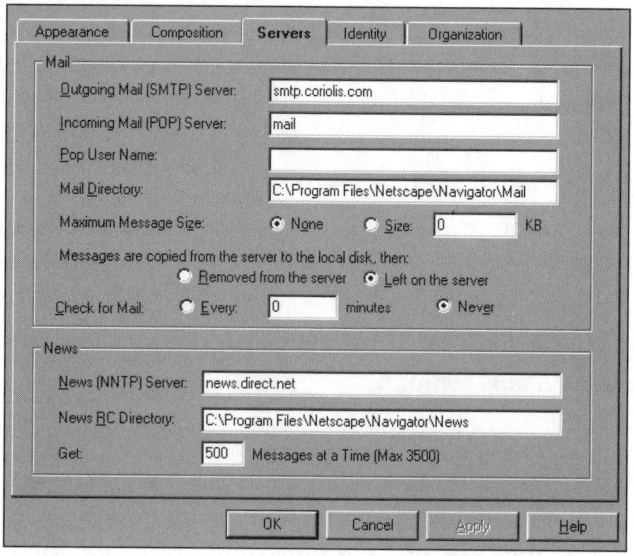

Figure 2.3 Use this main dialog to set up your Netscape Mail.

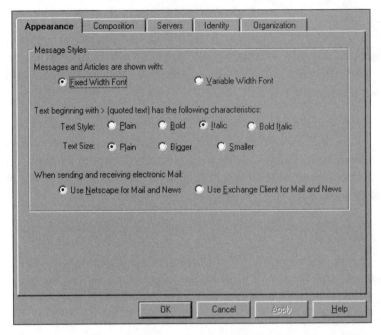

Figure 2.4   You can set up formatting for your mail in the tabbed dialog.

@ Include URLs in your mail messages and allow recipients to click on the URL to go directly to a Web site.

@ Attach fully formatted HTML pages the recipient can view in Netscape Mail exactly as if they were in the browser. (But be careful; if the recipient is using an ordinary, non-HTML mail reader, the result will not be pretty!)

@ Flag incoming mail as important while you scan through titles, then go back and read those flagged items first.

@ Automatically send and file carbon copies and blind carbon copies of messages.

@ "Thread" your incoming email so that all of the messages on a given topic are grouped together, sorted by whatever criterion you choose, to create easy-to-follow "conversations."

Netscape Mail has lots of other features that I won't go into here. All in all, it's a powerful mail tool, particularly considering that it's included free with the Navigator. If you're not already heavily invested in using Eudora or some other capable mail tool, you might want to consider using Netscape Mail.

People who have been on the Internet for a little while generally subscribe to one or more "mailing lists." Subject-specific mailing lists exist for almost everything you can think of (and a lot of stuff you can't think of!). Mailing lists function somewhat like topical bulletin board systems. You can read mail, questions, and answers submitted by other list members, and you can answer their questions or pose questions of your own, all as email.

If you subscribe to a mailing list, all of your interaction with other subscribers can take place through the Netscape Mail interface. Because Netscape Mail, unlike many other mail programs, supports threading of messages, following conversations within a mailing list becomes quite easy.

Newsgroups

Internet newsgroups differ only slightly from mailing lists, at least from the perspective of the user. One key difference is that anyone can put together a mailing list, host it on his or her server, and manage it completely. An Internet newsgroup is somewhat more carefully controlled. Starting a new newsgroup requires that the subject be clearly defined, the idea of starting the group be posted widely, and a certain minimum number of people vote in favor of establishing it. This approach goes back to the earlier days of the Internet when most of the participants were researchers, scientists, and college students; the idea was to prevent duplication of group topics. The utility of such groups is somewhat less clear today.

Still, there are thousands of newsgroups, and they're not going to go away. Netscape Navigator includes an integrated News service that allows you to read and respond to messages posted in these groups. Figure 2.5 shows the Netscape News interface.

This window looks a lot like the Netscape Mail window, doesn't it? That shouldn't surprise us, in view of what I just said about the many similarities between mailing lists and newsgroups.

Subscribing to a newsgroup in Netscape News is easy. If you know the name of the newsgroup (which you generally do), you can just select the File | Add Newsgroup option and type the name of the group. Netscape will open that newsgroup and display the pending messages for the group. (You can designate the maximum number of messages you want it to retrieve by setting a value in the setup options.) Once the group appears in the upper left pane of the Netscape News window, you can subscribe to it by clicking in the "Subscribe" column, denoted by a checkmark.

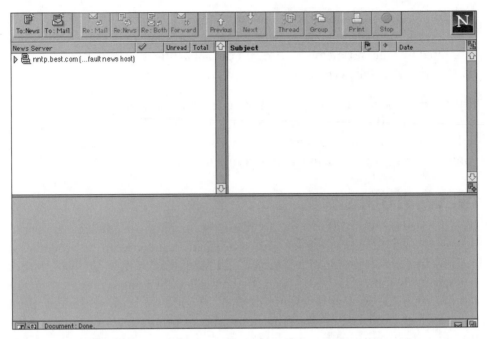

Figure 2.5   The Netscape News window provides access to newsgroup messages.

When you are getting started with newsgroups for the first time, you might want to ask Netscape to show you all available groups (by choosing Options | Show All Newsgroups). This option takes quite a few minutes to complete. Then you can scroll through the list and click under the "subscribe" column for those groups that sound interesting. (Don't start this task unless you have a big block of free time, however, because it can take a long while!) Figure 2.6 shows the first portion of this huge listing. As you can see, there are both individual newsgroups and collections of related newsgroups. You can open a collection by clicking on the little triangle to the left of the name; you'll see a list of all the individual newsgroups in this collection.

Some of the individual collections of groups are themselves huge. For example, the newsgroup sub-collection called "alt" (for "alternative") had, at the time I wrote this chapter, 4,196 individual newsgroups. You might want to buy an Internet Yellow Pages or White Pages book and use it to help you decide what newsgroups you want to join. Be forewarned: Newsgroups can turn into significant time sinks!

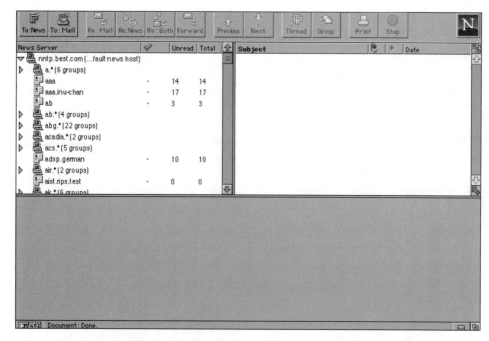

Figure 2.6   You can see all newsgroups in the News window.

File Uploads

With the new Netscape Navigator, you can upload files using the widely standardized File Transfer Protocol (FTP), which was previously supported only for downloading of files from other places to your system.

To upload files to an Internet server, you'll need permission from the owner of the site to write files using FTP. You usually need a previous agreement with the person or company that owns the server to allow this privilege. Servers that allow anonymous FTP access so that anyone can download files from them almost never allow unrestricted writing of files to their sites. Unrestricted writing of files on these servers could be an invitation to disaster.

You access an FTP site with a URL that begins like this:

```
ftp://ftp.coriols.com/freestuf
```

This URL is generally followed by the domain name of the server and, optionally, a path to a directory where you wish to place a file or from which you wish to retrieve a file.

Once you are granted access to an FTP site, your browser displays a directory of files and folders on the site, like that shown in Figure 2.7. You can navigate as usual to move around within the directory and download files. In addition, again assuming you have appropriate permission, you can drag and drop files into the browser window or choose File | Upload File to transfer files from your desktop or network to the FTP site.

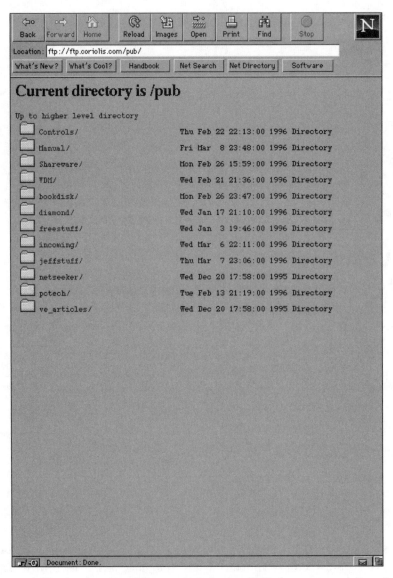

Figure 2.7   The Navigator allows you to display FTP directories within the Browser.

Enhanced Bookmarks and Addressing

Finding your way around in the World Wide Web's vastness can be a complicated and confusing experience. The earliest browser designers recognized this problem and created the concept of a "bookmark" to facilitate the browsing process. Using bookmarks (which go by other names in other browsers), you can keep track of URLs you've visited that you may wish to revisit.

In Netscape Navigator 1.x, maintaining these bookmarks—editing them, moving them around in the context of the menu where they are stored for easy access, and other activities—was difficult and cumbersome. In Version 2.0, Netscape has addressed this problem with a new approach that is much more intuitive and user friendly.

Again, a detailed explanation of using and managing bookmarks is beyond the scope of this book. But Figure 2.8 will give you some idea of the ease of use embodied in the new design. You can create new folders (which in turn correspond to hierarchical menu options) and use drag-and-drop techniques to move the folders and other items.

You can also select a URL entry and edit it using the dialog shown in Figure 2.9. This editing capability enables you to give a bookmark a meaningful name and correct any errors that may arise after the bookmark has been placed (for example, if the person maintaining the site moves or renames things).

The equivalent in Netscape Mail to bookmarks in the Web browser is the newly implemented Address Book feature. You can use this capability to store the names and email addresses of people with whom you correspond frequently. This feature makes addressing email much easier. To send a message to someone, you simply open the Address Book and double-click on the person's name; a new mail composition window opens with the address already completed.

As you can see in Figure 2.10, you can even include lists of people to whom you often send mail as a group. The list called SALON Staff contains three people, each of whom also has an individual entry. (The individual entry is required; a person cannot exist only in a list.) Adding people to a group requires only that you drag and drop their name entry into the list entry.

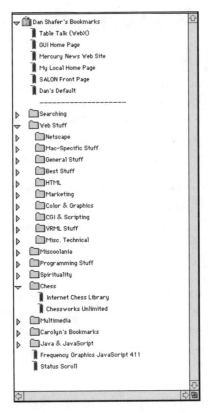

Figure 2.8   Bookmarks can help you track URLs you have visited.

Extended Multimedia Display

Netscape Navigator 2.0 adds built-in capabilities for the browser to deal with multimedia objects in some new and intriguing ways. In addition to support for plug-ins (see Chapter 5), which allow you to use and display a wide range of multimedia objects, you can use the following types of multimedia data in Netscape Navigator 2.0 without additional software or hardware:

- progressive JPEG image display
- animated GIF images
- multiple streaming data types
- client-side image maps

We'll have a lot more to say about client-side image maps in Chapter 4, so I won't cover it here. I'll discuss the other three enhancements in the order in which I listed them.

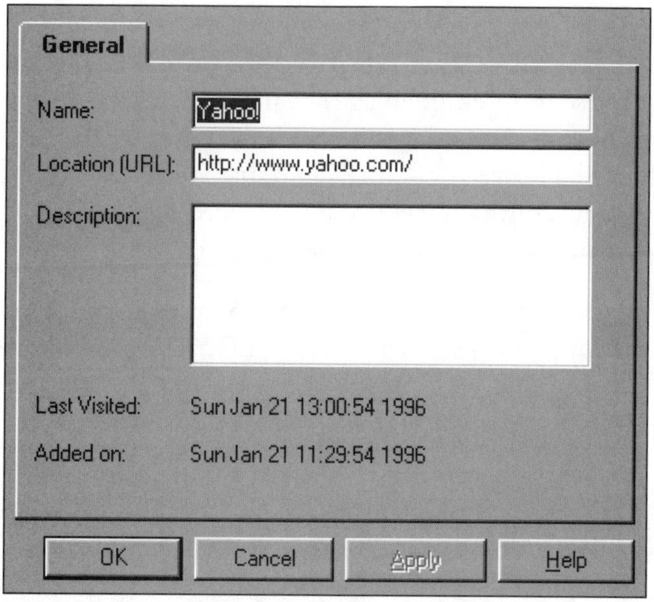

Figure 2.9   Use the Editing dialog to manage your bookmarks.

Progressive JPEG Images

One of the two commonly supported types of graphical images on the Web is JPEG images. JPEG stands for "Joint Photographic Experts Group," an industry-wide study group that created the JPEG standard. Images stored using JPEG's "baseline" format (which is the only format that was supported during the early days of the Web) are stored with the data describing their pixels (picture elements) from top to bottom. The figure reveals itself gradually, with each line of the picture being filled in complete detail before the next line loads.

One problem with JPEG is that the user often has no clue what the image is until most or all of it is displayed. How will the user know whether to wait and

Figure 2.10   Use the Address Book window to easily address email messages.

see the image in its entirety or to simply click the mouse and terminate the download? With Progressive JPEG (also referred to as P-JPEG), images are stored in layers that represent the entire image at various degrees of resolution quality. The first portion of an image the user sees is the entire image, but using fairly low quality. Still, the image is often recognizable at this level of display. Then, over time, the details of the image are downloaded and layered on top of the existing image until, finally, the clear image emerges.

P-JPEG is no faster than JPEG. In fact, it may be a tad slower, but it gets more useable information to the user faster than JPEG, which is why it is becoming so popular.

Not all browsers support JPEG at all. On some browsers, only GIF images (discussed in the next section) are supported; JPEG images appear as "broken" picture icons. Be judicious in the use of JPEG and P-JPEG.

Figure 2.11 shows how a baseline JPEG image would appear over time in your Navigator window. Figure 2.12 shows the same image displayed using P-JPEG over the same period of time.

GIF Animation

GIF (Graphics Interchange Format) is the other popular type of graphic image format used on the Web. This format, created by CompuServe for use in transferring images rapidly over their online service, is now in widespread use in many computing communities and is the most widely supported Web format.

| Time = 0.2s | Time = 1.0s | Time = 4.0s |

Figure 2.11 A baseline JPEG image reveals itself slowly.

Figure 2.12   You can distinguish the content of a Progressive JPEG image more quickly.

The two GIF standards are called GIF87 and GIF89a. GIF89a has been in place for almost seven years (the 89 refers to the year of its initial promulgation) but is not yet widely supported by Web browsers. GIF87 supports a single, static image. GIF89a allows a GIF image to contain multiple copies of the same image, each slightly different from the others. It then supports "playing" the series of GIF images as an animation sequence.

Netscape Navigator 2.0 added support for GIF89a animated images. They are used exactly the same way as static GIFs; you just use the IMG tag and include a SRC attribute that points to the file. Netscape recognizes that the GIF in question is a GIF89a standard format and instead of just displaying the first or last image statically, it loops through, displaying all of them repeatedly.

This sequence is hard to show in the book, but the CD-ROM accompanying this book has quite a few GIF89a images you can incorporate into your Web page. Look in the directory IMAGES\GIF89a.

Multiple, Simultaneous Streaming Data Types

In most browsers, sound, movie and other data types are handled synchronously. When your browser encounters such a file, it first downloads the entire file to your hard disk and then launches the helper application you've identified with that file type so that the information can be presented. These long delays have annoyed millions of Web users during the first few years of widespread use of the Web. Even if you have a high-speed connection to the Internet, downloading these files, which often occupy multiple megabytes on your drive, can be terribly time-consuming.

To deal with users' ever-increasing expectations for motion, animation, sound, and other interactive excitement on the Web, a new technique called "streaming" was developed. Streaming is a method to deliver large, complex files to Web browser desktops.

Using this technique, the data being delivered to the user desktop informs the browser at the start that this information can be displayed before all of it is actually downloaded to the user's desktop. The sound or movie begins to play as soon as the data begins arriving at the user's system. The application responsible for reproducing the sound or animation launches and begins to play the data at the same time as it downloads and stores the data on the user's desktop.

Netscape Navigator 2.0 added support for this streaming type of data. It allows the simultaneous download of several types of streamed data at one time.

Using Macromedia Shockwave, RealAudio, Voxtools, and other streaming plug-ins (see Chapter 5), the multimedia experience on the Web can be brought to your desktop with something resembling real-time immediacy.

Client-Side Image Mapping

Before Netscape Navigator 2.0 arrived on the scene, the server handled all of the interaction between a user clicking on a graphic image and the user's browser pointing at a new URL. This approach has a number of disadvantages, not the least of which is performance.

With the advent of Version 2.0, Netscape Navigator implements an alternate strategy for dealing with image mapping. Map information is stored in the HTML document. Navigation to other URLs based on mouse-clicks is managed from the user's desktop, as well.

We'll have much more to say about this subject in Chapter 4, which is devoted exclusively to this topic.

FRAMES
III

As we learned in Chapter 1, frames are probably the easiest of the new Netscape additions to understand. This enhancement will likely have the greatest impact on the way your World Wide Web pages look to people who visit your site.

We'll discuss frames in two sections. In the first section, we'll look at how to use frames: How they look on your site's pages, how users interact with them, and what purpose they serve. In the second part, we'll delve into how to create HTML pages for Netscape 2.0 and other frame-capable browsers. We'll also look at supporting the older style "frame-challenged" browsers.

Looking at Frames

Figure 3.1 shows a sample page with frames as it looks in a Netscape 2.0 browser. As you can see, the difference between this window and the previous standard Netscape look and feel is the sub-windows, or frames.

The window in Figure 3.1 contains three frames:

- One pane at the top of the window extends the entire width of the window and contains a banner heading to let users know which site they are visiting.
- A second pane extends the height of the window below the banner frame and occupies about one-quarter of the width of the window. It contains what appears to be a group of nested lists that make up a Table of Contents.
- A third pane extends the height of the window below the banner frame and occupies the remaining three-quarters of the width of the window; it contains a page of text from an apparently larger document.

Each of these three frames is essentially a separate document. The user can click into any of these frames and make it the currently selected one. Then, the user can activate links that potentially change the contents of the current pane or one or more of the other panes.

For example, if the user clicks into the Table of Contents frame in the window shown in Figure 3.1 and selects a new heading, the page corresponding to that entry is displayed in the largest frame in the window. Figure 3.2 shows you what can happen when the user clicks on a link in the Table of Contents frame of our sample window. Notice that the contents of the main document frame have changed from Figure 3.1 to Figure 3.2.

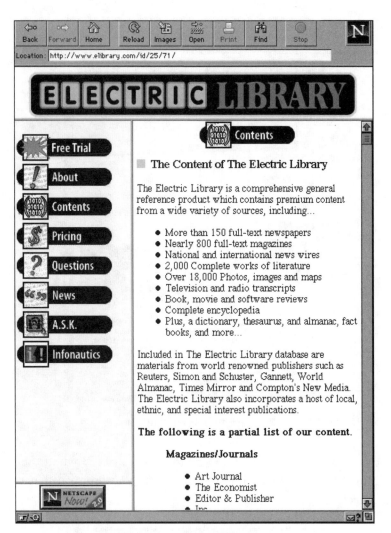

Figure 3.1   This sample window contains frames.

Similarly, the user can select one of the frames and ask to have it printed. To accommodate this change, Netscape has replaced the old "Print" option in the File menu with a new option labeled "Print Frame," as you can see in Figure 3.3. This option is present only if the page being viewed contains frames.

You may have noticed that the Table of Contents frame in Figures 3.1 and 3.2 has vertical and horizontal scrollbars. As the Webmaster, you are in charge of

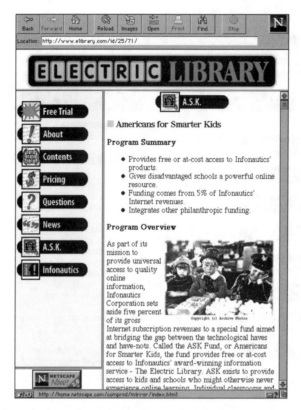

Figure 3.2   The contents of one frame have changed.

whether these scrollbars appear never, all the time, or only when the content's size demands that they appear. I'll explain how you accomplish that magic feat in the next section.

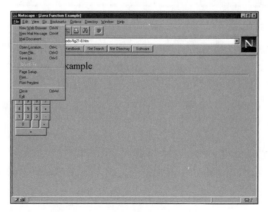

Figure 3.3   The File menu now prints frames.

Each frame on a page has its own URL. You can place any valid Web content in any frame of a Netscape-aware window that uses frames. This scheme gives you maximum flexibility in designing and presenting your frame-based Web pages to your users.

Navigation with Frames

Navigating in a multi-frame window obviously requires some new ways of thinking about the Web and how it works. Until frames came along, this navigation stuff was pretty easy. You opened one or more browser windows and, at any time, each window displayed the contents of a single URL. If multiple URLs were being accessed to display information, that fact was completely transparent to your users.

Frames present some special navigational problems, which Netscape has solved by two mechanisms.

First, if the user clicks on a navigational link in one of the frames in your multi-framed window and that link doesn't support or use frames, Netscape reverts to its old form. It allows the linked page to occupy the entire content region of the browser window, just as it has always done.

Second, the user may want to backtrack to some content within the context of a single frame. The "Back" button at the top of the browser window is, of course, not necessarily going to produce that result because it refers to the entire window. So Netscape's designers added a popup menu to each frame. (see Figure 3.4) from which the user can choose, among other options, "Back in Frame." This menu option has the effect of the "Back" button but only affects the contents of the frame in which the menu is selected.

Why Bother with Frames?

Frames are not without their downside, of course. Their major drawbacks from your perspective as a Webmaster are:

@ They are not understood by most browsers.

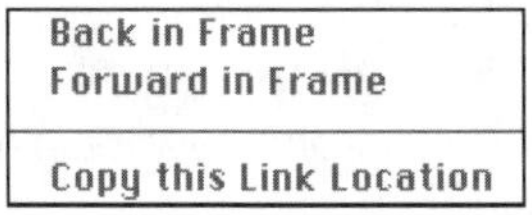

```
Back in Frame
Forward in Frame

Copy this Link Location
```

Figure 3.4   Users can use the frame popup menu to navigate.

- They take extra design and layout time and expertise.
- They require extra HTML coding of your site's content.
- For at least a few months after their introduction, they will almost certainly confuse some users.

So why bother to implement frames at all? There are a number of good reasons. I want to focus here on the three primary uses I see for frames on the sites I visit regularly or maintain as part of my life as a Webmaster. These uses are:

- context
- banners and advertising
- complementary content

Frames Can Provide Context

One of the most valid criticisms leveled not just at Web pages and sites but at hyper-linked information in general, is the observation that the user is often lost in a sea of hyperstuff. This absence of context can be quite disconcerting, particularly if the material the user is navigating is unfamiliar territory.

In the mid-1980s, Apple Computer popularized hypertext with the release of its highly successful HyperCard product. Developers building HyperCard "stacks" (or documents) experimented with many techniques to assist their users in locating themselves in the broader context of the information "space" in which they were navigating.

If this confusion was a problem in a limited sub-set of the universe such as that represented by a single HyperCard stack or even a small set of such stacks, think how much worse it must be when the navigation space represents potentially millions of pages and images on Web servers all over the world. You start out to find a recipe for chili that uses venison, click on a link that takes you to a site about deer, find an intriguing link to another page that discusses the history of hunting, and then click on a picture of an old hunting rifle. Suddenly, finding your way back to the chili may not be so easy and you may find yourself tempted to make some rather unpleasant use of the rifle.

With frames, you can provide your users with a clear context for navigation, at least as long as they stay on your site or on related sites for which you can provide some contextual links. You no longer are limited to showing a single page or site at a time in the Netscape browser. You can use one or more of the frames solely to give users a sort of anchor to which they can always return with a single click and that is always visible to them.

The sample framed window shown at the beginning of this chapter (Figure 3.1) is an example of this technique. The Table of Contents frame is designed so that users can glance at the outline and see exactly where they are in the context of the total content of the site. Another example of such frame use is in search-oriented Web sites and services. Such sites can use frames to enable you to see your search request at the same time as you examine the results of the search. I've seen frames implemented at a few lesser-known search sites already. I can confirm that their utility goes up dramatically when they can keep the search results in such a clear context.

Banners and Webvertising

You can use one or more of the frames in a Netscape 2.x browser window to display a constant (or even a constantly updated) banner that continually reminds users of the site they are browsing. This "flashing sign" approach may seem like shameless self-promotion, but it has value for your users, too. It is a subset of the context issue I discussed in the previous section.

A major potential use of frames is a particular flavor of banner. I speak, of course, of the ubiquitous advertisement, or, as these little morsels have come to be known in Webspeak, "Webvertisements." However you feel about them, one thing is clear: Frames will make their display and use more convenient and widespread.

(I should note here that I make my primary living working for an online magazine where Webvertising is a crucial part of our revenue stream. My position on the subject may therefore not be entirely objective. But at least you are forewarned.)

Before frames, advertisements were placed on a Web page but they could be scrolled out of sight. In any case they lasted only as long as users stayed on the page on which they appeared. This method made it difficult to design and place Webvertisements effectively. Companies that pay for such promotion expect their message to be readily visible, as it is in magazines and on television, but users—at least many of them—may try to avoid seeing them as much as possible. Using frames can keep the advertisements visible to the user.

Complementary Content

A third way in which frames will benefit your users is to enable them to see content that is complementary to your site without requiring them to leave your site.

Many Webmasters who have studied their statistical logs know that users seldom return to a site in a single session once they've left it, unless that site is a base of operations for them. To some extent, external links—hyperlinks that took users to other sites to explore information related to the subject at hand—were self-defeating if your purpose was to keep people at your site as long as possible. This may not be your primary purpose, depending on the motivation for your site, but commercial Web sites typically learn that they can sell more products or services, or persuade their users to give them more useful information, if they can keep them on their site for longer periods of time.

Yet it would clearly violate the underlying fundamental tenet of the World Wide Web if you were to copy related content from some other site to your site rather than providing a link to this other content. Not only would there be potential copyright issues (a really messy area, indeed!), but you'd be forced to maintain the imported information to keep your users current.

This dilemma is no longer an issue with frames. You can leave the complementary content on the original site, give your users a link to it, and display the related content in a frame on your site. The user never leaves your site; your banner, if any, remains displayed. The context remains unchanged. (This assumes, of course, that the page containing the related content supports frames. If not, you don't get the benefit. This effect will undoubtedly cause many people to support frames as a way of encouraging other sites to offer links to them.)

A Final, Speedy Note

There is a hidden advantage to the use of frames that may not be entirely evident. You might think that the addition of multiple frames to a window, each with its own URL, would slow down page serving, but the opposite seems to be true. Pages actually update more quickly in a frame-based window than in a single-paned window of the "old" style. (Amazing how quickly things become old in the digital culture, isn't it?)

To understand why this might be the case, let's return to the notion of the banner or Webvertisement at the top of a page of content. Let's postulate that the Webmaster of the site, under pre-frame browsers, organized the content of the site into 25 pages so that each would be small enough to avoid scrolling on most users' displays. This approach enabled the banner to remain visible on all the pages.

The downside to that design is that the banner image has to be reloaded with each page. Even if the browser is smart enough to cache the image (and not all browsers do cache individual images out of the context of the pages on which they appear), there is still a delay while the cached image is read and displayed as the user flips pages.

With frames, the Webmaster sets aside the top frame for the banner and only alters the content window. This hypothetical Webmaster, who no longer is concerned with keeping the banner on display by the artificial means of small page layouts, might now decide to put all the HTML for the content into a single document.

> The speed news is not necessarily all good. If the user resizes the window, Netscape will, in most circumstances, have to redraw some or all of its contents. The redrawing can get a little slow. The "old" Netscape had to do this as well, but it only had one window to manage.

Ultimately, even though more content may get shoved down the Web pipe by frame-enabled sites, the performance at the client and server sides of the conversation will probably improve, perhaps dramatically, as we start to take full advantage of frames.

So let's learn how to do just that.

Basic Frame Syntax

Think of frame documents as nearly identical to, but nonetheless slightly different from, "normal" HTML documents (the kind you've been designing and serving for longer than you might care to admit). I will sometimes use the term "frame document" to describe Web documents that implement frames.

If you've created many table structures in your HTML pages, you will find much in frames that is familiar. The Netscape designers who created the frame concept relied as much as possible on table concepts because of the similarities between the two design elements.

At its most basic level, a frame document simply substitutes a <FRAMESET> </FRAMESET> tag for the familiar <BODY> </BODY> tag. A minimal frame document looks like this:

```
<HTML>
<HEAD>
</HEAD>
<FRAMESET>
</FRAMESET>
</HTML>
```

Obviously, this minimal HTML isn't going to generate anything very interesting; it produces just what you'd expect: an empty document.

You can place a <BODY> in a frame document. If you do, however, neither the <BODY> tag nor any tags that would normally be placed in the BODY of a document can appear before the FRAMESET tag. If you make this mistake, Netscape will simply ignore the FRAMESET tag. So when you create frame documents in which nothing is happening with frames, check the order of your tags. Particularly if you are using a tool to generate HTML, you might find yourself starting with a template that violates this tag order rule. We'll see later in this chapter how to define a document so that people who browse your site with a browser that doesn't understand frames will not be greeted with either emptiness or chaos.

FRAMESET Essentials

Let's look further at the <FRAMESET> tag. It is the container object for frames; as such, it can contain two kinds of objects: other FRAMESETs and FRAMEs.

A FRAMESET can have two attributes: ROWS and COLS. In symmetrical layouts (for example, a layout with two rows of three columns where all the cells are the same relative size), you can put both attributes in a single FRAMESET definition. Irregular layouts require that you provide nested FRAMESETs where one set defines rows and another defines columns. We'll look at some examples shortly.

It is perfectly legal to define a FRAMESET with a ROWS attribute and no COLS, or a COLS attribute with no ROWS. In that case, Netscape creates a single row or column (depending on which attribute is missing) and allocates the entire available vertical or horizontal space to it.

The syntax for defining the attributes for a FRAMESET tag is the same for ROWS and COLS and looks like this:

```
<FRAMESET ROWS="rowspec1, rowspec2,...rowspecN">
```

If you define both ROWS and COLS attributes in the same tag, use a space to separate one string of specifications from the start of the next parameter, as shown here:

```
<FRAMESET ROWS="rowspec, rowspec" COLS="colspec, colspec">
```

The specifications for ROWS and COLS attributes tell the browser how to carve up the window to allocate the desired amount of space for each frame. These specifications are enclosed in quotation marks, and each individual entry is separated from the others by a comma. You can also use spaces between the elements (in addition to the required comma) for readability but it is not mandatory. Each entry in a row specification creates a row, and each entry in a column specification creates a column. (Nesting FRAMESETs makes this a little more complex; we'll look at that subject later in the chapter.)

Each element in a row or column specification can have one of three forms:

- @ a number of pixels to allocate to the row or column (fixed size)
- @ a number followed by a percent sign indicating the percentage of space to be allocated to the row or column (proportional size)
- @ an asterisk or a number followed by an asterisk defining how to allocate any space not allocated by fixed or proportional amounts (relative size)

FIXED SIZE SPECIFICATION

The fixed size specification for a row or column defines an exact number of pixels to allocate. You will probably find very little, if any, need for this specification. It is somewhat tricky to use correctly because you have no control over how large or small the user's browser window will be at any moment.

In no case should you use only fixed size specifications to define a frame document. If you do, the browser is liable to do some pretty strange things with your content (see the section "What About Unallocated Space?").

PROPORTIONAL SIZE SPECIFICATION

A number followed by a percent sign tells the browser to allocate the indicated percentage of the horizontal or vertical space in the window to the row or column with which it is associated. This proportion of the window's area is maintained if the user resizes the window. The frames will grow larger and stay in proportion to one another if the user makes the window larger, and will grow smaller proportionally if the user makes the window smaller.

RELATIVE SIZE SPECIFICATION

A relative size specification consists of an asterisk with no number or, alternatively, a number with an asterisk.

An asterisk alone tells the browser, "After you've allocated any fixed size and proportional size specification needs for the window, allocate all remaining space, if any, to this row or column." As long as there is only one asterisk in a specification, this concept is fairly easy to understand.

If you have two or more asterisks in a specification, you may wish to associate a number with one or more of them. This number forces the browser to allocate the remaining space by dividing it between these rows or columns, giving greater height or width to those elements with a higher assigned number.

Using and Combining Attributes

These three types of specifications for rows and columns in the FRAMESET tag interact with one another in carefully defined but potentially complex ways. In this section, I'll explain the basic rules by which these attributes affect each other, then provide a few examples that will clarify their use to accomplish your design goals.

ATTRIBUTES INTERACT

I said earlier that you should never define a row or column with only fixed size attributes, so I won't discuss such specifications here.

If you combine one or more fixed size attributes with one or more proportional size attributes, the browser allocates the fixed size regions of the window first. It then divides the remaining space in accordance with the proportional specification. For example, a tag like this one:

```
<FRAMESET COLS="300,50%,50%">
```

produces (with some additional markup to provide some cells and content) the effect shown in Figure 3.5. As you can see, the leftmost 300 pixels is occupied by one column while the rest of the space is divided equally into two columns. Resizing the window, as shown in Figure 3.6, demonstrates this principle even more clearly.

Combining one or more fixed size attributes with one or more relative size attributes has the same basic effect as using fixed and proportional size attributes together. The difference lies in how the browser divides any space not allocated by the fixed size attribute. For example, let's say you have a design that requires a 120-pixel banner at the top of the page and an 80-pixel navigation panel at the bottom of the page. The rest of the space should be used for content. To achieve that result, you can define a FRAMESET like this one:

```
<FRAMESET ROWS="120,*,80">
```

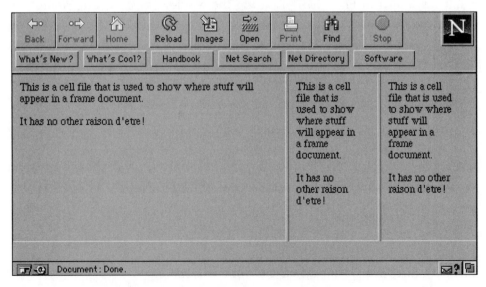

Figure 3.5   You can mix fixed and proportional sizes.

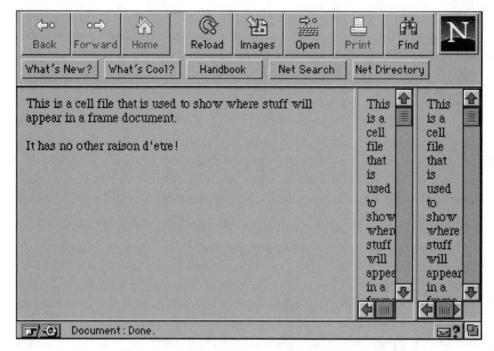

Figure 3.6   Here's an example of resizing a mixed fixed-proportional size frame.

The effect of this tag, with some additional markup coding to emphasize the results, is shown in Figure 3.7. Resizing the window, as shown in Figure 3.8, again demonstrates the effect more clearly. (Notice that in resizing the window, I made the center frame too small to show even a minimal amount of text, so Netscape produced a vertical scrollbar to allow the user to view all of the frame's contents. If I had made the window 200 or fewer pixels tall, the center frame would simply have disappeared.)

You can use proportional size elements alone in a FRAMESET to achieve a window with frames that always remain the same size in proportion to one another. For example, to divide a window into three rows, where the center row is always three times as high as the other two, you could write a tag like this one:

```
<FRAMESET ROWS="20%, 60%, 20%">
```

Figure 3.9 shows the result of this tag, and Figure 3.10 shows how the rows maintain their relationship when the window is resized.

You can achieve precisely the same effect with relative attributes and a little less typing:

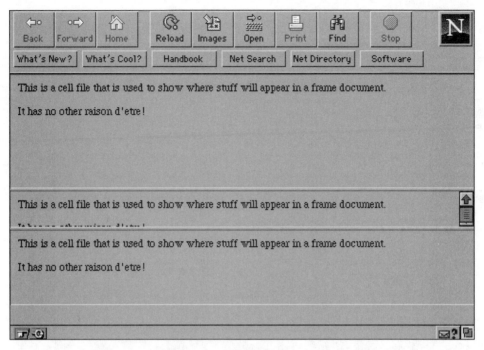

Figure 3.7 You can mix fixed and relative sizes.

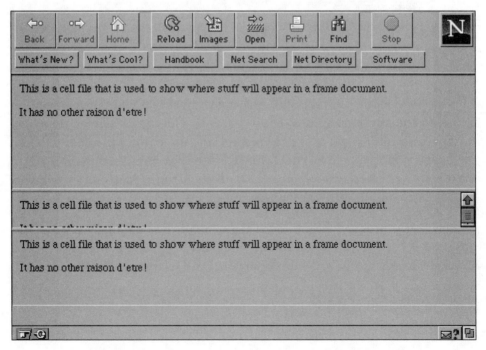

Figure 3.8 Here's an example of resizing a mixed fixed-relative size frame.

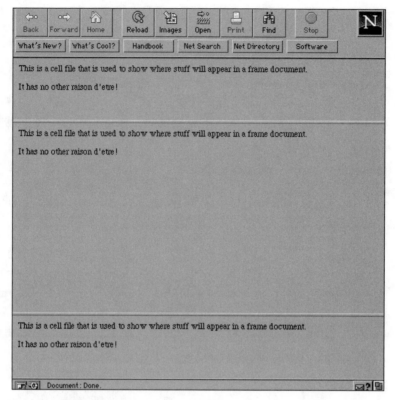

Figure 3.9 You can combine proportional size elements.

```
<FRAMESET ROWS="*,3*,*">
```

This strange-looking tag takes advantage of the fact that you can supply numbers with the asterisks. This essentially says to Netscape, "Divide the entire window into three rows. Make the second row three times as tall as either of the others, which should be equal in size." Whether you use this approach or the proportional percentage approach is a matter of individual taste and whether you're more comfortable with percentages or ratios.

By now you've probably begun to get the hang of this technique. It won't surprise you if I tell you that you can get the same result as the previous two examples by a judicious mixing of proportional and relative size frames:

```
<FRAMESET ROWS="20%,*,20%">
```

COMBINING ROWS AND COLS

Many of the layouts you want to create using frames will have more than one row and more than one column, requiring you to supply both types of attribute in a FRAMESET tag. For example, to create a fairly simple 2x2 layout that occupies an entire window with four equal rectangles, you might write a line like this:

```
<FRAMESET ROWS="50%,50%" COLS="*,*">
```

It may be obvious, but you could use the percentages throughout, the asterisks throughout, or mix them freely in this example because the desired outcome is so simple.

Let's try something a little more complicated. This time, we want three rows, where the middle one is three times as large as the other two, which are equal to each other, and three equal columns running through all three rows. Here's the tag that would accomplish this objective; Figure 3.11 demonstrates the result:

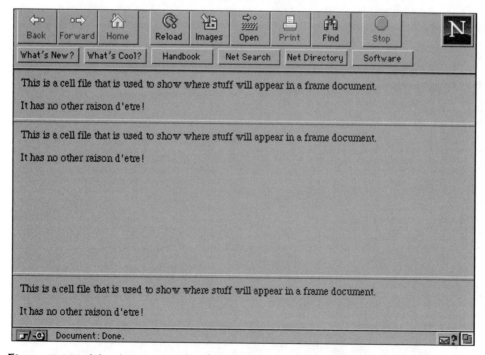

Figure 3.10   Here's an example of resizing a window with three proportional frames.

```
<FRAMESET ROWS="*,3*,*" COLS="*.*.*">
```

FRAMEs and Nested FRAMESETs

By now, you can imagine all sorts of permutations using ROWS and COLS in a FRAMESET tag. These combinations all work fine as long as you are doing reasonably regular layouts, but what if you want to try to accomplish something like Figure 3.12, with the top and bottom rows divided into three columns each and a single-column row occupying the center (and majority) of the screen? To create this result, you'll have to use nested FRAMESETs.

Before you can understand nested FRAMESETs, we have to deal with the other key idea in frame-based design, namely the FRAME tag. Until now, I've been

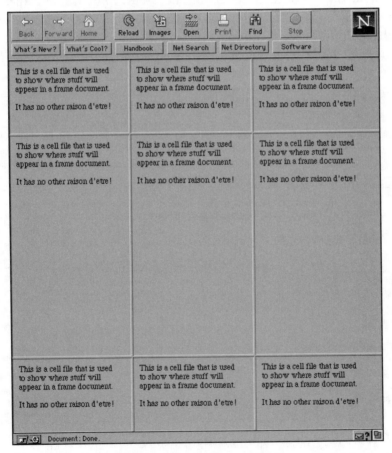

Figure 3.11   Let's combine three irregular rows with three equal columns.

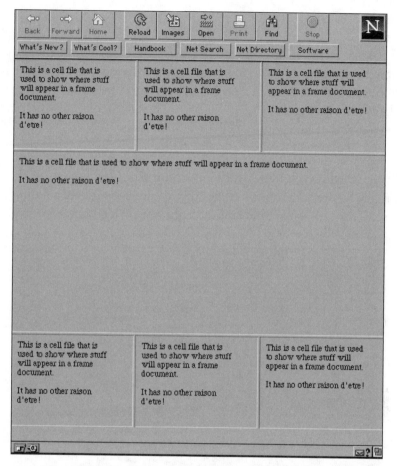

Figure 3.12 Use nested FRAMESETs to create these three rows and three columns.

filling in the FRAME tags for you (all with the same somewhat dull content), but now it's time to investigate this aspect of frame-based layout.

The basic syntax for the FRAME tag is:

```
<FRAME SRC="url of frame content">
```

(There are actually six attributes you can use with the FRAME tag. We'll focus on the SRC attribute for now and discuss the other five later in this chapter.)

If you looked at the source code for the previous examples, you'd see that each frame I created within a FRAMESET had a FRAME statement that defined its source as the file CELL.HTM. That tag looks like this:

FRAMES 43

```
<FRAME SRC="CELL.HTM">
```

Each FRAMESET defines one or more frames. Each frame defined in a FRAMESET tag must have a corresponding FRAME statement to tell the browser what to put into that frame. In a layout containing three rows of three columns each like we saw in Figure 3.12, nine FRAME statements must be placed between the <FRAMESET> and </FRAMESET> tags.

When you want to design less regular layouts, you need to use multiple, nested FRAMESETs, with each FRAMESET defining a regularized part of the design. For example, Figure 3.13 shows a layout that contains two equal columns, the left one divided into two equal rows and the right one divided into three equal rows.

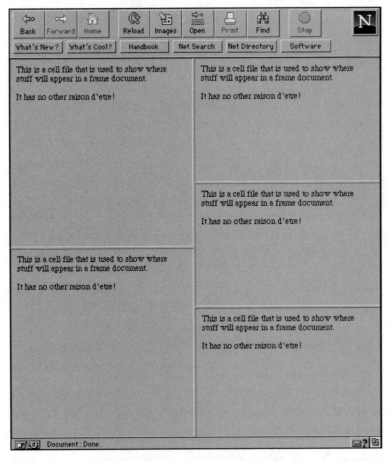

Figure 3.13   You can create irregular layouts with multiple, nested FRAMESETs.

In this case, we can view the window as a whole and see that the regularity in this illustration lies in the fact that the columns are the same throughout. So we'll define three FRAMESETs: one for the two columns that embrace the entire window and one each for the two row layouts. The resulting tags will look something like this:

```
<FRAMESET COLS="50%,50%">
  <FRAMESET ROWS="50%,50%">
    <FRAME SRC="cell.html">
    <FRAME SRC="cell.html">
  </FRAMESET>
  <FRAMESET ROWS="33%,33%,33%">
    <FRAME SRC="cell.html">
    <FRAME SRC="cell.html">
    <FRAME SRC="cell.html">
  </FRAMESET>
</FRAMESET>
```

The outermost FRAMESET container defines the two columns as each occupying half of the horizontal space in the window. It contains two other FRAMESETs. The first of these defines a set of two frames, each occupying half of the vertical space in the window. The second defines a set of three frames, each occupying one-third of the vertical space in the window.

Because the outermost FRAMESET defines two columns, it can contain at most two nested FRAMESETs. Each FRAMESET in turn defines the row format for one of those cells.

To turn this design on its side and have two rows, one of which has two columns and the other of which has three, we simply have to switch our COLS and ROWS attributes:

```
<FRAMESET ROWS="50%,50%">
  <FRAMESET COLS="50%,50%">
    <FRAME SRC="cell.html">
    <FRAME SRC="cell.html">
  </FRAMESET>
  <FRAMESET COLS="33%,33%,33%">
    <FRAME SRC="cell.html">
    <FRAME SRC="cell.html">
    <FRAME SRC="cell.html">
  </FRAMESET>
</FRAMESET>
```

The result is shown in Figure 3.14.

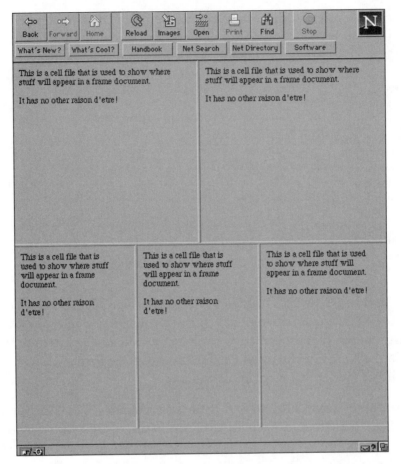

Figure 3.14   You can swap ROWS and COLS to create other irregular layouts.

The basic format for nested multiple FRAMESETs is fairly straightforward, even if it does sometimes feel confusing. The outermost FRAMESET must divide the entire window into ROWS or COLS. There is then one nested FRAMESET for each row or column created by the outermost FRAMESET. These FRAMESETs generally (but not always) contain only attributes of the kind not represented in the outermost FRAMESET. That is, if the outermost FRAMESET divides the window into COLS, the nested FRAMESETs it contains will define ROWS for those COLS.

Of course, it's not quite that simple. There is nothing (other than good taste, small size of frames, and tedium) to prevent you from nesting entire FRAMESETs defining both ROWS and COLS inside other FRAMESETs. (If there's a limit to this nesting, I haven't hit it yet, but I haven't tried dividing my entire screen into one-pixel-square grids, either!)

Just to demonstrate the flexibility of this scheme and the degree to which you can carry it, check out Figure 3.15.

The tag structure that creates the frames shown in Figure 3.15 looks like this:

```
<FRAMESET ROWS="*,3*,2*">
<FRAMESET COLS="*,*,*,*">
   <FRAME SRC="CELL.HTM">
   <FRAME SRC="CELL.HTM">
   <FRAME SRC="CELL.HTM">
   <FRAME SRC="CELL.HTM">
</FRAMESET>
<FRAMESET COLS="10%,10%,*,10%,10%">
   <FRAME SRC="CELL.HTM">
   <FRAME SRC="CELL.HTM">
   <FRAME SRC="CELL.HTM">
   <FRAME SRC="CELL.HTM">
   <FRAME SRC="CELL.HTM">
</FRAMESET>
<FRAMESET COLS="*,*">
   <FRAMESET ROWS="*,*,*">
      <FRAME SRC="CELL.HTM">
      <FRAME SRC="CELL.HTM">
      <FRAME SRC="CELL.HTM">
   </FRAMESET>
   <FRAMESET ROWS="*,*">
      <FRAME SRC="CELL.HTM">
      <FRAME SRC="CELL.HTM">
   </FRAMESET>
</FRAMESET>
</FRAMESET>
```

I could keep getting fancier, but by now you have the idea. Each FRAMESET generally deals with only ROWS or COLS except in highly regularly shaped layouts where they might well include both attributes in a single tag. Just remember: The number of FRAME tags that appear between FRAMESET container tag pairs must match the number of rows or columns into which the container divides its portion of the window.

Netscape 2.0 built one limitation into the way you can implement frames. This limitation is for your own protection. If you define the source of a frame to be an ancestor of the frame itself, you could wind up with an infinitely recursive situation. A cell's content would be defined as a parent's content, which in turn

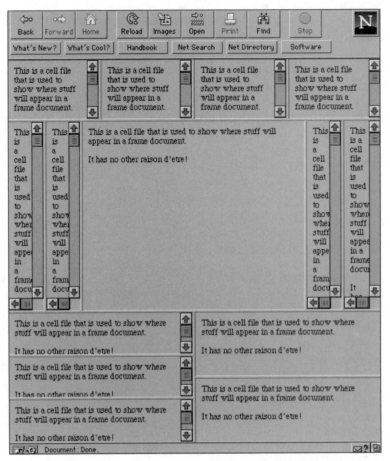

Figure 3.15   Using an arbitrarily irregular FRAMESET design gives you great
flexibility.

calls on itself, and so forth. As a result, if you create such a situation, Netscape
treats the frame as if it has no source of content (and is basically an empty
frame). This process prevents the recursion and the execution problems that
could accompany the situation.

Other Frame Attributes

As I mentioned earlier, a FRAME tag can define up to six attributes for a given
frame in a layout. The source ("SRC") is the most important of these attributes;
without it, the frame will be empty and the browser may not even draw an
empty frame.

The other five attributes you can define for a FRAME are:

- NAME
- SCROLLING
- NORESIZE
- MARGINWIDTH
- MARGINHEIGHT

Let's discuss each of these attributes in the order listed.

As with other multi-attribute Netscape objects, you'll find it easier to read and maintain your HTML markups if you adopt the convention of having one attribute or attribute-value pair per line.

The NAME Attribute

If you want to refer to a frame elsewhere in your HTML (or, for that matter, in a CGI application or other program), you must give it a name by which it can be referenced. The NAME attribute allows you to accomplish this task.

The value you assign to this attribute must be a string enclosed in quotation marks. It must begin with an alphanumeric character (no special symbols).

One of the primary reasons you might want to name a frame is so that you can use it with the newly defined TARGET attribute in a FORM or anchor (<A>) tag.

The SCROLLING Attribute

When the contents you assign to a frame with the SRC attribute are larger in either or both directions than the size of the frame, the user won't be able to see all of those contents. In some situations, this effect may be desirable (for example, to show only a selected portion of a larger graphic image to save display refresh time). You control whether or not the frame will display scrollbars with the SCROLLING attribute.

This attribute has one of three values:

- @ yes means the frame should always display scrollbars
- @ no means the frame should never display scrollbars
- @ auto, which is the default value, means that the browser should add scrollbars to the frame when the content demands it

Unless you have a good design reason for changing it, you should leave this attribute in its default state and let the browser do the right thing for the user.

The NORESIZE Attribute

Unless you were daring and experimented with some of the layouts I showed you earlier in this chapter, you may not realize that the user can resize all of the frames. (This seems kind of weird, doesn't it? You go through all this work to apportion the space very carefully and then the user gets to muck with it!)

You can turn off this default ability of the user to resize a frame by including the NORESIZE attribute in the FRAME tag. This attribute does not require or accept a value. If it is included in a FRAME definition, the frame cannot be resized. If it is omitted, the user can resize the frame by positioning the cursor over any interior edge and clicking and dragging the border to the desired new location.

The Margin Attributes

You can control the amount of "white space" between the contents of a frame and its borders with the MARGINWIDTH and MARGINHEIGHT attributes of the FRAME tag.

As their names imply, MARGINWIDTH regulates the amount of space between the left and right edges of the contents of a frame and its border, while MARGINHEIGHT controls the amount of space between the top and bottom of the contents and the horizontal borders.

Each of these attributes takes a number value that tells the browser how many pixels you wish to insert between the content and the appropriate border.

If you supply a value of less than 1, the browser will use 1 pixel as the margin. This value is also the default value for the margin.

Supporting Older Style Browsers

If you use frames extensively on your Web pages, you may wish to accommodate visitors to your site who are using browsers that don't support frames. Netscape includes the <NOFRAMES> </NOFRAMES> content tag pair to facilitate this support.

A frame-capable browser ignores all of the content that these tags bracket. The HTTP specification requires a browser to ignore any tag it doesn't understand. A browser that doesn't understand frames will ignore all of the content between the first <FRAMESET> and the last </FRAMESET> tag it encounters, as well as ignoring the <NOFRAMES> tag. It then correctly displays the content that follows the <NOFRAMES> tag.

The general structure for providing support on a single page for both frame-capable browsers and what Netscape marketers have dubbed frame-challenged browsers looks like this:

```
<FRAMESET attributes>
<NOFRAMES>
content for frame-challenged browsers goes here
</NOFRAMES>
<FRAMESET attributes>
</FRAMESET>
</FRAMESET>
```

You can, of course, nest the FRAMESETs as deeply as you like within this framework.

CLIENT-SIDE IMAGE MAPS IV

Since the debut of the Web, image maps have been among the most widely used types of interactivity on Web sites. An image map is a graphic object that has been converted into a clickable area (or a group of clickable areas) by the page designer or Webmaster.

Before the release of Netscape 2.0, image maps were handled strictly from the server side of the Web equation. The HTML used to define an image map and handle user clicks within its boundaries was minimalist. It relied on the presence of a special file (which bore an extension of .MAP) to help the server decide what to do with the user's mouse-clicks, depending on where those clicks took place.

This approach has some disadvantages, as we'll see shortly. As we learned in Chapter 2, Netscape, in designing a new approach to image maps for Version 2.0, created the concept of client-side image maps. All of the code to handle the user clicks and route actions correctly is encoded in the document in HTML.

In this chapter, we'll look briefly at how image maps were created in the past, how they were handled by the Web server, what the user saw, and what the problems were with this approach. Then we'll see how Netscape 2.0 addresses image maps, how they are handled, and what the user sees. Along the way, we'll talk about some of the primary advantages of this client-side approach.

Old-Style Image Maps

The original approach to image maps, which I somewhat irreverently call "old-style," uses a slightly oblique method of trapping and routing user mouse-clicks within a graphic designated as an image map. It requires the separate creation, using a design tool, of a .map file that contains information the server can use to decode and respond to mouse-clicks.

This old-style image mapping is still relevant despite the release of client-side maps with Netscape 2.0. It may be a long time before many of your Web site's visitors use a browser that supports this extension to HTML. (Some browsers, in fact, may see this as an unwarranted extension and never support it.)

Creating an Old-Style Map

To create an old-style image map, you open a graphic file using a program designed to convert the image into a clickable map object. Several of these programs exist for both the Windows and Macintosh platforms. The programs essentially provide tools with which you can draw regions in the graphic that you wish to be "hot," that is, linked to another location. The location can be within the document or outside the document on the Internet, on your site or any other accessible location.

For each of these clickable regions that you create by drawing with the tools provided, you must supply the URL to which the user's browser will point when the user clicks on that location. After you create all of the regions in your image map, the program generates the .map file.

The .map file contains an entry for each region you have drawn. (It is, of course, perfectly acceptable for the entire graphic image map to be a single clickable object so that the graphic acts more like a button than a typical map.) The entries have this basic syntax:

```
method URL coordinates
```

The first entry in the line is one of several pre-defined keywords for the shape of the clickable region to which it corresponds. (I don't know why it's called "method" instead of "shape," but I'm sure there's an interesting reason.) Table 4.1 summarizes the possible method (or shape) types and describes the coordinates that each method requires.

All of these shapes are fairly self-explanatory except, perhaps, default. If you have an image map whose entire region is not enclosed within a clickable area, you must define a default method in your .map file. This action will be taken if the user clicks outside any of the defined clickable areas.

Table 4.1   Image Map Shapes and Coordinate Requirements

Method (Shape)	Required Coordinates
circle	One pair for center, one pair for edge
oval	One pair for upper left corner of bounding rectangle, one pair for lower right corner of same rectangle
rect	One pair for upper left corner, one pair for lower right corner
poly	Up to 100 pairs, each defining a point, or vertex, in the shape
point	One pair
default	None required or allowed

A typical .map file, then, might look like this:

```
default contents/toc.html
circle contents/products/list.html 110,50 145,60
circle contents/services/list.html 120,70, 145, 90
rect contents/clients/cl_list.html 200,100 230,130
```

Actually, the process for creating and managing old-style image maps is somewhat more complex than I've presented here. The program you use to create image maps also has to deal with a database of its own. Except in rare circumstances, however, you never see or use this additional information directly, so I'm simplifying by ignoring it here. If you suffer from interminable curiosity and wish to know more about it, check out the explanation in WEB PUBLISHER'S DESIGN GUIDE FOR WINDOWS.

Handling Old-Style Image Maps

The HTML for inserting an image map into a document is fairly straightforward. It is identical to that used for any graphic image, using the IMG tag, with two additions:

- @ a URL reference to the .map file, containing the mappings as described above
- @ the inclusion of an ISMAP attribute to the HREF

Let's assume the graphic in the example at the end of the preceding section is called "locator.gif" and the .map file is stored in a file called "locator.map". The following HTML statement would be used to incorporate the map image and set it up for management by the Web server:

```
<A HREF="contents/images/locator.map"><IMG SRC="locator.gif" ISMAP></A>
```

What the User Saw

A major drawback of the old-style image maps is that when the user positions the mouse over such an image, the status bar at the bottom of the browser window doesn't reflect the URL to which the image is linked. Instead, it contains a cryptic-looking reference to the image map file and the mouse coordinates at which the user is about to click. If the image itself is not clear about what will happen when the user clicks at a particular point, this feedback is necessary. To the extent that the feedback is meaningless, it will frustrate the user who is exploring your page.

The status bar might look something like this when the user places the cursor over an image map that links an advertisement to a customer's site:

```
http://www.mysite.com/ads/ad3.map?180,43
```

This information doesn't tell the user much, although it may be more informative than most such status lines because at least the file path names give us some clue.

Other Problems

Apart from user confusion and inconvenience, old-style image maps place a fairly significant burden on the server, which presumably has a lot of activity. As World Wide Web bandwidth becomes an increasingly important issue in the next year or two, anything that can remove some of the server's work will be an important part of site management.

When the user clicks on an image map under the old-style approach, the server has to do all of the following processing:

- retrieve the click location
- open its map file to find out what this click location corresponds to
- consult its internal map database to determine what action to take
- invoke the appropriate URL

Each of these steps, of course, requires the server to operate on files and data, and each of them requires time and processor power.

The result is that the user waits longer than he or she might otherwise need to wait for something to happen, and the server becomes overburdened with relatively routine processing.

Another downside to the old-style image maps is that users cannot download and store pages and graphics for later off-line viewing. The image map mouse-clicks are not resolved until the server is back in the act. When people wish to make flexible decisions about where to store Web-related content they've down-loaded, licensed, or purchased, this drawback becomes a problem.

Client-Side Image Maps

With the introduction of client-side image maps in Version 2.0 of its Navigator browser, Netscape has overcome all of the disadvantages of the old-style image maps. As in all things, there is a trade-off. In this case, the HTML coder or Webmaster (that's probably you) will have to write more code directly into the HTML page to accommodate the new design.

Creating Client-Side Image Maps

The process of creating a client-side image map is virtually identical to that of creating old-style image maps. You use a map editing program, which generates a .map file that contains the location information for the map.

When you have this file, you open it with a text editor and copy the map loca-tions, so you can paste them into your HTML document as described below.

The HTML to create client-side image maps has two components:

- the IMG tag, which identifies the map
- the MAP tag, which describes each area in the image and its corresponding URL

We'll look first at the MAP tag.

THE MAP TAG

Each image map you wish to include in a document must have a corresponding MAP tag. This container has a syntax like this:

```
<MAP NAME="name">
<AREA [SHAPE="shape"] COORDS="x,y,..." [HREF=" reference "] [NOHREF]>
</MAP>
```

Let's look at this tag one line at a time.

The tag begins with the MAP keyword and requires that the map be named. (You wouldn't create it at all if you didn't plan to refer to it by name later.)

Following the opening MAP tag, you have one or more lines containing AREA tags. You need one of these tags for each clickable region designed to take the user to a different URL.

Each entry in the AREA tag has one required attribute: a list of the coordinates of the area, as described earlier in Table 4.1. If the SHAPE attribute is not included, a rectangular area is created. The third attribute of an AREA tag is either the HREF tag that contains the URL to which the user will navigate if he or she clicks on this area or the keyword NOHREF. NOHREF indicates that the browser should take no action if the user clicks in that region.

Any region of the image that is not encompassed in at least one AREA tag is treated as a NOHREF region, so you don't need to define such regions explicitly. It is not, however, wrong to do so, and it may add readability to your HTML pages where a particularly complex image map is defined.

If two AREA tags define partially or completely overlapping regions on the image map, the one defined first takes precedence in the overlapping area.

The coordinates defined for an AREA are inclusive. If you supply the coordinates "0, 0, 100, 100," you are actually defining a region 101 pixels by 101 pixels, which may well be exactly what you want to do. But, if you really want to define a region that is 100 pixels square, you would use the coordinates "0, 0, 99, 99."

HREFs are treated slightly differently in client-side image maps than in text links. Normally, a relative anchor specification URL (one that does not specify the entire path to the URL because it is local) is expanded to include the implied base HREF for the page. In the case of a client-side image map, though, the HREF is expanded from the URL of the map description, not from the base HREF. The exception to this rule arises if you explicitly define a BASE HREF for a page. In that case, image map relative paths will be built on that HREF, which overrides the path to the image.

An example will help to clarify this situation.

Assume we have mapping information stored in the directory /clients/clilist/ on a Macintosh disk called "maindisk" (the same principle, of course, applies to Windows drives with their letter designations). Here is a partial MAP listing:

```
<AREA SHAPE="RECT" COORDS="110,10,149,49" HREF="joe.html">
```

If the user clicks on this area of an image map, the browser will point at the location maindisk/clients/clilist/joe.html. If, however, you added a BASE HREF at the beginning of the file so that its partial contents looked like this:

```
BASE HREF="marketing/clients/"
```

The above AREA's HREF would take the user to "marketing/clients/joe.html."

THE IMG TAG

You are undoubtedly familiar with the standard use of the IMG tag to load a graphic into your HTML page, whether that graphic is "hot" (an image map) or static. To create a client-side image map, you use the same HTML to which you are accustomed, but you add the USEMAP attribute to it, with a pointer to the named MAP image to use. Here's a sample:

```
<IMG SRC="../clients/clilist/clipict.gif" USEMAP="#mapname">
```

Notice that since the .map file is in the same HTML document, the named anchor syntax, in which the name of the map is preceded by a pound sign, is used. You may, of course use a separate file for this definition and reference it with a full path and anchor reference.

BEST OF BOTH WORLDS

It would, of course, be problematic for you to rush out and convert all of your old-style image maps to the new client-side image map technique. All the browsers that don't yet (and, for all we know, may never) support this proposed HTML 3.0 extension would encounter this information with unpredictable and almost certainly unpleasant consequences.

To avoid this problem, you can code both an ISMAP and a USEMAP attribute for an IMG tag. The result would look something like this:

```
<IMG SRC="../clients/clilist/clipict.gif" USEMAP="#mapname" ISMAP >
```

What the User Sees

When users position their mouse over a client-side image map, the status bar reflects the URL to which they will navigate if they click the mouse. This method is consistent with the other uses to which the Navigator browser puts the status bar, and is therefore more comfortable and informative for users.

Other Advantages

Relocating a URL to which a segment of an image map points is difficult and time-consuming if you are using old-style image maps. The designer must re-open the .map file and edit its contents to reflect the new URL, then replace that .map file. With client-side image maps, the editing takes place entirely in the context of the HTML file from which the navigation takes place. This approach makes the change easier, more accessible to non-technical Web site developers, and less error-prone. You can immediately see the URL in the status bar of the window without clicking on the image map (only to find that you misspelled part of the URL).

USING
PLUG-INS
V

By including a plug-in architecture in of the new Navigator, Netscape allows software developers to create tightly integrated and seamless interactions between the World Wide Web and various kinds of information. This support goes beyond the original notion of "helper applications" and shows signs of becoming the preferred method for developers to use to integrate their technologies into your Web browser.

In this chapter, I'll explain the plug-ins, how they differ from helper applications, and how you as a user can put them to work for you. I'll provide a few examples of cross-platform plug-ins that are already available at this writing. I'll also point you to some URLs where you can track and locate new plug-ins as they become available.

What's a Plug-In?

The world in which the Netscape Navigator browser works is changing rapidly. It would be impossible for its designers to keep up with new kinds of data, interfaces, and other technologies if they had to do all of the new development themselves. Designers must deal with the difficulty of knowing what to do and the complexity of actually doing it. If they added every possible new type of information to the browser the Navigator would bloat to a size that users would not appreciate.

It Starts with Helper Applications

Netscape Navigator's developers understood this fact from the beginning. In the first release of the product, they provided support for helper applications. These applications were completely external to the browser. The browser could call upon them when the user downloaded certain types of data.

For example, Figure 5.1 shows part of the Helpers section of the Navigator Preferences window as it might appear on a Macintosh. The scrolling list at the top of the window contains numerous entries for various "Mime Types." For each mime type the list tells the Navigator browser:

- what application to use when the type is encountered
- whether to launch the application or just save the document in a format understood by that application
- the file extensions to which the mime type should be applied

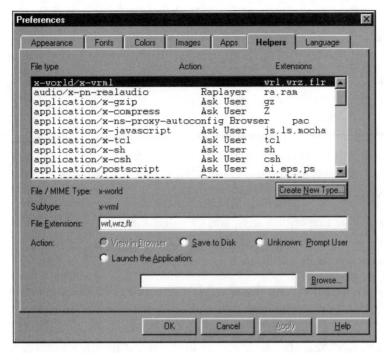

Figure 5.1 Helper applications are listed in the Navigator Preferences window.

The word "mime" is an acronym meaning "Multipurpose Internet Mail Extensions." It is an Internet standard for defining how Internet viewer applications should handle specific types of data. It is used not only in conjunction with Web browsers but also with Internet mail programs such as Eudora.

There are several standard mime types, including:

- application
- image
- text
- audio
- video

Each of these mime types, in turn, has a number of extensions. The addition of new mime types is pretty rare, but the definition of new extensions for mime types happens frequently. For example, the image mime type has a number of defined extensions, including:

- @ JPEG
- @ GIF
- @ PICT
- @ TIFF
- @ x-bitmap

There are actually more than a dozen such extensions to the image mime type, each of which deals with a different type of data. All of the extensions ultimately produce a visual image on the user's display, assuming the user's display supports bitmapped graphics.

Each mime type that your system and browser support must have an associated application. These mime types are all separate, stand-alone programs that Netscape simply launches on demand.

Let's say, then, that your browser is configured to launch the popular PKUNZIP.EXE program when it encounters a file whose extension is .ZIP. You are surfing along the Web, minding your own business, when you click on a file called COOLNESS.ZIP. Your browser looks at the data file, detects its extension, and checks to see if you've told it what to do with such files. If so, it simply follows your instructions, downloading the file and automatically launching PKUNZIP.EXE to handle the file.

If, however, you click on a file with an extension that you haven't told your browser how to handle, Navigator will display a dialog asking you what to do with the file. You can choose to download it anyway because you know what you want to do with it, or you can cancel the download. Under some circumstances, you may also be able to identify a helper application you haven't yet told Navigator about.

The Downside of Helper Applications

Helper applications are very useful. Without them, we wouldn't be able to view many kinds of images, look at QuickTime or other multimedia movies, or listen to sounds within the Navigator.

But they have one major disadvantage: They are fairly inconvenient. The inconvenience arises because helper applications require the following:

- @ The user must pre-configure the browser to deal with each data type in advance. The user does not necessarily know what data types will be encountered on the Web or what application is best suited to handle each data type.

◎ The user must remember what these applications are and where they reside on the disk. The user needs this knowledge to transfer the browser from one machine to another or to offer a colleague a URL to examine.

The user's hard disk needs to store an external application, which is potentially large.

◎ The helper application needs its own application space and windows in which to execute, cluttering the user's display and occupying significant additional memory.

Helper applications typically, though not always, reside outside the directory in which the browser is stored. Many of these applications were around before the user installed the browser, and most users don't design their directory structures around any one application.

Along Came Plug-Ins

To address at least some of the drawbacks of helper applications, Netscape developed the plug-in architecture for Version 2 of the Navigator application.

Plug-ins, unlike helper applications, are not true stand-alone programs. They are, rather, individual program modules with little or no user interface. As a rule, they run within the browser page. This design enables them to be much smaller than the equivalent program would be if it had to consider the user interface and manage the user's interaction with the environment.

A plug-in is developed for a specific operating system and environment. Making a plug-in work across platforms requires additional design and programming effort. Traditional programmers working in languages like C/C++, Pascal, and Visual Basic write plug-ins.

The key to the plug-in architecture is the seamless integration between the plug-in and the browser. Because the plug-in is written not to be an independent program but to require the presence of the browser, it can do things a helper application couldn't do. Some of the helpful things it can do include:

◎ drawing into the browser window directly

◎ receiving events from the browser window directly

- obtaining data from the network to which the browser is communicating,
- using the URLs the browser recognizes
- generating data that Netscape or other plug-ins can use
- overriding existing communication protocol handlers and even implementing new ones

Obtaining and Using Plug-Ins

Now that you understand the advantages of plug-ins over helper applications, where can you get your hands on some of them? And once you have a handful of them, how do you get your browser to acknowledge their existence and use them?

Sources for Plug-Ins

The most logical place to look for a specific plug-in is at the Web site of the company that markets it. Most, but not necessarily all, plug-in developers allow you to download their plug-ins from their Web pages. Developers that don't make it available directly on their Web site will have an order form there.

Netscape (http://home.netscape.com) maintains an area that lists the plug-ins about which they know, and links to the developer Web sites. Several other vendor-neutral places exist on the Web where you can find out about plug-ins and how to obtain them. One of my favorites is the BrowserWatch site (http://www.browserwatch.com/plug-in.html). This site (see Figure 5.2) lists the plug-in along with a brief description and a link to the site where you can obtain it. It even includes a graphical way of determining whether the plug-in is available for the system you run. This feature is helpful, particularly if you need to stay with cross-platform plug-ins or if you are looking for a plug-in for a friend, colleague, or client who uses a different system from yours.

Placing Plug-Ins

For Netscape Navigator to make use of a plug-in, of course, it must be able to find it. Netscape solved this problem in a traditional, if somewhat arbitrary and annoying way: Netscape simply limits you to where you can store plug-ins. The plug-ins must be in a directory or folder called PLUG-INS (case sensitivity depends on your platform).

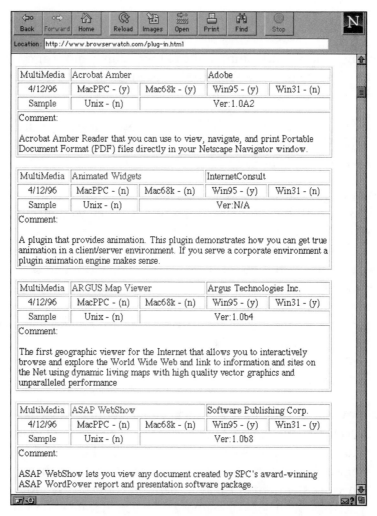

Figure 5.2   The BrowserWatch Plug-In page provides helpful information.

One of my pet peeves is software that requires you to arrange your desktop and file system to suit its view of the world. Why can't the software allow you to put things where they make sense to you and simply inform the program of your decision? It's my computer system, not theirs! I've written enough software to know that allowing the user this flexibility is not so difficult to do that there is any real excuse for this behavior.

After you download and de-compress the plug-in, simply move or copy it to the appropriate directory or folder. You need not re-launch Netscape Navigator or restart your system to use the new plug-in.

Incidentally, you can find out which plug-ins the Navigator has available to it by choosing "About Plug-Ins" from the system (Apple) menu on the Macintosh or the Help menu on a Windows system.

No effort at all is needed to actually use the plug-in once you've installed it correctly. Just as with the old helper applications, when you encounter a data type for which a plug-in has been installed, Netscape Navigator detects this situation and automatically loads the appropriate plug-in. In most cases, the plug-in will execute within the open browser window (though some plug-ins begin execution by creating a new window for their use). A few plug-ins might execute outside the browser window, but that event should be a rare experience. (Just because Netscape allows plug-ins to work within the browser window doesn't prevent a programmer from deciding not to take advantage of that feature for some reason.)

A word of caution is in order. While writing this chapter, I used Netscape Navigator 2.01 for the Macintosh. I found that plug-ins did not work as reliably as I would have liked. Sometimes, the plug-in loaded but the resulting file either didn't download or didn't display or perform correctly. By providing Netscape with gobs of memory (I finally allocated 10MB) and restarting often (there seems to be a memory leak, at least in the Macintosh version), I was able to get the plug-ins all to work at least some of the time. But this situation feels a little experimental at the moment. Hopefully, by the time you read this, things will have become more stable!

Some Sample Plug-Ins

The rest of this chapter describes five specific plug-ins that were available at the time I wrote this chapter. Except where indicated, all of these plug-ins are on the

CD-ROM accompanying this book. See Chapter 13 for a discussion of where they are stored.

I applied three criteria in choosing the plug-ins to include here, but I do not have space to discuss all of the plug-ins that met these conditions:

- The plug-in must work on both Windows and Macintosh systems. I'm a strong believer that the Web should remain as platform-neutral as possible.
- The plug-in must be useful in my experience. Some undoubtedly useful plug-ins didn't make the cut simply because they support activities for which I have not had a use on the Web.
- In the case of plug-ins with duplicate or largely overlapping functionality, I chose the one from the more established company or the one that complied best with real or de facto industry standards.

With these criteria in mind, I will describe the use of the following plug-ins:

- Acrobat Amber from Adobe Systems
- Lightning Strike from Infinet
- QuickTime Player from Apple Computer (along with a brief look at an interesting variation, MovieStar from Intelligence At Large)
- RealAudio from Progressive Networks
- Shockwave Director from Macromedia

Acrobat Amber

Adobe Systems has long been an advocate and developer of cross-platform tools of various kinds. They originally developed Postscript, the graphic description language used in most laser printers and on some computer displays (notably the Next machines). Adobe introduced the Acrobat product line and document format a few years ago.

Acrobat documents are typically created by users who simply "print" documents created in any application to an intermediate file that uses the cross-platform PDF (portable document format) specification. This document preserves fonts and other layout attributes and makes the resulting document viewable across platforms, even if the reader does not own the application with which the document was originally created.

Acrobat Reader, the application that makes it possible to read documents created in the PDF format, is available free from Adobe's World Wide Web site (http://www.adobe.com/Acrobat/readstep.html). Millions of Web surfers have downloaded Acrobat Reader and installed it as a helper application in their browsers so that they can read PDF files from the Web. When you encounter such a document and click on its URL, your browser downloads the document and then launches Acrobat Reader and opens the document.

As with all helper applications, this approach results in a new application window opening outside the Netscape browser. It also requires that the entire PDF document be downloaded before the reader can view even the first page.

In early 1996, Adobe introduced a new technology named Amber, a plug-in for Netscape 2 that opens PDF documents within the Netscape window and uses streaming technology. When you locate a PDF document on the Web, you can begin reading it moments after it starts downloading. You can also use Amber to read a single page at a time, jump to random pages even during the download process, and otherwise treat the document on a page-by-page basis. This approach to reading nicely formatted documents online is a major improvement over Acrobat Reader (which is itself a fine tool that many people find useful).

Figure 5.3 shows a page from a pictorial tribute to Baltimore Oriole baseball star Cal Ripken. Adobe provides the document as a sample of the use of Amber technology. This document contains a large number of sizable graphical images, But the reader does not need to wait for all of the images to download before beginning to browse through the document.

Amber documents can also embed hyperlinks, so that they can act in some limited ways like Web pages in their own right.

Lightning Strike

Lightning Strike, a Netscape plug-in from Infinet, is a major league graphical image compression and decompression utility. It can immensely accelerate the speed with which even complex color images appear in your browser window. Compared to the popular standard compression algorithms such as JPEG, this plug-in goes one better.

Because Lightning Strike's compression algorithm isn't a standard, however, it is unlikely the plug-in will gain widespread use. The server from which you are downloading material has no way to know in advance if you have a particular

Figure 5.3   With Amber you can browse a document before it finishes downloading.

plug-in. You may end up looking at broken-image icons if you frequent sites that make use of Lightning Strike and other, non-standard plug-in technologies that you don't yet own.

On the other hand, you can always decide that enough of the sites you visit do use Lightning Strike, or some other non-standard, plug-in, that it's worth having the plug-in on your system.

Figure 5.4 shows a portion of the Infinet Web page containing the Lightning Strike plug-in. The most interesting column in the table is the second one, labeled "Compression Ratio." The figures there sound astonishing, but in the testing I did for this book, I found they were accurately stated.

For example, the Sally image started life as a bitmap of 1,179,704 bytes. By the time Lightning Strike finished with it, it was only 10,891 bytes in size. By com-

Original Images	Compression Ratio	Lightning Strike	GIF/L.S.	JPEG 6.0
flower3.gif	71:1	flower3_71 inline	flower3_71.gif	flower3_71.jpg
cow.gif	75:1	cow75 inline	cow75.gif	cow74.jpg
eagle.gif	77:1	eagle77 inline	eagle77.gif	eagle77.jpg
cowboy.gif	89:1	cowboy89 inline	cowboy89.gif	cowboy89.jpg
laura.gif	100:1	laura100 inline	laura100.gif	laura97.jpg
lena.gif	100:1	lena100 inline	lena100.gif	lena100.jpg
sally.gif	108:1	sally108 inline	sally108.gif	sally107.jpg
cheetah.gif	122:1	cheetah122 inline	cheetah122.gif	cheetah121.jpg
fly.gif	124:1	fly124 inline	fly124.gif	fly124.jpg
wine.gif	165:1	wine165 inline	wine165.gif	wine165.jpg
bill.gif	170:1	bill170 inline	bill170.gif	bill170.jpg

Figure 5.4   This table shows Lightning Strike's compression ratios.

parison, the GIF version of the image was 226K in size; the GIF L.S. image (which retains its GIF structure but has some Lightning Strike technology applied) is 5K smaller than the original GIF.

As the Web becomes glutted with more and more graphical content, animation, movies, sound, and other multimedia types, the kind of compression represented by Lightning Strike will become essential. We need to keep the whole Internet from bogging down to unacceptably slow levels.

QuickTime Player and MovieStar

Apple Computer, Inc., has developed a number of technologies that it has deployed across platforms in the past few years. This largely unrecognized aspect of Apple's software development strategy has become more important with the emergence of the Web and the accompanying demand for cross-platform technologies.

One of Apple's most successful cross-platform products is QuickTime, a set of system extensions that enable computers to play full-motion video. QuickTime players for Apple's Macintosh line and for Microsoft Windows-equipped Wintel systems have been around for some time. Apple has recently been expanding the

QuickTime product line to include three-dimensional viewing, interaction, and virtual reality (VR) support. As it completes those technologies on the Macintosh, it will extend them to the Windows world as well.

Apple has announced that it will ship Netscape plug-in QuickTime movie players for both Macintosh and Windows soon. Probably by the time you read this, they'll be available. You can check their status at http://quicktime.apple.com.

Meanwhile, a third party supplier, Intelligence At Large, has issued pre-release versions of their product, MovieStar. This Netscape plug-in is available at their site: http://130.91.39.113/Trial/mspi-down.htm. The plug-in requires QuickTime Version 2.1, which you can download free from Apple's site if you don't already have it.

Once the MovieStar plug-in is safely nestled in your Netscape Plug-Ins folder, you can view QuickTime movies in streaming form. The movie begins playing almost instantly when it starts to download. This approach is much simpler than downloading the movie in its entirety and then launching the QuickTime Movie Player helper application from Apple (or one of several other QuickTime-compatible players from commercial, shareware, and freeware developers).

Figure 5.5 shows a still from a QuickTime movie playing directly in a Netscape browser window using MovieStar. (I tried to capture a movie for you, but, alas, the limitations of the flat printed page intervened. The movie itself, along with the alpha release of MovieStar, are on the CD-ROM accompanying this book, though, so you can see the movie in full motion if you wish to do so.)

The surfer movie running in the small, upper region of the window shown in Figure 5.5 comes complete with a driving-beat music segment. You can move the slider back and forth to view specific parts of the movie, and you can stop it to get a better look. Its postage-stamp size is a function of QuickTime limitations and technical decisions made by the people who created the movie and placed it on the Web. Bandwidth limits are the only reason that the movie couldn't be four to eight times as large.

RealAudio Player

One of my personal favorite Netscape plug-ins is the RealAudio Player plug-in from Progressive Networks. I like to listen to National Public Radio's talk show, "All Things Considered," but I don't always get time. Even when I do have time, I don't generally enjoy all of the segments. Well, RealAudio has

Figure 5.5   QuickTime movies can stream into your Netscape browser window.

solved this problem for me. I'll have more to say about how they did that in a moment. First, let me explain the RealAudio technology.

Audio, like other multimedia data types, required a helper application and a complete download of the file in some standard audio file format (AIFF, WAV, SND, and so on) before it could be played. The performance of sound-enhanced Web sites was a little uneven. You couldn't hear the narration of an illustration or an animation as it was playing. It wasn't real-time.

Along came RealAudio. In its first incarnations, it was a helper application, too. It handled audio in a streaming format so that even before Netscape 2.0's plug-in architecture was revealed, Netscape browser users could hear audio played in real time. With the plug-in, this process is faster, simpler, and more automatic. It also takes up less memory. Version 1.0 of the RealAudio tool produced AM-radio quality sound. Version 2.0 delivers FM-quality audio to your desktop; CD-ROM quality sound is in the offing as the Progressive Networks engineers work on continuing to improve the technology.

With the RealAudio plug-in safely installed in your Netscape Plug-Ins folder or directory, you can enjoy real-time sounds from a number of sources. Figure 5.6 is the Web page at Progressive Networks where you can select the audio segments for your listening pleasure.

Figure 5.6 You can select sample audio segments from the RealAudio Web page.

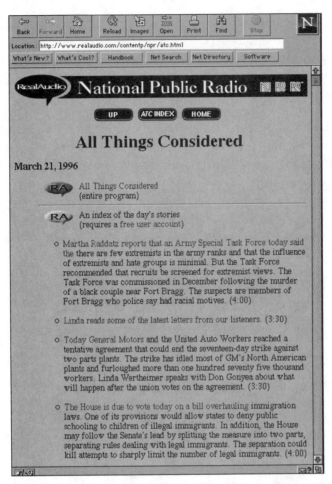

Figure 5.7   Pick the segments that interest you from "All Things Considered."

Figure 5.7 depicts a good example of using RealAudio. Each day, National Public Radio's "All Things Considered" is presented on this page. You can elect to hear the entire show replayed, or you can select one or more segments that sound interesting to you.

When you select an audio file for download, you will see a control panel like the one shown in Figure 5.8. You can use this panel to change the volume, "slide" forward and backward in the file, and even return to the browser while the sound plays in the background!

So far, all the RealAudio techniques I've described are independent of whether you're using the plug-in or the stand-alone player. Now comes the cool stuff. Look at Figure 5.9. This part of the page describes and demonstrates the plug-in

Figure 5.8   The RealAudio player lets you control the audio file.

version of the RealAudio player. The HTML needed to include RealAudio sounds into your Web pages is presented as well, and it is amazingly simple.

RealAudio's compression format is not yet a standard in the industry. However, with more than three million downloads of its players and plug-ins, Progressive Networks is certainly making a strong bid to become the standard for Web-based streaming sound.

Shockwave

The last plug-in we'll look at in this chapter is perhaps the most impressive of the lot. Shockwave, from multimedia conglomerate Macromedia, Inc., allows you to stream-view movies and animations created with Macromedia's Director program. Director, the massively dominant tool for multimedia development on desktop computers, allows you to create animations, embed sounds, and create both Director and QuickTime movies.

Once you have created a movie using Director, you can run it through the AfterBurner filter, which Macromedia provides free. You can convert the movie to a format that can then be read and displayed by the Shockwave plug-in, which Macromedia also distributes free.

The animations and movies you can create for Web distribution know no real bounds with Director and Shockwave technology available to enable your users to see this artistry in real-time. You can do such simple things as create animated logos (see Figure 5.10) and user interfaces that respond even to mouse movement in real-time. (You simply can't do this with Netscape, or even with JavaScript, but it is quite trivial with Director and Shockwave.)

You cannot, of course, tell that the logo in Figure 5.10 is rotating, but it is. You'll find this logo, as well as the Shockwave plug-in, on the CD-ROM accompanying this book. Try it out for yourself!

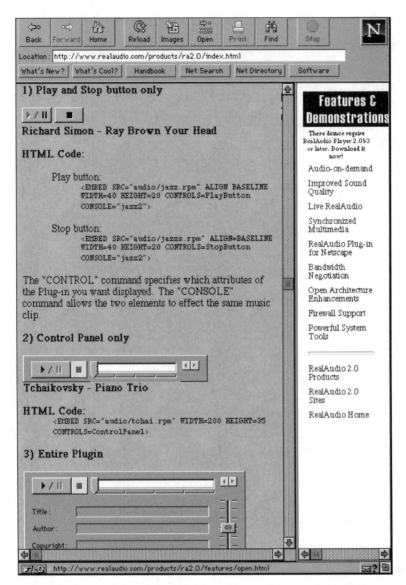

Figure 5.9   Check out this cool RealAudio plug-in demo and HTML page.

One of the most mind- and technology-stretching and bending places on the Web, if you're into Director movies, is Marc Canter's Mediaband site (http://www.mediaband.com). It's hard to describe the zaniness and frenetic creativ-

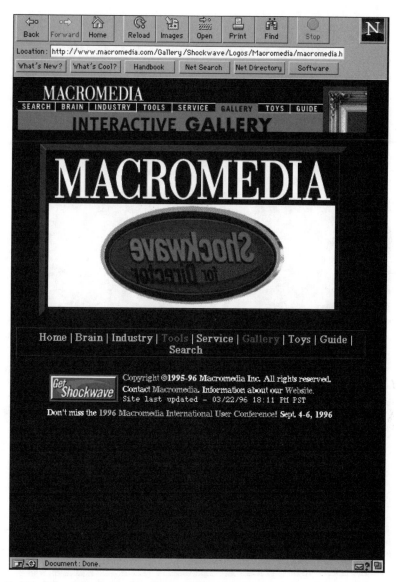

Figure 5.10   The Macromedia animated logo rotates in 3-D space.

ity embodied in this site. Figure 5.11 gives you some sense of the location; check it out yourself, though. You'll see some amazing stuff. ("Macaroni Man," for example, shows you the potential of cartooning on the Web in ways that a book full of technical descriptions could not describe.)

Figure 5.11   Marc Canter's Mediaband site uses Shockwave in creative ways.

(By the way, it figures that Canter would be a major exploiter of this technology. He created Director and its predecessor, and is in many ways the unsung founder and father of affordable and accessible computer-based animation.)

JAVASCRIPT OVERVIEW VI

From your perspective as a Webmaster, JavaScript is the most important addition to Netscape Version 2. The built-in scripting language. It will dramatically increase your control over the pages you serve, as well as users' experiences with your Web site.

We'll look at JavaScript in this chapter and the following three chapters. In the process, we'll take a fairly comprehensive look at this scripting language and its use in Netscape documents.

This chapter provides an overview of JavaScript. I begin by describing what JavaScript is and what it is not, differentiating it from the Java programming language with which it is often confused. Then I discuss the mechanics of JavaScripting: How scripts are included in your pages, and when and how they are executed. The chapter concludes with a brief discussion of the basic rules of JavaScript's syntax and usage.

Along the way, I'll provide examples of JavaScripts in action. The pages containing these examples are, as usual, contained on the CD-ROM accompanying this book. Use these CD-ROM files if you want to avoid typing the text in the chapter.

What Is JavaScript?

We expect scriptability in modern software applications. Word processors, spreadsheets, databases, and personal information managers often enable a reasonably knowledgeable end user with no formal programming background to script them. In the process, users adapt the behavior of these applications to their own needs, a direction in software I heartily applaud.

The earliest scriptable applications were telecommunications programs that allowed the user to write scripts to automate online sessions. For the most part, these scripting interfaces were arcane, accessible only to the technically sophisticated user. Over time, and spurred largely by Apple Computer's introduction of HyperCard in 1987, scripting became more approachable. Microsoft included a Visual Basic Application edition (VBA for short) in several of its programs in the early 1990s.

World Wide Web browsers are among the most ubiquitous of software programs ever offered. Strangely, at least to those of us who keep an eye on the software industry and champion the cause of scripting, these browsers did not include scriptability until the release of Netscape 2.0.

When the Netscape engineers began working on Version 2.0, scripting was very high on their list of features to implement. Originally, they called the scripting language in Netscape LiveScript. Before LiveScript could be brought to life, however, Sun Microsystems announced and released their full-blown Internet-capable programming language, Java. Quickly, Sun and the up-and-coming Netscape forged marketing and technical alliances. One offshoot of these relationships was the renaming of LiveScript to JavaScript. The result has been increased confusion among the Web browsing public.

I'll begin my definition of JavaScript, then, by emphasizing that it is not Java. The Java programming language, which bears a close resemblance to the widely used C++ professional programming language, is a completely separate entity from JavaScript. We'll take a brief, top-level look at Java in Chapter 10, but more than an overview is beyond the scope of this book. To write useful, even fairly complex JavaScripts, you do need not to be a programmer capable of dealing with all of the scope, power, and complexity of Java.

Table 6.1 summarizes the main differences between Java and JavaScript.

Table 6.1   JavaScript Compared to Java

JavaScript	Java
Interpreted by client; not interpreted by and not visible to server.	Compiled on server, then transmitted to client for execution on desktop.
Object-based. Language includes pre-defined objects that are extensible in limited ways, but there are no classes or inheritance	Object-oriented. Applets and applications consist of classes of objects with full single inheritance.
Creates scripts, which are embedded directly into HTML.	Creates applets and applications, which are called from HTML but are not embedded in it.
Variables need not be declared as to their type.	Variable types must be declared.
Usable by non-programmers and "power" users with no professional training or experience.	Requires programming training or experience to use efficiently and effectively.
Uses dynamic binding, meaning that objects can be unknown or unresolved until the script is actually executed.	Uses static binding, meaning that objects must be known when the application or applet is compiled.

As time goes on, we will see many complex, interactive Web pages that combine the strengths and capabilities of Java with the power and simplicity of JavaScript. The JavaScripter will make use of applets created by Java programmers, who in turn will design their applets so that the objects they contain make their properties accessible to JavaScript. The combination is going to be powerful and an incredible amount of fun!

With that clarification out of the way, let me attempt to put JavaScript into context for you. Here is a concise, if somewhat oversimplified, definition: JavaScript is a scripting language based on an object model that allows you to control many aspects of user interaction with your HTML pages.

Now let's take this definition apart and examine it in greater detail.

JavaScript as a Language

The first thing you should notice is that JavaScript is a scripting *language*. In this respect, it is completely different from HTML, which is a collection of markup tags. Creating HTML documents is often incorrectly characterized as HTML programming. Marking up documents for display by HTML browsers like Netscape is really quite unlike programming. It's much more like editing and a little like desktop publishing design.

At the same time, JavaScript is different from scripting *environments* such as HyperCard, AppleScript, UserLand Frontier, Microsoft Basic Script, and VBA. These languages include not only linguistic elements but also things like editors, debuggers, browsers, and other tools to make your scripting life easier. At least in its first incarnation, JavaScript doesn't have any of these tools.

JavaScript is, however, a very capable scripting language. Its syntax borrows a little too heavily from C for my taste, but it isn't hard to get used to, and it is quite readable for the most part.

As a scripting language, JavaScript includes or supports such features as:

- @ objects, which have properties you can set with JavaScript statements
- @ looping constructs for repeating actions
- @ conditional constructs for choosing among two or more courses of action depending on some value or situation or input
- @ events, which are generally user-triggered activities that can in turn cause a JavaScript to begin executing

From even this partial list, it should be clear that JavaScripting is potentially somewhat more complex than HTML mark-up. Don't be put off by this list, even if some of the terms are unfamiliar to you. You don't have to be a trained professional programmer to use JavaScript.

I need to make one final point about JavaScript before we delve further into it. JavaScript is not a "standard." At this writing, it is not included in any of the drafts for upcoming releases of HTML standards, and it's not likely that it will be. Also at this writing, it isn't clear to me how or whether Netscape plans to encourage, facilitate, or even allow other WWW Browser publishers to use JavaScript in their browsers. So when you include JavaScript in your Web pages, you are doing something that is and may remain completely outside the capability of any non-Netscape browsers (including earlier versions of the Netscape browser itself). I won't beat this one to death; I said enough about it in Chapter 1 to make the point. But JavaScript is the clearest non-standard extension to the HTML world embodied in Netscape 2.0, and I would have felt remiss not to point it out one last time.

The JavaScript Object Model

If you have any experience with AppleScript or Frontier on the Macintosh or with Visual Basic or Delphi on Windows, the existence and use of an object model is old hat. The JavaScript implementation of the object model is necessarily different in the details from other implementations you may already know, but the fundamental idea remains the same.

The basic idea behind the JavaScript object model is that the world in which JavaScripts execute is made up of objects. An object can be a window, frame, URL, document, form, button, or some other item. Each of these objects has properties associated with it. They may have names, locations (on the user's screen or within a window), colors, values, and lots of other attributes.

Most, but not all, of what you do in JavaScript involves manipulating these objects. You will either create new objects, or use those that are created for you by the user's interaction with the Web browser. You will script most often by examining these properties, making decisions about what to do based on their values, and altering those values to change the user's experience.

The object model is sufficiently important that I've devoted all of Chapter 7 to it, so I won't spend a lot more time on it here. If you understand the object model at least at a surface level, you're going to get value from the rest of this chapter.

Objects and their properties are referred to using the de facto standard "dot notation" that Visual Basic promoted. For example, if you want to work with the name of a document, you'd expect to use a construct something like this:

```
document.name
```

Similarly, if you have a form in a Web document and you want to work with the value of a checkbox in that form, you might have a line like this:

```
document.OrderForm.PaymentCheckBox.value
```

The above example illustrates the importance of a new feature in Netscape 2.0 that is useful primarily (though not exclusively) when you write JavaScript. Many objects, including forms and documents, that existed in earlier versions of Netscape, have a new NAME property. This property allows you to give the objects internal names you can use when referring to them in your JavaScripts. Here, we have named a form "OrderForm" and a checkbox (Option) object "PaymentCheckBox." We can then use those names in object references using dot notation.

The object model has a hierarchy. Windows contain all other objects, including documents, which in turn contain forms, links, and anchors. Form objects, in turn, contain form elements. I'll describe the entire hierarchy in Chapter 7.

Controlling the Document with JavaScript

Ultimately, the reason for writing JavaScripts is to control the user's interaction with and experience of your Web pages in ways that aren't possible without scripting. You can think of these new abilities as falling into three rather broad and not mutually exclusive categories:

- tailoring the experience
- extending the experience
- validating user input

As we move through the next three chapters—and particularly in Chapter 9 when I present some fleshed-out examples of using JavaScript—you'll see examples of each of these types of JavaScript use. Let's explore each of them briefly here, just to provide a context for our broader discussion of scripting Netscape.

Tailoring the Experience

JavaScript includes language elements that would permit you, for example, to alter the appearance or content of a Web page based on such things as the day of the week, date, time, or user domain.

Maybe you run a Web site in a company where one of the items posted is the company's cafeteria meal menus. You could set up your page to show only today's menu, or to display today's menu differently from others. If your network identifies users as they open a page, you could even greet them personally.

Similarly, you can determine what browser the user is using. Then you can display different content or pages to present your material in the best light possible, given each browser's limitations.

Extending the Experience

JavaScript allows you to perform some dynamic page modifications that previously would have required programming CGI scripts in conventional programming or scripting languages outside the Netscape browser.

For example, you can easily add a button or link text to a Web page that would allow the user to ask your page to show its type in larger or smaller characters. You do not need to pre-tag the page appropriately or build multiple pages with the same content, in different font sizes. I'll show you how to easily change type in Chapter 9.

Validating Input

If you used forms in a pre-Netscape 2.0 experience, you probably wished for an easy way to ensure that the data the user gave you was appropriate. For example, you ask the users to enter a number between 1 and 10 to indicate how strongly they feel about some subject. Instead, they type "Very Strong" or "Nine" or even a number larger than ten. If you're passing the gathered data to a database program, it is going to be somewhat unforgiving of such data mistakes.

With JavaScripts, you can easily validate data, not only as to its type but even its range in the case of numeric values. You can help the user complete the information correctly and catch potentially serious data errors before they ever get in your database's way.

Adding JavaScripts to Your Pages

OK, enough background. Let's get our hands dirty on some JavaScript. In this section, I'll show you:

- the general mechanism for adding JavaScripts to your Web pages
- how to ensure that browsers that don't "grok" JavaScript won't choke on your scripts' presence
- the various ways in which a JavaScript can be triggered

We enclose JavaScripts within two new HTML tags: <SCRIPT> and </SCRIPT>. Everything that appears between these two tags defines some JavaScript code that will execute at an appropriate time.

The <SCRIPT> tag has an optional attribute called LANGUAGE where you can define the scripting language you are using. We are using only JavaScript, which is the default value for this attribute, so we can safely ignore its existence.

You can put JavaScripts anywhere in your Web documents. As we'll see shortly, you can apply some guidelines to help you decide the most effective place for them.

Here is the modern-day equivalent of the traditional C "hello, world" program, done in JavaScript:

```
<HTML>
<HEAD>
<TITLE>A Silly Page</TITLE>
</HEAD>
<BODY>
This is the default page for my local server.<P>
<SCRIPT>
document.write ("This is a JavaScript talking to you!")
</SCRIPT>
</BODY>
</HTML>
```

When the user opens this document, the window will look like Figure 6.1. The JavaScript contained between the <SCRIPT> and </SCRIPT> tags executes

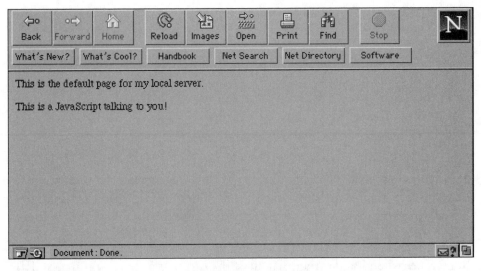

Figure 6.1   Let's say "Hello" with the simplest JavaScript execution.

immediately when it is encountered in this case. (I'll explain later how you can change this basic behavior.) As a result, the reader sees both lines in the browser window.

If you open the same document in a browser that does not understand the <SCRIPT> tag, in theory, nothing bad should happen. I say "in theory" because bad things sometimes do happen when you present Web browsers with content they don't understand. For example, opening this simple page in a script-un-aware browser might result in a display like that shown in Figure 6.2. The scripting line itself displays as if it were simply part of the document's content. This result is clearly not what we intended.

Hiding Scripts

The specifications for the HTML standard dictate that a browser should simply ignore tags it doesn't understand. Not all browsers follow this rule. To hide a JavaScript from a browser that otherwise might display a result like the one in Figure 6.2, we can use comments. The following example is the same as the previous HTML markup, except for the addition of comments:

```
<HTML>
<HEAD>
<TITLE>A Silly Page</TITLE>
</HEAD>
<BODY>
```

```
This is the default page for my local server.<P>
<SCRIPT>

<!--
document.write ("This is a JavaScript talking to you!")

//-->
</SCRIPT>
</BODY>
</HTML>
```

This syntax is probably familiar territory to you, but one new wrinkle was added that you may not immediately understand. The standard comment symbols in HTML markup are <!-- and -->. So why did I use the double slashes before the comment closure?

Remember when I said earlier that all of the text that appears within a SCRIPT container is being interpreted as JavaScript code? If you leave out the double slashes, the JavaScript interpreter built into Netscape will try to interpret the -->" symbol as a language command. This process will fail. When that happens, an error message like the one shown in Figure 6.3 displays.

We use the double slash to indicate a comment within JavaScript. When the JavaScript interpreter encounters this symbol, it stops looking at the contents of the line and moves on to the next line.

You might be tempted by this comment-within-a-comment observation to try to put the HTML comment markers outside the <SCRIPT> container tags, thus avoiding the problem. Don't do it! Even a JavaScript-aware browser will skip over the JavaScript, because when it sees the start of a comment, it ignores everything until it sees an end of comment symbol.

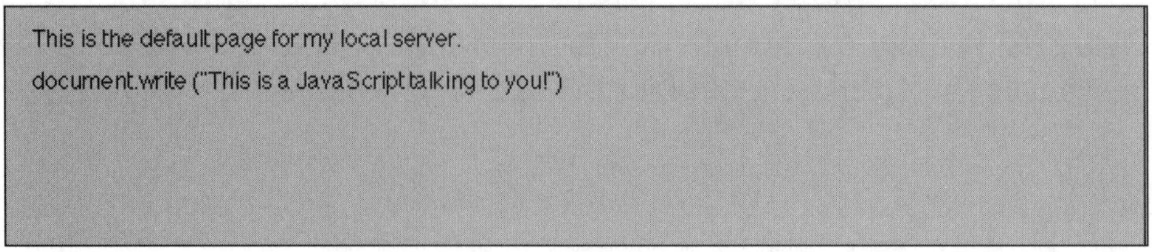

This is the default page for my local server.

document.write ("This is a JavaScript talking to you!")

Figure 6.2   A script-unaware browser may view JavaScript incorrectly.

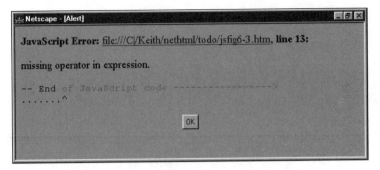

Figure 6.3   An error dialog can result from using incorrect syntax.

When JavaScripts Execute

Now that we know how to define JavaScripts in our Web pages, we need to understand what causes them to execute. Do they all run as soon as the browser encounters them? Or is there some way we can control when they are carried out?

The answer to these questions is yes. Or, maybe I should say, it all depends.

The two types of JavaScripts are scripts and functions. So far, we've looked only at scripts. Scripts execute as the browser encounters them during the process of loading the page and interpreting the HTML codes. Functions execute only when a script asks them, or when an event triggers them. (I'll have more to say about events shortly.)

You can easily tell a function from a script because a function begins with the word "function." Once defined, a function just hangs around waiting for its name to be called by an event, a script, or another function. Only then does it spring into action.

As a rule, you will define functions in the <HEAD> portion of your document. This practice ensures that they are always available to be called from any script or event on the page, because the head must load before the <BODY> content by design. It is not mandatory that you define functions in the head of a document. It is, however, mandatory that you not attempt to call a function before it has been defined; doing so will produce errors.

A function will almost always appear on a given page at least twice: Once when it is defined with the word "function," and at least one other time when its name is used to call it into action. Functions often are called more than once in a given document.

Defining and Calling Functions

Let's look at a couple of examples of functions. First, we'll work on a mathematical function. Here is the HTML for a page that will define a function called "square" and then invoke that function when the user opens the page. I've hard-coded the call to the function so that it produces the square of the number 5. Later, we'll see how we can enable the user to enter the number to be squared.

```
<HTML>
<HEAD><TITLE>Square Tester</TITLE>
<SCRIPT>
<!--
    function square (i)
    {
        return ("The number " + i + "  squared is " + i*i)
    }
//-->
</SCRIPT>
</HEAD>
<BODY>
<SCRIPT>
document.write (square (5) + "<P>" )
</SCRIPT>
Done!
</BODY>
</HTML>
```

When the Netscape browser displays this page, it will look like Figure 6.4.

Notice that the function "square" appears in two places in this HTML. The first time, it is in the HEAD portion of the document. Here, it is preceded by the word "function." This occurrence is called the function's "declaration." In other words, we are not yet causing the function to do anything; we are simply notifying the browser that later we may want to call a function called "square."

The second time the function's name appears, it is in a different SCRIPT block. Here, it is the argument to a "write" function (one of Netscape's built-in functions, about which we will have more to say in Chapters 7 and 8). Briefly, this script line tells the browser to:

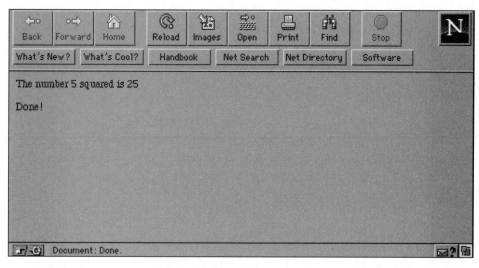

Figure 6.4   This window shows the square function after execution.

- Calculate the square of 5 using the function we just declared
- Add a "<P>" tag to the end of the result
- Write that content to the document

We finish by writing the word "Done!" to the window without using a JavaScript line. Remember, we are creating a standard HTML document here, so we can output any text (or embed images or whatever) simply by coding it as we would in any HTML page.

Calling Scripts Directly

The example we just saw uses the technique of calling a JavaScript by invoking it directly in the HTML document using a <SCRIPT> tag. The script has one statement. It uses the built-in `write` function associated with Netscape document objects (which will become much clearer in the next chapter).

Either the function itself or the call to the function must include one or more script statements that actually produce output. Otherwise, the result isn't very satisfying. For example, try changing the script call in the previous listing so that it calls the function but does not use the document.write function, like this:

```
square(5)
```

Now load the page again. You see the word "Done!" but no output from the function call. The function call itself simply returns a value. Because the script that calls the function doesn't tell it what to do with that result, it simply grabs it and holds onto it.

I originally coded the example so that the call to the function handled the output. If you were going to call the function from several places in the page, however, you might want to do something more efficient. You could change the square function so that it generates the appropriate output to the page, simplifying the function call itself, as shown here:

```
<HTML>
<HEAD><TITLE>Square Tester</TITLE></HEAD>
<SCRIPT>
<!--
    function square (i)
    {
      document.write("The number " + i + "  squared is " + i*i)
      document.write("<P>")
    }
    //-->
</SCRIPT>
<BODY>
<SCRIPT>
square (5)
</SCRIPT>
Done!
</BODY>
</HTML>
```

Now, if you wanted to print out the squares of the numbers from 5 to 10, you could do it more efficiently than you could have in the earlier example.

```
<HTML>
<HEAD><TITLE>Square Tester</TITLE></HEAD>
<SCRIPT>
<!--
    function square (i)
    {
     document.write("The number " + i + "  squared is " + i*i)
     document.write("<P>")
    }
    //-->
</SCRIPT>
<BODY>
```

```
<SCRIPT>
square (5)
square (6)
square (7)
square (8)
square (9)
square (10)
</SCRIPT>
Done!
</BODY>
</HTML>
```

Using Events to Call Scripts

The other way you can execute a JavaScript is to connect it to an event. User actions generally cause events.. Most often, the user clicks on a button in a form, clicks on some linked text, or perhaps chooses an item in a form. Some events are more like system events. For example, an event is generated when the user opens or closes a document.

You can easily create functions in the HEAD sections of a page that are invoked by an event. The definition of the function itself is the same as we just saw for functions called directly from within an HTML page.

One of the events you can use to trigger a JavaScript is called onLoad. This event is created each time the user's browser loads a document. Here is a variation of our number-squaring example that calls the script when the user loads the page:

```
<HTML>
<HEAD><TITLE>Square Tester</TITLE></HEAD>
<SCRIPT>
<!--
    function square (i)
    {
     document.write("The number " + i + "  squared is " + i*i)
     document.write("<P>")
    }
    //-->
</SCRIPT>
<BODY onLoad="square(9)">
</BODY>
</HTML>
```

Notice that the <BODY> tag includes a definition of what to do when the document loads (when the onLoad event is generated). The value assigned to the onLoad event must be enclosed in quotation marks. (This subject creates much consternation and not a few errors; we will have more to say about this requirement shortly). This argument need not be a call to a previously defined function; it can be a full script in its own right. If it is a full script, each line of the script must be separated from the others with a semicolon.

The same formatting holds true for multiple function calls being made in response to an event. (If you think about it, the two ideas—a multi-line stand-alone script and multiple calls to pre-defined functions—are almost identical. Thus, we can modify the above example so that we call the square function twice when the page loads:

```
<HTML>
<HEAD><TITLE>Square Tester</TITLE></HEAD>
<SCRIPT>
<!--
    function square (i)
    {
     document.write("The number " + i + "  squared is " + i*i)
     document.write("<P>")
    }
    //-->
</SCRIPT>
<BODY onLoad="square(9); square(11)">
</BODY>
</HTML>
```

You may, but are not required to, end the argument to the onLoad event with another semicolon. Figure 6.5 shows the result of loading a page with the HTML shown above.

So far our scripts have been one-sided events with the page loading and carrying out functions without our help or input. Using the **onClick** event, we can get more interactive with these scripts.

You can use linked text to manage a user's mouse clicks. With Netscape 2.0, you can include in an anchor hypertext reference (or "href") an event handler similar to the one we saw earlier for the onLoad event. The general format for this addition looks like this:

```
<A HREF=" "  onClick="doSomething()">TEXT TO CLICK</A>
```

The anchor argument is usually blank, because you want to carry out some function when the user clicks this text, as opposed to opening a URL, but you

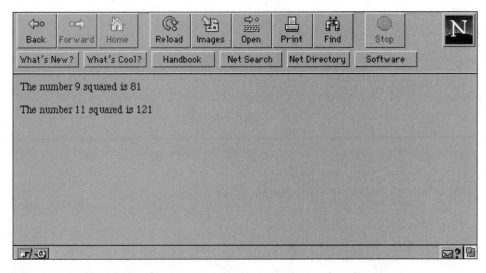

Figure 6.5 The square function is called twice in an onLoad event.

can certainly do both if it makes sense.

Now, let's make things a little more interesting with our square function. Look at the following HTML page design:

```
<HTML>
<HEAD><TITLE>Square Tester</TITLE></HEAD>
<SCRIPT>
<!--
    function square (i)
    {
     newWindow = window.open ("", "n")
     newWindow.document.write("The number " + i + "  squared is " + i*i)
     newWindow.document.write("<P>")
    }
    //-->
</SCRIPT>
<BODY>
Click on the number whose square you want to calculate:<P>
<UL>
<H2>
<LI><a href="" onClick="square(5)">5</A>
<LI><a href="" onClick="square(6)">6</A>
<LI><a href="" onClick="square(7)">7</A>
</H2>
</BODY>
</HTML>
```

The first change you notice is that the square function definition opens a new window before it displays the square of the requested number. This order is necessary because you can't modify the contents of an HTML document once it's opened. (Actually, that's something of an oversimplification. You can change the contents of the page after it's open but only with fairly sophisticated means that go beyond what JavaScript supports or what normal HTML allows.) If you tried this same approach without modifying the function to open a new window, you'd probably get a system crash as the script tried to update its own window. We can achieve some very interesting results with the combination of JavaScript and frames, as we'll see in Chapter 9.

The second change is that each of the text items in the unordered list is now a link with no HREF but with an **onClick** behavior. In each case, we just call the square function and pass it the value requested by the user.

Now we're starting to get a little more interactive! Using events, particularly events like **onClick** that are caused by the user taking some deliberate action to trigger a response, lends an air of real-time interaction to your Web pages. This interaction was difficult to obtain before JavaScript. As you'll see in the next several chapters, you can do a great deal with the combination of JavaScript and events.

Rules of the JavaScript Road

Because JavaScript is a scripting language, it has a certain number of rules that define its syntax and usage. I'll explain the most common ones in this section; others will pop up from time to time as we further explore the language in the next few chapters.

JavaScript is case-sensitive. Statements are separated from one another using the semicolon. Blocks of statements are grouped using curly braces to begin ({) and end (}) them. White space is ignored.

JavaScript has two types of comments:

⚜ Single-line comments begin with a double-slash (//). The slashes can be the first characters on a line or can appear anywhere within a line. The JavaScript interpreter ignores everything following a // until it reaches the end of the line.

◎ Multi-line comments begin with a slash-asterisk combination (/*) and continue until the interpreter encounters the ending asterisk-slash combination (*/). The interpreter ignores all text between these two delimiters.

Many scripting errors, particularly while you are learning the language, arise from the improper use of quotation marks. The rules aren't so complicated, but applying them takes care. Here are the basic rules to keep in mind:

◎ Values assigned to event names must always be enclosed in double quotation marks.

◎ You must alternate double and single quotation marks.

◎ Quotation marks must occur in pairs.

When you need to assemble strings to pass as arguments or parameters, and some elements of the string are variables, use the "+" operator to concatenate items. Here, keeping track of the quotation mark situation is vital.

JavaScript uses "dot notation" to separate objects and identifiers from properties and function names. For example, a window called testWindow automatically has a document associated with it. This document is referred to in your JavaScript as "testWindow.document." If you want to do something to this document (for example, write some information into it), you add another dot and the name of the method or function to execute, along with any required parameters. Here's an example:

```
testWindow.document.write("Hello, world!")
```

The equal sign operator (=) is used to assign values to variables and properties. For example, documents have a background color property named bgColor. You could assign the special color value "chocolate" (which is actually a defined name in the new color values associated with Netscape 2.0) with a statement like this:

```
document.bgColor="chocolate"
```

The JavaScript Object Model VII

The central idea in JavaScript is that you work with objects. Your scripting work will focus almost entirely on altering the characteristics of objects and executing functions that perform various operations on and with objects. The aggregation of objects, characteristics (which are formally called properties), and functions (also referred to as methods) that make up the Netscape universe comprises the JavaScript Object Model.

In this chapter, I will explain the JavaScript object model, first in the general, or abstract, sense, and then in specific detail. I will describe each object in the JavaScript Object Model, define its properties and how to work with them, and explain its built-in functions, or methods, and what they do. Along the way, I'll offer lots of sample HTML pages, which, as usual, are stored on the CD-ROM accompanying this book.

First, let's distinguish between the objects in Netscape that we work with using JavaScript and the broader world of objects you may have heard about in the context of object-oriented programming (OOP). While OOP is all the rage in business programming these days (and with good reason), JavaScript is not an example of OOP. JavaScript is, rather, object-like, or object-based. You work with objects, but your involvement with and control over them is minimal compared to the interaction between an OOP programmer and the objects in languages such as Java, C++, and Smalltalk.

I like to explain the difference between OOP and object-based programming or scripting using a manufacturing model. As a scripter, you are like a computer manufacturer who buys printed circuit boards, power supplies, fans, disk drives, keyboards, monitors, and chassis from other manufacturers and "snaps" them together into computers that your customers order. A customer decides which CPU to buy, how much memory to put in, how big a monitor to get, and other similar options. Selecting from a group of component parts, you assemble the computer. To the user, you are the manufacturer.

You might not even think of yourself as a manufacturer, though. When you visualize a manufacturer, you might think of someone with a big factory where they create integrated circuits, printed circuit boards, power supplies, monitors, and all the other pieces you need. These people have tons of money invested in tooling equipment, people, quality assurance teams, packaging, inventory, warehousing, and a bunch of other stuff you don't even want to know about. These people are the equivalent of Java programmers. They make the components that you assemble into a finished product.

Like all analogies, this one will break if you stretch it far enough. But you get the idea. As a JavaScripter, you are going to be able to deal with Netscape Navigator activities at a pretty high level, but you can't avoid learning some technical-sounding material to be really good at scripting.

For the rest of this book, every time I make a statement about objects and their usage, you should automatically read the phrase "from your viewpoint as a scripter" because that's the only viewpoint I'll be discussing. The only exception to this comes in Chapter 10 where I take a quick peek under the hood of Java.

The World of Objects

Objects are an inherent part of how Netscape Navigator is designed. You may consciously create objects in your scripts, but even if you don't, objects are everywhere in the Netscape world.

The simple act of loading a page in Netscape Navigator, for example, creates the following objects, at a minimum:

- at least one window object (more than one if the window contains frames, which you can think of as "child" windows for object purposes)
- a location object (the current URL)
- a history object (previously visited URLs)
- at least one document object (one per window or frame)

When the window contains a document that has a JavaScript in it and that script creates objects, then those objects are also instantly created when the page loads.

Objects are fairly dull by themselves. What makes them interesting is their characteristics. Every object is associated with properties; many objects also have functions, or methods. Properties describe what an object looks like or what it contains. Functions, or methods, describe what an object can do.

Most of this chapter is a description of the built-in objects defined by Netscape Navigator and accessible from JavaScript. As I explain each object, I'll describe its properties and built-in methods, but you should keep in mind that the concepts of objects, properties, and methods are much broader than the built-in objects. When you create your own objects, you can give them properties and methods. Java applet objects that you include in your Web pages by calling them from JavaScript also have properties and methods. You will use these properties and methods in exactly the same way you use built-in objects.

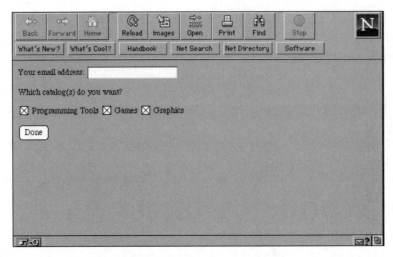

Figure 7.1   This sample page contains a simple form.

A Sample Page's Objects

Figure 7.1 shows a simple Web page viewed in a Netscape Navigator browser. As you can see, the page has a simple form consisting of a text box for the user's email address, three checkboxes to choose various types of catalogs, and a push-button to order the catalogs.

Here is the HTML that created the page in Figure 7.1:

```
<HTML>
<HEAD><TITLE>Simple Sample</TITLE></HEAD>
<BODY>
<FORM NAME="subscribeForm" ACTION="UpdateSubs()" METHOD="GET">
Your email address: <INPUT TYPE=text NAME="reader">
<P>
Which catalog(s) do you want?<P>
<INPUT TYPE="checkbox" NAME="catalog" VALUE="progTools" CHECKED>Programming
Tools
<INPUT TYPE="checkbox" NAME="catalog" VALUE="Games" CHECKED>Games
<INPUT TYPE="checkbox" NAME="catalog" VALUE="Graphics" CHECKED>Graphics
<P>
<INPUT TYPE= "button" NAME="button1" VALUE="Done"
onClick="UpdateSubs(this.form)">
</FORM>
</BODY>
</HTML>
```

When the user loads this form, a relatively large number of objects come into being, including a window, location, history, and document object. These objects might have properties such as the following:

- ◎ location.href = "http://www.widgetland.com/orders/catalogs.html"
- ◎ document.title = "Simple Sample"
- ◎ document.fgColor = #000000
- ◎ history.length = 2

Netscape Navigator would also create the following objects based on the contents of the page:

- ◎ document.subscribeForm
- ◎ document.subscribeForm.catalog
- ◎ document.subscribeForm.button1

These objects in turn would have properties such as:

- ◎ document.subscribeForm.action = "http://www.widgetland.com/cgi/ UpdateSubs()"
- ◎ document.subscribeForm.method = GET
- ◎ document.subscribeForm.catalog = "(progTools, Games, Graphics)"

The complete list of objects and properties that would be created even by this relatively simple page is substantial (far more than I am willing to bore you with here!). Generally, you'll find yourself working with a fairly small subset of all the objects and properties available on a given page.

THE OBJECT HIERARCHY

When I described some of the objects and properties in the previous section, I used the dot notation I described earlier. The first object listed in most cases was the document; that's because most of the properties you want to work with are related to the document or to things the document contains, such as text or form items.

Some of the object and property names have two or three elements connected by dots. (And you thought you had outgrown connect-the-dots!) You might be curious about the rules for composing object names. This task turns out to be simple and straightforward. Objects are arranged in a hierarchy that corresponds to the hierarchy of the HTML page itself. The window contains the document, which in turn contains the form, which in turn contains a button, for example.

To name an object, then, you start with its top-level "ancestor" or container and then name each of the relevant objects in turn, separating each item with a dot. The exception to this rule is that in the case of a single-frame window, JavaScript doesn't require you to use the window as the first object, even though it is technically part of the structure.

Figure 7.2 depicts the hierarchy of built-in Netscape objects.

The Navigator Object

The remainder of this chapter describes each object in the Netscape Navigator, beginning in this section with the Navigator itself. In each section, we'll discuss a specific object (or in some cases a group of very closely related objects). The discussions all follow a pattern:

- overview of the object and its role in the Navigator world
- description of each of its properties

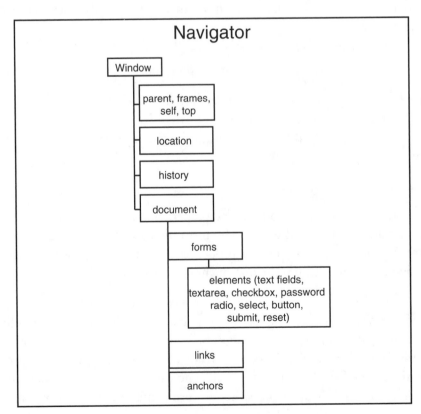

Figure 7.2   The Netscape Navigator uses an object hierarchy.

@ description of each of its methods

@ notes and comments

Not all objects will include all of these topics; some objects don't have methods, for example, and many will not require additional notes and comments. I am not including event handlers as part of the object descriptions because events seem to me to be separate from properties and methods. I will talk about events and their management in Chapter 8.

The Navigator object is a little on the boring side. It will become more useful in the future when other browsers support JavaScript and its Object Model. For now it can only tell us things we could easily deduce without its help: the name, version, and code name of the browser application.

NAVIGATOR PROPERTIES

The Navigator object has four properties:

@ appName, which stores the name of the Navigator application (which returns "Netscape" predictably)

@ appVersion, which stores the version of Netscape Navigator being used (in a string that looks like this: "2.0 (Macintosh; I; PPC)")

@ appCodeName, which stores the code name for the browser (in the case of Netscape Navigator, this is currently "Mozilla")

@ userAgent, which stores the code name and version of the user's browser (for example, "Mozilla/2.0 (Macintosh; I; PPC)")

If JavaScript is implemented by other browser publishers, the use of the Navigator object could become more interesting. For now, there is at least one potentially interesting use for the appVersion or userAgent property. You can use the built-in substring function to determine what type of computer the user is running and, based on that information, open different URLs. This might come in handy, for example, if you have a lot of sound files on your site and you want to take the user to a page where the sounds are available in a format supported by his or her system.

The Window Object

As you know, the window object is the top-level client-side object in the object hierarchy. The window is the base reference point for the document it contains, as well as for the URL, history of previously visited URLs, and a few other more or less interesting properties.

Because JavaScript can't exist outside a document and a document can't exist outside a window, the existence of the window is assumed. You can ignore the window itself in defining an object with the by-now-familiar dot notation. It is perfectly legal to use the window in the object's name, but experienced JavaScripters seldom use it. The lone exception to this rule arises when you have a window object whose name (for example, "status") could be misinterpreted to refer to a property of the current window. In that case, to make your code clearer and your intent precise, you may wish to include the window in your object reference.

Window Properties

Windows define seven properties, two of which serve identical (and not very useful) purposes. These seven properties are:

◉ defaultStatus, which contains the string that will be displayed in the window's status area if nothing requires it to be replaced. When the user positions the cursor over a link object, for example, the Navigator's behavior dictates that the link be displayed in the status window. If you have set the defaultStatus property, the contents of that property are replaced as long as this link is required to be displayed. The default status string returns when the user moves the cursor to a place where no status display is required by the browser's design

◉ frames, which contains an array of descriptive items, one for each frame defined in a window (we discuss arrays in JavaScript later in this chapter)

◉ parent, which contains an identifier for the window's parent, a value that is useful only in the case of frames, where the window defined in the FRAMESET tag is the parent of all of the FRAMEs defined within that FRAMESET

◉ status, which contains the string currently displayed in the window's status area

◉ top, which contains an identifier for the topmost window in the current parental hierarchy. The window identified in top is its own parent. If you've only opened one window, it is the top window.

◉ self and window, which simply refer to the current window and are useful only for clarity of code or for resolving ambiguous references

The frames property is unusual in that, rather than having a single value like the other properties in this list, it potentially has more than one value. After all, as we saw in Chapter 5, a window can have multiple frames. If it does contain multiple frames, this property has one entry for each frame. A JavaScript array (which we'll look at in greater depth in Chapter 8) is an ordered collection of information or properties concerning an object. The frames property of a window contains one entry for each frame defined in the window with a <FRAMESET> tag as described in Chapter 5. Information about the first frame defined in a window is stored in the property frames[0] because the first element of all arrays always bears the number zero. The second frame's information is in the window's frames[1] property, and so forth. The specific contents of an array are defined by the properties of the object involved. Later in this chapter, we'll look at frames (which are very much like windows) and you'll see what information each entry in the frames property stores.

Window Methods

Window objects implement seven methods. Three of them deal with displaying dialog boxes to permit some interaction with the user, two of them deal with creating and closing windows, and two deal with controlling the timing of actions.

Dialog Box Methods

The window object defines three methods that result in dialog boxes being displayed to the user. These methods differ in terms of the input the user can provide to each.

The alert method is the least interactive. It requires a string argument that tells the window what message to display in the dialog. It then displays that string and a single OK button, as shown in Figure 7.3. As you can probably tell from its name and this description, the purpose of this dialog is simply to alert the user that something has happened or is about to happen. The user doesn't have a choice in the matter.

Figure 7.3   An alert dialog tells the user that something happened.

If you want to give users a chance to change their minds about what is about to happen, use a confirm method. This method, like the alert method, requires a string argument that is the message to be displayed to the user. But the dialog displays two buttons: OK and Cancel (see Figure 7.4). You can determine in your script whether or not the user clicks "OK", and take appropriate action depending on the user's response.

The last of the three dialog box methods defined in a Navigator window is called prompt. This dialog, shown in Figure 7.5, asks the user to enter a piece of information. It requires a string that is the prompt to pose to the user. You will almost always wish to supply a second argument containing the default response to be used if the user simply clicks the "OK" button. If you don't supply this second argument, JavaScript supplies a default response (the string <undefined>), which is almost never what you want.

The two arguments that create a prompt dialog should be enclosed in quotation marks and separated by commas. The quotation marks are unnecessary if a numeric response is supplied as the default answer.

Methods to Create and Close Windows

You create a new window with the open method. You close a window with the close method.

Figure 7.4   A confirm dialog allows the user to respond.

Figure 7.5   A prompt dialog allows the user to enter some information.

The open method works with no arguments, but it doesn't do anything very interesting until you give it at least one argument. The three optional arguments you can pass to the method are, in this order:

@ the URL of the content you wish the window to display
@ the name by which you wish to refer to the window later
@ a list of options that define the window's appearance

All of these arguments are strings, which means they must be enclosed in quotation marks.

The URL is self-explanatory. You supply the name of a file or the full URL of an HTML document stored elsewhere, and the window searches for that URL as it opens.

The second argument is useful only in an event handler, which we'll discuss in Chapter 8. When you are defining a new window in a script, you can leave this blank. You'll have to assign the new window a name with the = operator in any case.

Ignoring for the moment the third argument, this is a simple window-creating statement in a JavaScript:

```
newWindow = open ("http://www.mySite.com/index.html")
```

The window is created and open, then the Navigator tries to find the URL. If it can't find it, or if something goes wrong, the window remains open on the user's screen.

Notice that I didn't supply the second argument, naming the window. You can refer to the window by the name it is assigned as a result of its creation, in this case, newWindow.

The third argument is a comma-separated list of names of window options. These options determine how a window will look on the user's screen; their names are reserved words in JavaScript. They must be supplied exactly as listed here:

@ toolbar (determines whether the standard Navigator toolbar, containing
@ buttons such as "Back" and "Reload," is included in the window)
@ location (determines whether a Location entry field is included)
   directories (determines whether to display the standard Navigator "What's New?", "What's Cool?" and other buttons below the Location field)

- status (determines whether to include a status area at the bottom of the window)
- menubar (determines whether to show or hide the system menubar)
- scrollbars (determines whether to add horizontal and vertical scrollbars if the document's size exceeds the current boundaries of the window)
- resizable (determines whether the resize box in the lower right corner of the window will be displayed and whether the window is otherwise resizable)
- copyhistory (determines whether the newly created window should carry forward the URL history of the window containing the JavaScript from which it is generated)
- width (specifies the width of the window, in pixels)
- height (specifies the height of the window, in pixels)

All but the last two are "Boolean" values; they are either true or false. The interaction among these elements is critical.

If you omit the list entirely, all of the Boolean values are true, so the window appears in the usual way. The width and height are system-dependent. For instance, the user may have opened the window previously in a particular size and location, and Netscape may remember that information.

If you wish to eliminate any of the items from being included in the window, you must do two things: Turn off the ones you wish omitted and specifically name the ones you wish included. Otherwise, excluding even one of the options and failing to mention the others results in none of the options being true. (I find this strange, but it is how the current release works.)

To specify any changes in the default set of window options, you must supply a string enclosed in quotation marks, with items separated by commas and no spaces. (This last point is important.) To include an item, all you need to do is supply its name. To exclude an item, type the item's name, followed by an equal sign and the word "no". Here's an example that will result in the top of the window showing the toolbar and location box, but not the directory buttons:

```
window.open("","","directories=no,toolbar,location")
```

If you have the following line in an HTML document, none of the top portions of the window—directories, location, or toolbar—will display:

```
window.open("","","directories=no")
```

The menubar option is meaningful only on platforms other than the Macintosh; the Navigator has no in-window menubar on the Macintosh.

You can close only the current window. The simple command close() will accomplish this, but for clarity you may wish to use one of the alternative forms:

```
window.close()
self.close()
```

CONTROLLING TIMING OF ACTIONS

The last two window-related methods we'll look at deal with controlling the timing of actions that take place in a window. The first method sets up a timed event; the second clears the timer.

Timed events are delayed, but not repeated. If you set up a timer so that something happens after five seconds, for example, the event takes place five seconds after the script executes, but it executes only one time. (We'll talk in Chapter 8 about how to cause scripts or portions of scripts to execute more than once.)

The window method that sets up a timer for an event is called setTimeout. Its syntax looks like this:

```
timerID = setTimeout("action to take", delay)
```

The result of setting the timer, which in this case is assigned to the variable timerID, is useful later if and when you wish to clear the timer. This action is useful only if you want to clear the event before it is triggered; once it has executed, clearing the timer has no effect.

The first argument to the setTimeout method is a string enclosed in quotation marks that defines the action to be taken when the timer expires. The delay is a number that defines the number of milliseconds that should elapse before the action is taken. A millisecond is 1/1000 of a second, which is almost always far too fine a precision for mere mortals like us. Just remember that if you want to delay for a certain number of seconds, put three zeros after the number of seconds and that's the value you need in the delay setting.

Here's an example of the use of the setTimeout method. We're giving the user five seconds after pressing the "submit" button on a form to change his or her mind and cancel the submission. (Note that the function called holdForCancel must have been defined in the <HEAD> portion of this document for it to be called here. I'm not showing that function because my purpose here is to explain the use of the setTimeout method.)

```
<BODY>
<FORM>
After you click on the "Submit" button, you'll have five
seconds to change your mind by clicking the "Stop" button.<P>
<INPUT TYPE="submit" VALUE="Send Form"
   onClick="timerID=setTimeout('holdForCancel ()',5000)">
<INPUT TYPE="button" VALUE="Stop!"
   onClick="clearTimeout(timerID)">
</FORM>
</BODY>
```

As you can see from the above example, the "Stop" button has an event called "clearTimeout" associated with it. This is the second of the two window methods we're talking about in this section. It takes a single argument, which is the result of a previously called setTimeout method. Here, we assigned the result of the setTimeout method to the name timerID, then used this name as the argument to the clearTimeout method. After five seconds, this button has no effect because the holdForCancel function will have been executed and, presumably, the form will have been submitted.

(We've had to get a little ahead of ourselves in this example to show the meaning of the two methods. The onClick syntax for the two buttons in the form in this example are event handlers. We'll cover events in the JavaScript world in Chapter 8 and their use here will become clear. For now, you can just understand that these script components define what happens when a certain event, in this case, clicking with the mouse, happens to a certain object, in this case, one of two buttons. They are actually only slightly more complicated than that.)

The Document Object

The document object is easily the most often used and most powerful object in the JavaScript object model. It contains all information about the current document.

A document object has 13 properties and defines five methods. It is also the repository for the definition of two event handlers that are technically part of the window object. We'll get into that subject in Chapter 8.

As you'd undoubtedly expect, you define a new document object with a <BODY> tag. Everything that appears between that tag and the </BODY> tag constitutes the document, as far as JavaScript is concerned.

Document Properties

The 13 properties associated with a document object can be divided into three broad categories:

@ color-related properties
@ descriptive properties
@ content properties

We'll look at these three types of properties in turn.

All document properties can be accessed by placing the word document, followed by a dot, before the name of the property. It is not necessary, but also not incorrect, to include the "window" specifier and another dot before the word "document". But, unlike window properties, you must include the word "document".

COLOR-RELATED DOCUMENT PROPERTIES

When you work with a document in a <BODY> tag, you can define five types of colors. Each of these colors corresponds to a property you can access in JavaScript. Here are the five color-related properties of a document:

@ alinkColor (contains the color used in links that have been activated by the user)
@ linkColor (contains the color used in links that have not been activated by the user)
@ vlinkColor (contains the color used in links that have been followed by the user)
@ bgColor (contains the color used as the background for the document's display)
@ fgColor (contains the color used as the default text color, as well as for other non-graphical objects such as horizontal rules, displayed on the page)

The difference between an activated link and a followed link may not be evident. The user can activate a link without following it by, for example, copying it to a clipboard or adding it to the navigator's bookmarks. A followed link is one that has been activated and navigated to, or from which a file transfer has occurred.

All of these properties have the same kind of value associated with them: a color. Colors in JavaScript come in two flavors (if you'll pardon a very bad mixed metaphor):

- an RGB triplet (which has the format "#rrggbb" where rr, gg, and bb, are two-digit hexadecimal values that tell the computer display how much red, green, and blue, respectively, to include in making up a color)
- a string literal describing the color based on the newly defined color names in Navigator 2.0

The string literal is much easier to use. For example, typing the color name "antiquewhite" is easier on the brain than typing "#FAEBD7". The problem is that no other browser understands Netscape's color name mapping (at least not yet), so for now you're better off staying with the RGB triplet.

DESCRIPTIVE DOCUMENT PROPERTIES

Four of the properties associated with a document describe the document as a whole. They are:

- lastModified (containing the date the document was last changed)
- location (containing the document's URL)
- referrer (containing the link from which this document's URL was accessed)
- title (containing the contents of the <TITLE> </TITLE> tag in the docu-
- ment window's definition)

All of these properties have strings as values.

CONTENT DOCUMENT PROPERTIES

The remaining four document properties relate to the contents of the document rather than to the document taken as a whole. These properties are:

- anchors (containing an array of objects describing all the named anchors in the document, in the order in which they appear in the source document)
- cookie (containing some advanced, embeddable information that is beyond the scope of this book)

@ forms (containing an array of objects describing all the <FORM> definitions in the document, in the order in which they appear in the source document)

@ links (containing an array of objects describing all the links in the document, in the order in which they appear in the source document)

Document Methods

Document objects define five methods. All are involved with modifying the content of the document itself. These five methods are:

@ open
@ close
@ clear
@ write
@ writeln (pronounced "write line")

Before you can understand the meaning of the open and close methods, you need a little background in dynamic document creation. When you are creating a document in JavaScript (or by any means other than simply opening a URL and displaying its HTML), you are working with what computer professionals call a "stream." That concept threw me for a loop when I was learning programming, but it's really simple. A stream is just a bunch of information traveling serially from one place (your script in this case) to another place (the page where the content will be displayed).

When you open and close a document, then, you are really opening and closing this stream. If you aren't doing any dynamic document modification or creation, you don't need these methods. Simply opening a window with the appropriate URL opens and displays the document and closes the stream displaying the document, all transparently to you.

In fact, you generally don't have to open a document explicitly if you open a window with no URL. You might want to get into the habit of doing this anyway, but it isn't essential.

You must, however, call the document.close() method when you finish writing your output to a dynamic HTML document. If you don't, the information you think you are writing to the document will never be displayed. (This one drove me nuts when I was learning JavaScript before any real documentation was available.) Some actions, such as any font-change tags, <P> and <BR> tags, effectively also perform a document.close() for you, but I always explicitly close a document when I finish adding content to it in a JavaScript.

You can completely empty the content of a document with the document.clear () method. Whether the document contains only HTML loaded from a URL, dynamically generated content, or a mixture of both, this method erases everything.

Adding information to a document in JavaScript requires you to use either the document.write() method or the document.writeln() method. They are exactly equivalent, at least for now; the latter is designed to add a carriage return at the end of the line it writes. Because this white space is ignored by the Navigator, the effect of using either of these methods is the same at the moment. As a result, I save my fingers a little typing and always use document.write().

The argument to a write method is a string that contains the information to be written to the window. Any valid HTML, as well as display text, links, anchors, GIF references, and any other element that can be placed on a Web page can be added with this approach. Since white space isn't important, you can gather the strings in almost any arbitrary way.

There is one major exception to what you can write to a document: You cannot add a script to the document using a JavaScript. Remember that JavaScripts are executed as they are encountered in the window's contents. Because the window is already open when you write to the document, the script would be ignored even if you could add it, which you cannot.

You've seen lots of examples of the use of the write method in this chapter, so I won't bore you with more simplicity here. We'll work with this method more than any other, and it will quickly become second nature.

The Form Object

The form object is always contained within a document object. As you saw in the previous section, a document object has a property called forms, which contains an array of information describing each form in the document. The form objects in this array are arranged in the order in which the forms are defined in the document.

A form, of course, is defined by a <FORM> tag terminated by a </FORM> tag. A document may contain a theoretically unlimited number of forms, consistent with things like memory limitations.

Forms allow your Web pages to interact, on at least a limited basis, with your users. Users can enter and edit text, and make choices from such input devices as checkboxes, radio buttons, and popup menus. Forms typically have one or two push buttons associated with them. Users click to submit the contents of the form to your server or to cancel the contents of a form and start over.

When you want to refer to a form's properties or initiate a form action, you do so by referring to the form as:

```
document.formName.property
```

or

```
document.forms[n].property
```

where "n" is a number reflecting the order in which the form appears in the document, with the first form being identified as forms[0].

Form Properties

Forms have five properties.

- ◎ action (containing a string that specifies the URL of the server to which the form's contents are to be sent when the user submits the form)
- ◎ elements (containing an array of objects that represent the form elements, such as radio, button, checkbox, and text objects, arranged in the order in which the elements appear in the form; later we'll discuss the properties that define each form element)
- ◎ encoding (containing a string that defines the MIME type used to encode the form)
- ◎ method (containing either "post" or "get," which defines the method by which form input information will be sent to the server)
- ◎ target (containing the name of the window to which form contents will be sent for display after the server has received the information)

These properties are self-explanatory with the possible exception of the encoding property. The MIME (Multipurpose Internet Mail Extension) type of an object determines how a browser will deal with its contents and, in some cases, how a server will handle it as well. The MIME standard concerns itself with the physical format of the data to which it relates. Most of the time in Web pages, we're dealing with the "text/html" MIME type. We don't need to specify it because by telling the world that we are an <HTML> document, MIME encoding is assumed.

There are times when we want to use some other encoding type. For example, you might be preparing data to be uploaded or downloaded as a binary file, or maybe you are putting data into a format to be used directly by a database. To encode a form's contents as other than text/html, you include the MIME parameter in the form's definition.

Form Methods

A form only defines one method: submit. This method has the same effect as clicking the generally present "Submit" button. It transmits the form's content to the server using the method and action defined for the form.

You could use this method, for example, to enable the user to click on some text that appears at the top of a form area (perhaps even outside the form itself; location is unimportant). This method permits the user to submit a form without scrolling to the bottom of the form where the "Submit' button traditionally is placed. You'd simply define an onClick behavior for the link object. (We'll get into event handlers and behaviors in the next chapter.) The code might look like this:

```
<A HREF="" onClick="document.forms[1].submit">Send the order</A>
```

Objects Contained in Forms

As you know if you've built many forms in HTML, you can put a variety of items within a form layout. Each of these items corresponds to an object in JavaScript. The items are:

- anchors
- buttons
- checkboxes
- hidden objects
- links
- password fields
- radio buttons
- reset button

- select lists (also known as popup menus)
- submit buttons
- text fields
- textarea fields

Because various combinations of these objects share properties and methods, I'm going to discuss them in groups in the following sections. I've divided them into three groups:

- those that deal with hypertext navigation
- those that contain or represent data
- those that cause some action to occur

Hypertext-Related Form Objects

The two hypertext-related form objects are anchors and links. You probably are familiar with them. An anchor is a named place in a document to which a user can

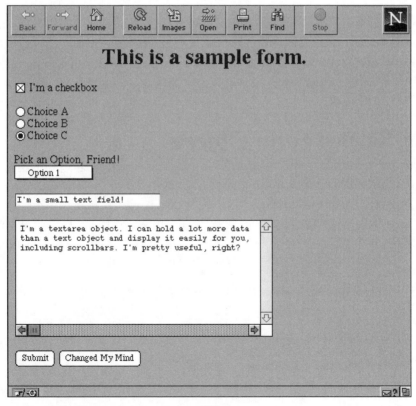

Figure 7.6   This form shows data-related objects.

be taken with a link that uses a pound sign ("#") preceding the anchor name. A link is a connection to a URL containing other hypertext or a file to transfer or some other information.

If, for example, you have a document in the current directory called recipes and it has an anchor called KillerChili, the anchor would look like this:

```
<A NAME="KillerChili">Steve's Killer Chili
```

and the link to it from within a different document would look like this:

```
Here's a great <A HREF="recipes#KillerChili">hot chili</A> recipe for you!
```

THE ANCHOR OBJECT

An anchor object has no properties and defines no methods.

THE LINK OBJECT

A link object has only one property and defines no methods.

The lone property of a link object is called target. It specifies the window into which the link is loaded when activated. This window can be an existing window other than the current window, or a frame in the current window. It can also use one of the "magic" frame names (_top, _parent, _self, or _blank) that we will discuss in greater detail in Chapter 8.

Data-Related Form Objects

The checkbox, hidden, radio, select, text, and textarea objects are all involved in or representing data in a form on an HTML page. All of these objects are displaying created with an HTML <INPUT> tag in which you can define the TYPE of object you wish to create. Figure 7.6 shows an HTML page with an example of each of these types of form objects, with the exception of the hidden object, which wouldn't be visible even if I *had* defined one.

Here is the HTML that created the form shown in Figure 7.6:

```
<HTML>
<HEAD><TITLE>Sample Form</TITLE></HEAD>
<BODY>
<H1 ALIGN=CENTER>This is a sample form.</H1>
<FORM ACTION="test1.acgi" METHOD="GET">
```

```
<INPUT TYPE="checkbox" NAME="cb1" CHECKED>I'm a checkbox<P>
<INPUT TYPE="radio" NAME="Radio Button 1" VALUE="A" >Choice A<BR>
<INPUT TYPE="radio" NAME="Radio Button 1" VALUE="B" >Choice B<BR>
<INPUT TYPE="radio" NAME="Radio Button 1" VALUE="C" CHECKED>Choice C<P>
Pick an Option, Friend!<BR>
<SELECT NAME="select1">
<OPTION> Option 1
<OPTION> Option 2
<OPTION> Option 3
</SELECT><P>
<INPUT TYPE="text" NAME="text1" SIZE=30 VALUE="I'm a small text field!"
><P>
<TEXTAREA NAME="text2" ROWS=10 COLS=50>I'm a textarea object. I can hold a
lot more data
than a text object and display it easily for you,
including scrollbars. I'm pretty useful, right?
</TEXTAREA><P>
<INPUT TYPE="submit" VALUE="Submit">
<INPUT TYPE="reset" VALUE="Changed My Mind"></FORM>
</BODY>
</HTML>
```

COMMON PROPERTIES

All six of the objects, with the exception of the select object, have both a name and a value property. The select object has a name property but no value property.

The name property refers to the object in JavaScripts. As a rule, you need not name objects to which you don't expect to refer in JavaScripts. Experienced programmers and scripters, however, have learned to err on the side of naming too many things to avoid trying to figure out later why you can't reference some object that you failed to name when you created it.

Depending on the specific type of object, the value property can mean slightly different things. In general, it contains what you'd expect to find if you wanted to determine what a particular form object contains or is trying to tell you.

For a checkbox, this property contains a string that describes the state of the checkbox: "on" if item is checked; "off" if it is not checked. The value property for a radio object is a string reflecting the VALUE attribute. This value will be assigned to the radio object when a given radio button is on. In the form example above, this would be "A", "B", or "C", depending on which of the three radio buttons the user selected.

For select objects, the value property describes the string that will be sent to the server as the value of the object when the "Submit" button is clicked. For text and textarea objects, this property contains the contents of the field. The value property for a hidden object is the contents of the VALUE parameter when the object was created. This string generally conveys some information about which the CGI program that processes the form is aware.

You can dynamically modify the contents of a text or textarea object, and they will be updated when you execute the change. None of the other form objects is dynamically modifiable, however.

Additional Checkbox Object Properties

In addition to the common name and value properties described in the previous section, checkbox objects have two other properties:

- ◉ checked (containing a Boolean value that indicates whether this button is presently checked)
- ◉ defaultChecked (containing a Boolean value that indicates whether this button is checked when it is displayed, before the user has clicked on it)

Additional Hidden Object Property

The hidden object has one property besides the two common properties, name and value. Its defaultValue property defines the value this object will have when it is first created. You can change the value of the object dynamically, but the next time the form is loaded, the hidden object takes on its defaultValue property's value.

Additional Radio Object Properties

Radio objects have four properties in addition to the two common properties described earlier. Two of these, checked and defaultChecked, have the same meaning as they have for Checkbox objects, described earlier in this section. The other two properties are:

- ◉ index (containing a number that indicates the ordinal position of the presently selected radio button in a given radio button set; the first button is 0)
- ◉ length (containing a number that indicates how many radio buttons are contained in the radio object)

Additional Select Object Properties

Select objects are the most complex form objects. As we learned earlier, they are the only data-related form objects that lack a value property. As it turns out, that's not completely true, but we'll deal with that problem in a moment. First, let's describe the three properties a select object has in addition to a name property:

- length (containing a number that indicates how many choices are in the list from which the user may select)
- options (containing an array of other objects that I'll explain in a moment)
- selectedIndex (containing a number that indicates the ordinal position of the currently selected item in the list; the first item is item 0)

As you have shrewdly deduced by now, the options property holds the key to the mystery of the misplaced value property. The options property of a select object contains an array for each choice in the object. Each of these entries in the array contains the following five properties:

- defaultSelected (containing a Boolean that indicates if this particular choice is selected by default when the select object is drawn on the screen)
- index (containing a number that indicates this particular choice's ordinal position on the list of choices; the first choice is index 0)
- selected (containing a Boolean that indicates if this particular choice is currently selected by the user)
- text (containing a string that is the contents of the choice as the user sees it on the screen)
- value (containing a string that is the information to be passed to the server when this particular choice is selected by the user clicking the "Submit" button)

Strictly speaking, then, the select object does not have a value property; rather, each of its choices has a value property.

ADDITIONAL TEXT, PASSWORD, AND TEXTAREA OBJECT PROPERTY

Text, password, and textarea objects have one additional shared property that is not common to the other data-related form objects. This property is called defaultValue. Like the other properties with this name, it contains a string that is the value this object holds and displays when it is drawn, until and unless it is explicitly modified.

CHECKBOX AND RADIO OBJECT METHOD

Checkbox and radio objects define a single method: click. This method behaves slightly differently for these two form objects because of the different nature of the objects.

If a checkbox object's click method is called, the checkbox state is toggled. If the checkbox was checked before the method was called, it will be unchecked after the method executes; if unchecked, it will be checked.

A radio button, however, can never be turned off by clicking on it. When a radio object receives a click method, the button is turned on; if it was already on, the method has no effect. If the radio object is one of several radio buttons in a set (as it generally should be, if user interface guidelines are followed), the button that is presently turned on in that set will be turned off.

TEXT, PASSWORD, AND TEXTAREA OBJECT METHODS

Text, password, and textarea objects share three methods in common. We expect to use these objects in a similar manner. The key difference lies in how much text you expect them to display (and, in the case of a password object, how user input is echoed back to the screen).

The three methods all have to do with the concept of the current state of a text, password, or textarea object.

Call the select method for a text or textarea object to highlight their entire contents.

If you want to make sure the user's next input (or your program's next output) is displayed in a particular text or textarea object, you must make sure that the proper object has the focus. To do this, you invoke that object's focus method.

The opposite of the focus method is called blur. You call this method to remove the focus from a particular object.

As a rule, the user's actions—clicking into and out of various form objects—determine the focus of a form. You can control the focus programmatically if you wish to do so. For example, perhaps by clicking on a particular button, the user has indicated a desire to enter a product code. You can ensure that the text object where you want the product code entered is where the user's typing will appear by sending that object a focus message.

If you are still alert after reading all these pages about the JavaScript object model, you noticed that the last sentence introduced the idea of sending an object a message. This is, for all practical purposes, the same as invoking or calling an object's method of the same name. The whole method-calling structure of an object-like language like JavaScript is based on one idea: A message with a certain name will cause a method of that same name to be invoked, if the object to which the message is sent has a method of the same name. This idea will become clearer in Chapter 8 when we talk about events and messages.

Action-Triggering Form Objects

There are three action-triggering form objects, all of them some form of a pushbutton. (A pushbutton is one that, when clicked or pushed, triggers an action and whose state generally changes momentarily while it is being clicked. This action distinguishes them from state buttons such as checkboxes and radio buttons, whose state changes permanently when clicked.)

JavaScript defines three types of pushbuttons:

- reset (which clears the values on a form and returns all form objects that have default values to those values)
- submit (which invokes the form's submit action when clicked)
- button (which provides a general-purpose way for you to connect JavaScript actions to pushbuttons you define on a form)

COMMON PROPERTIES

All three of these buttons have the same two properties that all but one of the data-related form objects shared: name and value. Their name property is used to refer to them in JavaScripts. For button, reset, and submit objects, the value property is the label that appears on the screen.

Common Method

Each of these buttons defines one method: click. When this method is called for a submit or reset button, that button's action is taken. This action is defined as part of the standard Netscape interface. The "Submit" button passes the data on the form to the server and invokes the CGI application defined in the FORM's definition. The "Reset" button resets the values of all form objects to their default values and empties all text and textarea objects that don't have default values.

On buttons you define, the click method invokes the script or action you define in the button's "onClick" handler. We'll look at this subject in depth in Chapter 8.

The String Object

The most widely used and versatile object in Netscape is the string object. It is one of three built-in, or native, object types. The others are Date and Math objects, which we will look at later in this chapter.

You can create string objects implicitly by enclosing a series of characters in double or single quotation marks, as in "Albert Schweitzer" or 'Albert Einstein'. (Of course, not all strings start with the word "Albert," although some of my favorites happen to do so.)

Most of the strings you create in an HTML page do not have names associated with them because you create them dynamically, or implicitly. But you can create a string explicitly and, in the process, give it a name. Here's an example:

```
var cool_name = "Albert"
```

Having created a name explicitly, you can now use the single method and 19 properties associated with string objects to find out about and manipulate the string.

String Object Property

String objects have one property: length. It contains the number of characters in the string, including spaces and other special characters. Specially encoded characters preceded by a percent sign or an ampersand for the decoding required by the HTML specification do not count as one character. Each character counts as a separate individual character. Thus the commonly used "%20" that encodes spaces counts not as one character for the space it represents but as three characters.

String Object Methods

String objects define 19 methods. Thirteen of these methods deal with the appearance of the string in the user's browser. Two are concerned with the behavior or nature of the string in the context of the browser. The remaining four involve retrieving information about or from the string object.

APPEARANCE-RELATED METHODS

Most of the 13 appearance-related methods that a string object implements have HTML equivalents. Where those equivalents exist, I'll point them out as I discuss each of these methods.

Three of the methods that string objects understand involve the size of the font in which text is displayed. These methods are:

- big
- small
- fontsize

Neither big nor small requires an argument; they are called as shown in this example:

```
var stringToShow = "JavaScript is cool!"
document.write (stringToShow.big())
document.write ("<P>" + stringToShow.small ())
```

Figure 7.7 shows what a document looks like when the above script fragment is executed.

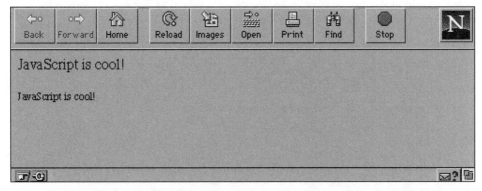

Figure 7.7   Both big and small methods are demonstrated in this document.

Netscape defines HTML extensions that are equivalent to these methods. The following HTML produces the same result as the above script fragment:

```
<BIG>JavaScript is cool!</BIG><P>
<SMALL>JavaScript is cool!</SMALL>
```

The <FONTSIZE> HTML tag has a method equivalent in JavaScript called, logically enough, fontsize. It takes a single argument, which is a number. An unsigned number between 1 and 7 indicates the font size to use. A number preceded by a plus (+) or minus (-) sign indicates how much larger or smaller than the document's BASEFONT size the font should be. You can use a tag in the HEAD portion of the document to set the size of a document's BASEFONT. If you don't set the size, Netscape uses a default BASEFONT size of 3.

If you don't define a BASEFONT size in your document's HEAD, asking Netscape to use a FONTSIZE of "+2" is equivalent to asking it to use a font size of 5 (the default 3, increased by the requested 2).

In no case can a font size of larger than 7 be generated. If you have a BASEFONT size of 4 and attempt to increase it by 4, you will end up with a font of size 7.

The <BIG> tag and its corresponding method produce text that is one larger than the BASEFONT size, while the <SMALL> tag and its corresponding method produce text that is one smaller than the BASEFONT size. If a BASEFONT declaration is absent from the HEAD of your document, BIG means a font size of 4, and SMALL means a font size of 2. This type of font size is demonstrated in Figure 7.8, which was generated by the following HTML:

```
<FONT SIZE="+1">This font is up one in size.</FONT><BR>
<BIG>This was created with a &lt;BIG&gt; tag.</BIG><BR>
<FONT SIZE="-1">This font is down one in size. </FONT><BR>
<small>This was created with a &lt;SMALL&gt; tag.</small>
```

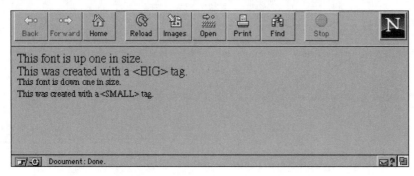

Figure 7.8 This document demonstrates BIG and SMALL type.

The next six methods we'll look at affect text formatting. These methods are largely self-explanatory:

- bold
- fixed
- italics
- strike
- sub
- sup

Figure 7.9 demonstrates the use of these methods by means of the following script:

```
<HTML>
<HEAD><TITLE>Styling of Strings</TITLE>
<BASEFONT SIZE = 4>
</HEAD>
<BODY>
<SCRIPT>
var boldWord = "bold"
var italWord = "italics"
var strikeWord = "strike-through"
var superWord = "superscript"
var subWord = "subscript"

document.write (boldWord.bold())
document.write ("<BR>"+italWord.italics())
document.write ("<BR>"+strikeWord.strike())
document.write ("<BR>"+"The next word is above the line"+superWord.sup())
document.write ("<BR>"+"The next word is below the line" + subWord.sub())
</SCRIPT>

</BODY>
</HTML>
```

The next two methods are of somewhat limited use. The blink method causes the affected text to flash on and off on an inverse background. Most browsers don't support this capability, and most readers don't like it very much. I make it a practice never to use it. The fontcolor method, on the other hand, has some value. Because most browsers allow the user to override your document's font colors at will, however, the impact of its use is unpredictable.

Finally, you can use two methods to switch the case of the text as it displays. The string itself is not changed in the process, unless you assign the changed text to

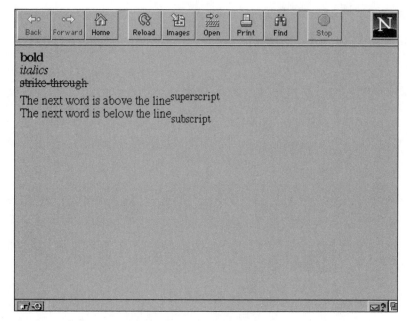

Figure 7.9   This document demonstrates font characteristics.

the variable containing the original string. These two methods are toLowerCase and toUpperCase. Their effect is self-explanatory.

BEHAVIOR-CONNECTED METHODS

There are two string object methods that alter the purpose of a string, converting it from a passive object that merely displays its contents to an active participant in the hypertext process. These methods are:

- ◎ anchor
- ◎ link

You can use these methods to create named anchors and hypertext links dynamically in your HTML documents. Here is an example of the use of the anchor method:

```
<SCRIPT>
 var myString="Table of Contents"
   msgWindow=window.open("","displayWindow")
   msgWindow.document.write(myString.anchor("contents_anchor"))
   msgWindow.document.close()
</SCRIPT>
```

And here's an example of using the link method:

```
<SCRIPT>
var hotText = "SALON Magazine"
var URL="http://www.salon1999.com"
document.open()
document.write("Click to return to " + hotText.link(URL))
document.close()
</SCRIPT>
```

CONTENT-RELATED METHODS

String objects understand four methods that deal with finding out information about, or retrieving the contents of, a string. These methods are:

- charAt
- substring
- indexOf
- lastIndexOf

The charAt method requires a single parameter, which is a number. It retrieves the character at that numbered position in the string object to which the message is sent. The first character is at position 0. To retrieve more than a single character, you would use the substring method. This method takes two numeric parameters and returns the string that is encompassed by the two indices, exclusive of the ending character.

Here are some examples; I've used comments to indicate the value that would be returned by each message:

```
var theString = "liberty and justice for all"
theString.charAt(1)
// returns "i", the second character in the string
theString.charAt(14)
// returns "u", the 14th character in the string
theString.charAt(255)
// returns an empty string since theString is less than 255 characters long
theString.substring(0,7)
// returns "liberty", the first seven characters of the string
theString.substring(7,0)
// returns "liberty" as well; if the first number is larger than the sec-
ond,
// string extraction is in reverse order
theString.subString(11,11)
// returns the empty string since both values are equal
```

The charAt and substring methods are useful if you know the positions of characters in a string. More often, perhaps, you know the character you want but you're not sure where it is in the string. In that case, you can use either the indexOf method or the lastIndexOf method. Both of these methods require one argument, the character or string for which to search in the target string. You may optionally supply a numeric argument, separated from the first by a comma, which tells JavaScript where in the target string to begin its search for the character or string..

The indexOf method returns a number indicating the start position in the string at which it finds the first occurrence of the search string. The lastIndexOf method returns a number indicating where the last occurrence of the search string starts.

Here are some examples; again, I've used comments to describe the return values:

```
var theString = "over and over and over again"

document.write(theString.indexOf ("and"))
// returns 5, the position where the first occurrence of the word
//"and" starts document.write(theString.indexOf("and",6))
// returns 14, the next start position for the word "and" after
//the 6th character document.write(theString.lastIndexOf ("over"))
// returns 18, the start position of the last occurrence of the
//word "over"
```

Math Objects

Strictly speaking, JavaScript has only one Math object. It, like the string object, is a built-in object type. All of its properties and methods are referenced by preceding their names with the word "Math" (and remember, case is important).

The Math object has six properties and defines 18 methods.

Math Object Properties

All six of the Math object's properties are constants that are often used in calculations. These constants are:

@ Math.E (a mathematical value known as Euler's constant, approximately 2.718)

@ Math.LN10 (the natural log of the number 10, approximately 2.302)

- Math.LN2 (the natural log of the number 2, approximately 0.693)
- Math.SQRT1_2 (the inverse of the square root of two, approximately 0.707)
- Math.SQRT2 (the square root of 2, approximately 1.414)
- Math.PI (the ratio of the circumference of a circle to its diameter, approximately 3.1415)

Math Object Methods

I've divided the 18 Math object methods into four categories:

- trigonometric methods
- comparative methods
- evaluation methods
- miscellaneous methods

TRIGONOMETRIC METHODS

JavaScript implements the six most common trigonometric functions as methods:

- acos (arc cosine)
- asin (arc sine)
- atan (arc tangent)
- cos (cosine)
- sin (sine)
- tan (tangent)

Angles are always expressed in radians.

COMPARATIVE METHODS

The Math object understands two comparative methods:

- max (which returns the larger of the two numbers supplied as arguments)
- min (which returns the smaller of the two numbers supplied as arguments)

EVALUATION METHODS

Four of the methods defined for a Math object involve evaluating the numeric argument and doing something with it. These methods are:

@ round (which rounds its argument to the nearest integer, raising its value to the next higher integer if the decimal portion is .5 or greater, or reducing it to the next lower integer if the decimal portion is less than .5)

@ abs (which removes a negative sign if there is one and ignores a positive sign, returning the numeric value of the argument without respect to its sign)

@ ceil (which raises the value of its argument to the next higher integer, regardless of the decimal portion)

@ floor (which reduces the value of its argument to the next lower integer, regardless of the decimal portion)

MISCELLANEOUS METHODS

The last three Math object methods defy classification.

The exp method returns the value of E raised to the power of the argument to the method.

The log method enables you to calculate the natural logarithm of a value. You supply the value as an argument.

Finally, the pow method takes two arguments, raising the first number to the power indicated in the second number. Thus, Math.pow(3,2) returns a value of 9 (three to the second power).

The Date Object

The Date object is another built-in JavaScript object. To create a Date object, you must use JavaScript's new operator. Any of the following forms will create a new Date object:

@ theDate = new Date () (returns the current date and time)

@ theDate = new Date ("month day, year hours:minutes:seconds") (returns a new date with the supplied values)

@ theDate = new Date (year, month, day) (returns a new date with the supplied values)

@ theDate = new Date (year, month, day, hours, minutes, seconds) (returns a new date with the supplied values)

You can omit any value from the lists of values supplied as arguments to the last three forms of the function above. If you do, you also must leave out all other values to the right of the omitted value. In other words, you can stop at whatever level of precision for a date and time that suits your needs. If you omit the time completely, JavaScript defaults to midnight.

The Date object has no properties.

Date Object Methods

The Date object understands 20 methods. To use all but two of them, you must create a Date object with a name as described in the previous section. Two of the methods use the syntax "Date.methodName" and I'll point them out when we discuss them.

Most of the methods (15 of the 20 to be precise) involve either getting or setting some portion of a Date object's value. You can think of a Date object as being divided into day, month, date, year, hour, minute, and second components. For all but one of these components there are two methods. One starts with the word "get" and returns the current value of that component for the Date object to which it is sent. The other one starts with the word "set" and changes the current value of that component of the Date object to which it is sent. The lone exception to this rule is the day component, which cannot be set (the day on which a given date falls is fixed by the calendar). This process gives rise to the following list of methods:

- getDate
- getDay
- getHours
- getMinutes
- getMonth
- getSeconds
- getYear
- setDate
- setHours
- setMinutes
- setMonth
- setSeconds

There are also two methods that retrieve and change the time as a single component:

@ getTime

@ setTime

The getTimeZoneoffset method returns a signed value that describes the number of minutes by which local time differs from Greenwich Mean Time (GMT). Notice that the "o" in "offset" is not capitalized, which is not consistent with other multi-word JavaScript keywords.

You can convert a given date to a string showing the date and time as GMT, using the toGMTString method. Conversely, you can convert a given date to a string showing the date and time in local terms, using the toLocaleString method. The latter approach is useful when you know that the date and time you're dealing with are expressed in non-local terms.

Two methods aren't addressed to Date objects you create. These two methods are part of the Date object's inherent behavior in JavaScript; they are parse and UTC. You invoke them as follows:

@ Date.parse (argumentList)

@ Date.UTC (argumentList)

The parse method takes a single argument that is a string containing a date and optional time. It returns the number of milliseconds that have elapsed between midnight January 1, 1970, and the given date. The UTC method takes a comma-delimited string that represents, in order, the year, month, day, hours, minutes, and seconds for a given date. It returns the number of milliseconds that have elapsed between midnight January 1, 1970, and the given date. These values can then be used in date calculations.

The Location Object

As you know, a document object has a location property. That property, in turn, is a location object. A location is a complete URL. Most URLs you deal with are simple, as in this example:

```
http://www.coriolis.com
```

But a full URL often contains either a search portion (beginning with a question mark) or an anchor reference (beginning with a hash mark), or both. Thus, a complete URL might look like this:

```
http://www.coriolis.com/cgi-bin/search?p=Esperanto#pagetop
```

Generally stated, the syntax for a full URL would look like this:

```
protocol//hostname:port/pathname?searchTerm#anchorTerm
```

A location object has eight properties and defines no methods.

Location Object Properties

A location object has properties that allow you to retrieve any of these individual elements of a URL, as well as specific groups of related elements that are treated together. These properties are directly related to the elements of a URL as described above, except for the last two in the following list:

- hash (returns the string following the "#", called a "hash symbol" and representing the anchor term for the URL)
- hostname
- pathname
- protocol
- port
- search (returns the string following the "?" representing the search term)
- href (returns the complete URL)
- host (returns the combination of the hostname and the port)

The port is seldom used. As a rule, port 80 is used for Web page services. Deviations from this practice are driven by local architectures and necessities, and you don't need to be concerned about them.

The History Object

The last JavaScript object we will look at is the history object. This object is a linked list of URLs the user has visited. This list is generally displayed by the user activating the Navigator's Go menu.

History Object Property

The only property a history object has is length, which returns the number of entries in the history list.

History Object Methods

The purpose of the history list is to enable the user to navigate freely among previously visited URLs, so it's not surprising that the methods this object defines all relate to navigation. There are three such methods:

- back (which returns the user to the most recently visited URL)
- forward (which takes the user to the next entry in the list of URLs from the browser's present position)
- go (which allows the user, under JavaScript control, to navigate forward or
- back by more than one entry at a time and even to locate a URL based on partial contents)

The go method is clearly the most interesting one. It can take one of two types of arguments. Given a signed numerical argument, the go method causes the browser to reposition at the URL that is later (for a positive number) or earlier (for a negative number) in the history list than the present position. Given a string argument, the go method will cause the browser to go to the nearest URL—forward or backward from the present position—that contains the string in its address.

JAVASCRIPT BASICS VIII

With a clear understanding of the objects, properties, and methods that make up the JavaScript object model, you are ready to tackle the rest of the basic concepts in JavaScript. This chapter will complete your JavaScript "boot camp" education by presenting the following topics:

◎ how objects are named and referenced in JavaScripts

◎ the built-in expressions and operators

◎ how functions and statements are formed and how they differ

◎ creating new user-defined objects

◎ conditional processing

◎ repeat loops

◎ using frames in JavaScripts

◎ events and event handlers, including built-in events understood by objects

Along the way, I'll use lots of sample HTML with JavaScript to demonstrate how these concepts work and how you can use them in your JavaScripts.

If some of the topics discussed in this chapter seem abstract and you have trouble figuring out where you might use them in JavaScripts, don't worry about it. Some of them really are a little obtuse. Others seem obtuse, but their role will become clearer in Chapter 9 when I use them in a few sample JavaScripts that will help you consolidate your understanding of this scripting language.

Referencing and Naming JavaScript Items

Much of the work your JavaScripts do involves manipulating objects and their properties. Obviously, before you can interact with an object or other item in a script, you must know how to identify it so that JavaScript will recognize it.

You can refer to three basic types of items in JavaScript:

◎ objects

◎ variables

◎ literals

Let's look at each type of item in turn.

Object Naming and Referencing

You already know everything you need to know about naming and referencing objects from your reading of Chapter 7. Using the object hierarchy as your template, you simply name each object in the hierarchy, starting optionally with the window (which is never required to be named explicitly) and continuing to the object of interest. You then append the name of the property you want to reference. The whole identifier is divided into segments using periods. To find out how many elements the first (or only) form in a document called "bookorder" has, for example, you might create a reference like this:

```
bookorder.forms[0].length
```

This naming process contains some subtleties that will come into play when we discuss frames and targets later in this chapter. But these nuances will constitute minor variations on this fundamental theme.

Variable Naming and Referencing

In Chapter 7, we used variables from time to time without really explaining them. In this section, we'll look at the uses for variables in JavaScript and how to name and reference them.

Why Use Variables?

A variable is a label that essentially names a container into which you put some information you will retrieve later and possibly change during the course of running your JavaScript. A variable is a data element whose value can vary during the execution of your script (which is why it's called a variable, of course).

Defining Variables

As long as you avoid the use of JavaScript keywords, you can define a variable merely by referencing it and giving it a value (by using the equal sign), as in this example:

```
userID = "beta_tester_42"
```

You may, if you wish, add the keyword "var" in front of such a declaration. This convention makes your code potentially more readable, but I've frankly come to view this as a "noise word" and almost never use it. The above declaration would look like this if you disagreed with me:

```
var userID = "beta_tester_42"
```

Once you've declared a variable, you can use its value in functions and expressions, including assigning it a new value, again by using the equal sign:

```
userID = "beta_tester_44"
```

(If you've already defined the variable and just want to assign it a new value, don't put the "var" keyword in front of it. Reusing "var" with an existing variable may result in an error.)

The process of creating a variable in JavaScript requires that you assign it a value. This step is often referred to as "initialization" of a variable.

DATA TYPES AND VARIABLES

As I will discuss in greater detail later in this chapter, JavaScript variables don't have a data type associated with them. Just because you create a variable and initialize it with a string value, for example, doesn't mean you can't later place a number or some other kind of value into it. Thus, you could define a variable like this:

```
size = "extra large"
```

and then later assign the variable size a new value like this:

```
size = 42
```

NAMING VARIABLES

A JavaScript variable must start either with a letter (upper or lower case) or an underscore character. It may not begin with a number or special symbol. After the first character, you can use any character, number, or symbol in your variable names (within some limits that we'll get to later) except spaces. Variables must appear to JavaScript to be one word.

Here are some legal variable names:

```
Number_of_users
t14
_author
```

The following variable names are illegal for the reasons given in parentheses after each:

```
Number of users (has embedded spaces)
14t (begins with a number)
*42 (begins with a special character)
break (is a JavaScript reserved keyword)
```

USING VARIABLES

You can find thousands of ways to use variables in JavaScript, as in any other scripting or programming language. Here's a simple example that shows how you might ask the user for some input and then display that input using a variable:

```
<SCRIPT>
defaultReply = 42
answer = prompt ("Gimme a number, please!", defaultReply)
document.write ("You said " + answer)
</SCRIPT>
```

If you run this example, the user will be presented a dialog box like the one shown in Figure 8.1. The user can either click "OK" and accept your suggested response of 42 or enter some other number. The number that the user enters will then be displayed in the window, as shown in Figure 8.2.

Literal Naming and Referencing

A literal is a piece of information in a JavaScript that is simply a value you intend the script to use "as is." In other words, you want it to be "taken literally." The three basic types of literals in JavaScript are:

- numbers
- Boolean values
- strings

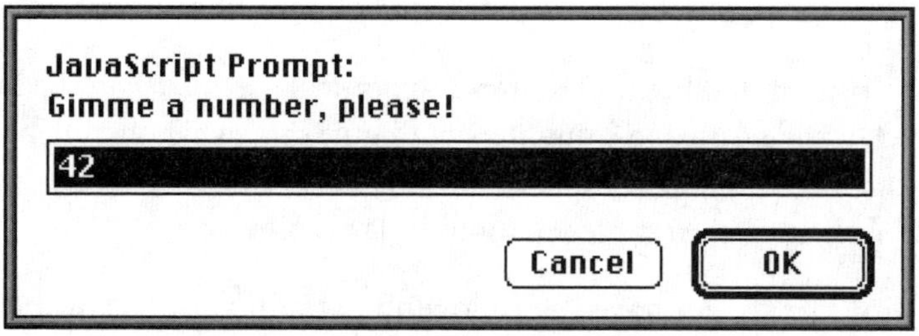

Figure 8.1   This dialog prompts the user to enter a variable.

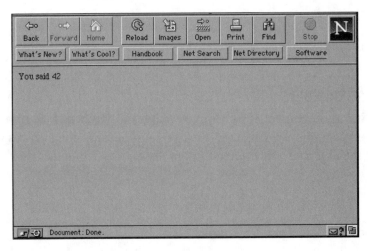

Figure 8.2   This window shows the user's response.

Because they are taken literally, literals are not named. They are referenced only when they are used directly.

NUMERIC LITERALS

Numeric literals consist of all-numeric values not enclosed in quotation marks. Here are some examples:

```
42
11.99999
-6.14E3
```

Two types of numbers can be represented directly in JavaScript. Numbers with no decimal points are called integers. All other numbers are called floating point literals (because the decimal point "floats" depending on the value of the power to which the decimal number is raised, as I'll explain in a moment).

Integers can represent numbers in the standard decimal base of 10, in the hexadecimal base 16 (which is widely used in computers), or in the somewhat obscure but occasionally useful octal base 7. Table 8.1 explains the differences among these types of numbers and the prefixes used in their representations in JavaScript.

Floating-point literals can have the following parts in various combinations:

@ decimal integer as described above
@ decimal point

Table 8.1   Decimal, Hexadecimal, and Octal Numbers

Value Type	Valid Characters	Prefix
Decimal	0-9	None; leading zero not allowed
Hexadecimal	0-9, A-F	0X (zero followed by upper case or lower case X)
Octal	0-7	0 (zero)

@ another decimal number after the decimal point (referred to as the fractional part)

@ an exponent symbol (upper case or lower case letter "e" followed by a decimal integer)

The number 3.14159, which is the approximate value of the mathematical constant known as PI, is a floating point literal consisting of a decimal integer, decimal point, and fractional part. It could also be expressed as .0314159E2 (which would be interpreted as .0314159 times 10 squared), which contains a decimal point, a fractional part and an exponent symbol. You could also represent it as 314159E-5 (314,159 times 10 raised to the minus-five power).

BOOLEAN LITERALS

The two Boolean literal values are true and false. They are used in conditional expressions, which we'll look at in greater detail later in the chapter.

STRING LITERALS

A string literal consists of zero or more characters enclosed in single or double quotation marks. A string must start and end with the same type of quotation mark, but the two types are equivalent. You create a string literal merely by supplying some characters between quotation marks, as in these examples:

```
"Krista"
'krista'
"2468"
```

If you start a string literal in a JavaScript and fail to close it properly, either by omitting the second quotation mark or by using a non-matching quotation mark, JavaScript will complain about an unterminated literal. Check the string to make sure you've started and ended it with the same type of quotation mark.

This issue of proper string termination becomes important when you write JavaScripts that involve event handlers, as we'll see later in this chapter. In writing such script elements, you often need to embed one string within another. When you do that, you must alternate the quotation mark types. Here's an example, but don't worry for now about what it means or how it works; just focus on the quotation mark usage:

```
<A HREF="http://www.mysite.com/"
   onMouseOver="window.status='Click this if you dare!'; return true">
Click me</A>
```

Here, we have a small two-line script (the two parts of which are separated by a semicolon). The script is enclosed in double quotation marks, which in turn contain a string parameter that must therefore be enclosed in single quotation marks.

If you need to display a quotation mark in text that you write to a document, you must precede the quotation mark with a backslash character ("\"). This technique is called "escaping" the character. Here's how it looks in practice:

```
document.write ("You should read \"Introductory Notes\" first.")
```

There are several special characters you can embed in a string literal, though most of them are not very useful because of the way HTML handles white space. These characters are all preceded by a backslash to avoid confusing them with their ordinary character counterparts:

- \b for a backspace
- \f for a form feed
- \n for a new-line character
- \r for a carriage return
- \t for a tab character

Data Types in JavaScript

JavaScript is, as I have indicated, a loosely typed language. Data type is largely irrelevant and you can safely ignore it. As a rule, JavaScript just converts numeric values to strings when both occur in an expression. You would expect this example to work:

```
x = 42 + 58
```

but in some programming languages an expression like this one would cause problems of varying severity:

```
x = 42 + " Thanks for All the Fish"
```

JavaScript will simply convert the number 42 to the string "42" and display the resulting combined string:

```
"42 Thanks for All the Fish"
```

What if you have a script that generates a string you want to treat as a number? (For now, let's not be concerned about how this might happen.) Here's a script that encounters a problem with this kind of design:

```
<SCRIPT>
defaultReply = "42"
answer = prompt ("Gimme a number, please!", defaultReply)
document.write (75 + answer)
</SCRIPT>
```

When this JavaScript executes, you might expect the window to display the value 117 (assuming, of course, that the user leaves the default response in place). But it doesn't; it displays "7542" (without the quotation marks). Why? Because of the rule I mentioned a moment ago: JavaScript tries to convert numbers to strings when it encounters mixtures of strings and numbers.

We clearly didn't want this, so what do we do? JavaScript's developers anticipated this problem and created three special functions, each of which takes a string argument (and in one case a second argument) and attempts to convert it as described:

- ◎ eval converts a string to a number
- ◎ parseInt converts a string to an integer using the base specified as the second argument
- ◎ parseFloat converts a string to a floating point number

If we apply the eval function to the example above that produced a surprising result, we find that it now does what we expected. It displays the number 117 in the window if we accept the default response of 42:

```
<SCRIPT>
defaultReply = "42"
answer = prompt ("Gimme a number, please!", defaultReply)
document.write (75 + eval(answer))
</SCRIPT>
```

Here are some additional examples of the use of these functions, with the results of their execution written as JavaScript comments:

```
eval ("42)"
//42
eval("57 + 42 - 11")
//88
parseInt("A8DF",16)
//43231 (the decimal equivalent of the hexadecimal value)
parseInt("A8DFJ13",16)
//43231 (returns value up to the first un-parsable character, in//this case
"J")
parseInt("A8DF",8)
//NAN(000) (error means "Not a Number"; Octal values must be 0-7)
parseFloat ("A8DF")
//NAN(000) (error means "Not a Number"; float can only contain //decimal
values, minus sign, plus sign, "E", and/or "e")
parseFloat ("37.25E2")
//3725
```

We also need to know one final datatype-related keyword. The word "null" stands for an item that has no value at all. It's not zero. It's not empty. It's null.

Expressions and Built-In Operators

All JavaScripts ultimately consist of expressions and statements. I discuss statements in the next section. In this section, we'll look at expressions and one of their primary building blocks, built-in operators.

Expressions

An expression in JavaScript consists of a combination of literals, variables, operators, and other expressions that ultimately evaluate to a single value. That value may be assigned to a variable or it may just have a value. For example, this expression simply has a value:

```
42 + 57
```

This example is a valid JavaScript expression (though as it stands it doesn't really do anything useful for us). Here is an assignment expression:

```
x = 15
```

It creates a variable called "x" and initializes it to have a numeric value of 15. If the variable already exists, the expression changes its value to 15.

Put these together and you have a single expression that contains both types of expression:

```
x = 42 + 57
```

(A third type of expression is called a "conditional expression." I'll discuss that idea later in this chapter.)

Built-In Operators

JavaScript defines six types of operators:

- assignment operators
- comparison operators
- string operators
- arithmetic operators
- logical operators
- bitwise operators

We'll take a look at each of these built-in operators in turn, except for the last category. Bitwise operators are complex and seldom used by anyone who isn't already an accomplished professional programmer. They are beyond the scope of things you need to understand to use JavaScript.

ASSIGNMENT OPERATORS

We use assignment operators to assign the values of expressions to other objects: variables, object properties, or other expressions. We've already used the most common assignment operator, the "=" sign. JavaScript, taking a page from the book of the C language, also defines four shorthand assignment operators, as follows:

- += (x = x + y)
- -= (x = x - y)
- *= (x = x * y)
- /= (x = x / y)

JavaScript also includes some bitwise assignment operators that are seldom used, but, as I indicated, we won't cover those in this book.

COMPARISON OPERATORS

The six comparison operators in JavaScript compare the values on either side of their symbols and return a logical (Boolean) value. The value indicates whether the comparison is true (in which case, it returns "true") or not (in which case, it returns "false").

While comparison operators are typically used with numerical values, they can be used with string values as well. Table 8.2 summarizes the comparison operators and their usage.

Table 8.2   Comparison Operators

Operator	Meaning	Examples
==	Are the two terms exactly equal?	9 == 9 returns true
		9 == 99 returns false
		"nine" = "nine" returns true
>	Is the left value greater than the right value?	9 > 9 returns false
		9 > 10 returns false
		9 > 7 returns true
		"a" > "A" returns true
		"9" > "a" returns false
		"9" > "A" returns false
>=	Is the left value greater than or equal to the right value?	9>= 9 returns true
		9 >= 7 returns true
		9 >= 10 returns false
<	Is the left value less than the right value?	9 < 9 returns false
		9 < 10 returns true
		9 < 7 returns false
		"a" < "A" returns false

Continued

Table 8.2	Comparison Operators (Continued)	
Operator	**Meaning**	**Examples**
<=	Is the left value less than or equal to the right value?	9<=9 returns true 9<=7 returns false 9<=10 returns true
!=	Opposite of ==. Are the two terms not equal?	9 != 9 returns false 9 != 99 returns true "nine" != "nine" returns false

If you are familiar with another programming or scripting language that uses the "=" sign to test for equality rather than the double equal sign, you will probably need some time to adjust to this new syntax. Interestingly, the designers of JavaScript came up with a really cool way to deal with this common mistake. If you use a single equal sign where you possibly wanted to use a double equal sign, JavaScript assumes the double equal sign. It alerts you to its assumption with a syntax error dialog like the one in Figure 8.3.

STRING OPERATORS

All of the comparison operators, as we just saw, can apply to strings. In addition, the concatenation operator (represented by a plus sign) combines the two string values on either side of it. As we saw earlier in the chapter, if you use the "+" operator with a string and a number, JavaScript converts the number to a string and joins them.

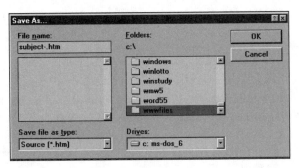

Figure 8.3   JavaScript displays this helpful syntax error dialog when you make a mistake.

If you join two strings with this operator and they need a space between them, you must supply it explicitly. You can make it the last character in the string on the left of the operator, the first character in the string on the right of the operator, or a separate concatenation character as shown here:

```
"Mailbox" + " " + "full." (which produces the string "Mailbox full")
```

You can combine the concatenation and assignment by using the "+=" shorthand assignment operator we saw earlier, as in:

```
statusMessage = "Mailbox"
statusMessage += " full."
```

It is not legal to use the other shorthand operators with strings. (If you think about it, it makes no sense to try.)

ARITHMETIC OPERATORS

JavaScript includes are eight arithmetic operators.

As you'd expect, the four basic operators—addition (+), subtraction (-), multiplication (*), and division (/)—are defined in JavaScript and work exactly as you'd expect them to work. In addition, unary negation (a fancy way of saying "put a minus sign in front of the number") has the effect of switching the sign of the numeric value to which it is applied. It is called "unary" because it has only one argument, while the other common operators have two arguments.

The modulus operator (represented by the percent sign, "%") returns the modulo (or remainder) generated by dividing the value on the right side of this operator by the value on the left side of this operator. Here are two examples:

```
x = 14 % 3 //returns 2 (14/3 =4, with a remainder of 2)
y = 99 % 3 //returns 0; there is no remainder
```

The last two operators are called increment (represented by two plus signs) and decrement (represented by two minus signs). Increment adds 1 to the value of its argument and decrement subtracts 1 from the value of its argument. Both of these operators can be placed before or after the variable whose value you wish to change. If it is placed before the variable, it is called "prefix;" if it is placed after the variable, it is called "postfix."

This notion of prefix and postfix incrementing and decrementing of variables is something for which I have had no use in my entire career. I've done scripting in several languages, some of which supported the concept and some of which did not. If you don't understand all of this, skip it. You won't be a less capable scripter for it.

Whether the increment or decrement operator is prefix or postfix affects the outcome only when the operator is included in an assignment statement. For example, if x begins life with a value of 42, the following statements produce the indicated result:

```
y = x++ //increments x to 43 and sets y to 42 because the //increment takes
place after the assignment
y = ++x //increments x to 43 and sets y to 43
y = x- //decrements x to 41 and sets y to 42
y = -x //decrements x to 41 and sets y to 41
```

LOGICAL OPERATORS

JavaScript supports three logical operators, which work with Boolean values (true and false) as operands. Logical operators return Boolean values as well.

Table 8.3 summarizes the three operators.

JavaScript uses the common "short-circuit evaluation" approach to carry out logical operations. If the left-hand expression evaluates to false and the next operator is &&, evaluation stops and false is returned. It doesn't matter what the next value is because both values must be true for the && operation to return true. The same is true if the first expression evaluates to true and the next operator is ||. In this case, JavaScript stops execution and returns a true because no false result can arise.

Functions and Statements

A JavaScript statement consists of one or more keywords. It can contain any or all of the elements of the JavaScript language that we've been looking at, including objects and properties, built-in operators, and expressions.

Table 8.3	Logical Operators	
Operator Symbol	**Meaning**	**Examples**
&&	AND	(3 > 2) && (5 < 4) returns true because both Boolean expressions are true
		(3<2) && (5<4) returns false because one or both of the Boolean expressions is false
‖	OR	(3>2) ‖ (5<4) returns true because at least one of the Boolean expressions is true (in this case, both are)
		(3<2) ‖ (5<4) also returns true because at least one of the Boolean expressions is true
		(3<2) ‖ (4>5) returns false because both Boolean expressions are false
!	NOT	! (3 < 2) returns true because the Boolean expression is false and the NOT operator inverts its value
		! (4<5) returns false because the Boolean expression is true and the NOT operator inverts its value

Scripts Contrasted with Functions

A JavaScript is made up of one or more statements enclosed between the <SCRIPT> and </SCRIPT> tags. A single statement can span multiple lines in the HTML document source. Conversely, you can place more than one JavaScript statement on a single line by separating individual statements from one another with semicolons.

Statements can be simple or compound. A simple statement carries out a single operation. A compound statement is a group of simple statements enclosed in curly braces, starting with "{" and ending with "}". As a rule, compound statements are found in two places:

◎ functions, where they are a required part of the syntax

◎ conditional and loop constructs (discussed later in this chapter) where more than one statement is to be executed repeatedly or under some specific circumstance

Recall from Chapter 6 that JavaScript functions are generally placed in the HEAD portion of a document while scripts that consist entirely of statements to execute immediately are placed in the BODY. This rule is not hard and fast. It is perfectly legal to define a function in the BODY as long as the SCRIPT in which it is defined appears before the SCRIPT that calls it into execution. You can even define a function within the same script where it will be called. Doing this makes the function inaccessible from any other script on the page, of course, because the function is known only inside the SCRIPT where it is defined.

The key differences between a function and a script of statements are:

- @ a function begins with the keyword "function"
- @ a function must return a value as its last executable step

As we saw in Chapter 7, JavaScript has many built-in functions, or methods. Each one returns some value, as all functions must.

JavaScript Statements

As you'll recall from Chapter 6, most of JavaScript consists of dealing with objects and their properties. The syntax of the JavaScript language defines 13 statements that provide the structure around which this object property manipulation takes place. We'll look at most of those statements in this section. We'll leave the statements that deal with creating new objects of your own design, looping, and conditional processing for a later discussion in this chapter.

FAMILIAR STATEMENTS

We've already encountered several of these functions, so they require little or no additional explanation here.

Comments are one type of statement in JavaScript. As we saw in Chapter 6, you can define two types of comments:

- @ single-line or partial-line comments that start with a double slash
- @ multi-line comments that begin with the special character pair "/*" and end with a matching "*/" pair

The keyword "var" is a statement type as well. I indicated that I tend not to use it because it is optional. Actually, I lied (well, I merely oversimplified, as some politicians would say). Inside a function, you must precede variable declarations with the "var" keyword if a variable of the same name is defined globally (outside the function). You can define and initialize more than one variable on a single line of JavaScript code. You simply separate each variable name and initial value (if any) from the others with a comma, as in this example:

```
var size_of_sample = 0, initial_score = 99, surveyID
```

We've seen the "function" statement several times. It marks the beginning of a function's definition. The statement requires a name for the function. As a rule, it also includes one or more parameters, enclosed in parentheses and separated by commas if there are more than one. Although it is not, strictly speaking, required, most functions include yet another JavaScript statement, "return." This statement results in the function returning a value to the script statement that calls the function. It is rare that a function wouldn't return a value. The argument of a return statement is any valid JavaScript expression.

THE "WITH" STATEMENT

We've dealt now with the familiar basic JavaScript statements with which we have had some previous experience. In this and the next two sections, I'll introduce three new statements. (Actually, only one of them—"with"—is really a statement in the JavaScript language definition. The other two—"new" and "this"—defy categorization and are placed here because they are for all practical purposes the same as statements.)

The "with" statement is a finger-saver. It lets you perform multiple operations on a single object's properties without having to retype the name of the object every time. You supply the name of an object as the argument to the "with" statement, and JavaScript implicitly places it in front of all the subsequent statements enclosed in the next set of curly braces. For example, assume you have defined a FORM object in your HTML page and this form has three checkboxes on it. Based on some user input or other script execution, you want to turn on all of these checkboxes. The checkboxes reflect musical preferences for the user and are called "classical," "pop," and "jazz." Here's how you'd write the script that would handle this task (from what we know so far):

```
<SCRIPT>
forms[0].classical.checked=true
forms[0].pop.checked=true
forms[0].jazz.checkedc=true
</SCRIPT>
```

Here's how that same script looks using the "with" statement:

```
<SCRIPT>
with (forms[0]) {
```

```
    classical.checked=true
    pop.checked=true
    jazz.checked=true }
</SCRIPT>
```

As you can see, even in this trivial example, using "with" saved us typing a dozen or more characters. Multiply this effect over many such situations in a complex HTML document and you can appreciate its value.

THE "THIS" KEYWORD

The keyword "this" can be used in an object whose script calls a function to refer to the object itself. As such, it is primarily useful in event handlers (which I discuss later in this chapter). Its real utility lies in the fact that it makes it possible for us to write highly reuseable functions.

One very useful place to apply this keyword is in form data validation operations. Let's say you have three different text objects in a form, each of which must contain numbers in a certain range, but the range differs with each of the text objects. You want to ensure that the age a person enters is between 18 and 99, that the number of items ordered is less than 100, and that the highest level of education attained is between 12 and 22. You could define a single function, which I'll call validateNumbers, that looks like this:

```
function validateNumbers (obj, minValue, maxValue) {
    if ((obj.value < minValue || (obj.value > maxValue))
        alert ("Value out of range!") }
```

Now you can define an "onChange" handler for each text field that calls the validateNumbers function and tells the function its object identity (using "this") and the two values it wants to use for validation. The three text fields would then include definitions like these:

```
<INPUT TYPE = "text" NAME = "age" onChange="validateNumbers (this, 18, 99">
<INPUT TYPE = "text" NAME = "numItems" onChange="validateNumbers (this, 0, 99">
<INPUT TYPE = "text" NAME = "education" onChange="validateNumbers (this, 12,22">
```

When the "age" object's value is changed and the onChange handler is called, it will in turn call the validateNumbers function, with its own identity as the first argument. The other text objects would work the same way.

Creating Your Own Objects

The built-in objects in JavaScript are adequate to the task of dealing with windows, documents, and other browser objects. But sometimes you will want to create new objects to deal with the kinds of data your documents need to manage. JavaScript makes that process fairly easy. It involves two steps:

1. Define the object type by creating a function.
2. Create instances of this new object type with the "new" statement.

Defining New Object Types

The function that defines a new object type looks like any other function. You define one parameter for the function for each property you want the new object type to have. Then in the body of the function you use "this" notation to assign each property to one of the incoming parameters.

For example, let's assume we're creating a document that keeps track of orders for clothing a customer might be ordering. Each article of clothing will have four properties:

- type (dress, slacks, shirt, socks, and so on)
- size
- color
- price

To define this new type of object, which I'll call "clothing," you'd write a function something like this:

```
function clothing (type, size, color, price) {
    this.type = type
    this.size = size
    this.color = color
    this.price = price
}
```

It may be obvious to you, but it wasn't to me the first time I saw this kind of construct, that the names of the parameters you pass to the function do not need to be the same as those used in the body of the function. We could just as easily, for example, have called the incoming parameters "theType" and "theSize." We would then have assigned the values in a statement like this:

```
this.type = theType
```

The way that you do this kind of scripting is a matter of individual taste. I generally use the same names, as I did in the example above, because the mapping between the incoming parameters and the data types is clearer when I read the script six months after I wrote it.

Creating New Objects

Having defined an object called "clothing," you can create a specific clothing object (called an "instance" of the clothing object) by using the "new" statement. Here's an example of such a statement:

```
newClothes = new clothing ("blouse", 34, "purple", 19.99)
```

That's all there is to creating an instance of an object. Just don't forget this step.

Accessing Properties

Once you've created a new object (such as our clothing object called "newClothes" in the previous section), you can reference its properties just as with JavaScript's built-in objects. To find out the price of the article of clothing, for example, you would refer to the object this way:

```
newClothes.price
```

Objects as Properties

Let's carry this process one step farther. The person for whom we are creating this Web site wants to keep track of where she stores her clothing. She has four closets, each of which has a number of racks, shelves, and bins. We could just add two properties to the "clothing" object, one for the closet number and one for the container identification (for example, "drawer 12"). But that would duplicate effort in many places because a given container will probably hold multiple pieces of clothing.

So we define a new "storagePlace" object (note that we couldn't call it "location" because that's a JavaScript reserved word) with those properties, like this:

```
function storagePlace (closetNum, containerID) {
    this.closetNum = closetNum
    this.containerID = containerID }
```

Then we can create new instances of storagePlace objects like this:

```
mainDrawer14 = new storagePlace (1, "drawer14")
```

Now go back to the clothing object and redefine it to include a storage location property:

```
function clothing (type, size, color, price, whereStored) {
    this.type = type
    this.size = size
    this.color = color
    this.price = price
    this.whereStored = whereStored
}
```

When you create a new clothing object, you would do it like this:

```
blouse1ForTrip = new clothing ("blouse", 34, "purple", mainDrawer14)
```

Notice that the last parameter is not enclosed in quotation marks. That's because it is an object identifier that points to another object (which happens to be a "storagePlace" object).

We could now refer to the storage closet for this article of clothing like this:

```
blouse1ForTrip.whereStored.closetNum
```

Objects Contrasted with. Instances

In the preceding section, we added a new property to an object type. You can also add new properties to individual instances of objects, though that is not generally what you want to do. If you add a property to an object type, all objects you create of that type will have that property. If you add it to a single instance of the object type, only that instance will have the new property.

Objects are like cookie cutters that stamp out identical objects on demand. Instances are like individual cookies with the same basic shape but with possibly different flavors, frostings, nuts, and the like.

Conditional Processing

So far, all of the JavaScripts we've written have been linear. Execution starts at the first statement and continues through the last statement in the script. While most of the JavaScripting you do will probably involve just this type of approach, you may want to choose other procedures depending on the value of some property.

To accommodate that need, JavaScript, like most programming and scripting languages, defines a statement called "if...else." Let's examine this statement.

Basics of If...Else Processing

The basic syntax of the if...else statement looks like this:

```
if (condition) {
    statement_group_1 }
```

The condition clause must evaluate to a Boolean value (true or false). In the basic construct shown above, if the condition evaluates to true, the statements in statement_group_1 will be evaluated. (Note that although I've shown this statement group as a compound statement, it may be a simple statement.) Here's an example:

```
if (cust.creditLimit < cust.currentBalance + cust.newOrder) {
    cust.currentBalance += cust.newOrder
    processOrder (cust.ID, cust.newOrder) }
```

This partial script adds the customer's currentBalance property and newOrder property to determine if this purchase is within the customer's credit limit. If so, it updates the customer's currentBalance property by adding the value of the newOrder property and then calls the "processOrder" function.

If this purchase would push the customer over his or her credit limit, the above script doesn't do anything; the rest of the if...else statement comes into play. Let's say we merely want to alert the user of the Web site to the problem. We could use the complete form of the if...else statement as follows:

```
if (cust.creditLimit < cust.currentBalance + cust.newOrder) {
    cust.currentBalance += cust.newOrder
    processOrder (cust.ID, cust.newOrder) }
else
    alert ("Credit Limit Exceeded!")
```

Now we've defined a path of action to be taken if the credit limit would be exceeded by the new order. (Of course, much more complex processing and a compound statement could be part of the "else" clause of the if...else statement, if needed.)

Most of the time in JavaScript when you use if...else statements, you will be checking the value of a property against some other value or property.

Repeated Execution in Loops

Conditional execution allows you to choose among different processing routes. Looping allows you to execute one or more statements repeatedly. JavaScript supports three types of loop statements:

- ◎ for (where you use a counter and loop a specific number of times)
- ◎ for...in (where you carry out an operation on each property defined by an object)
- ◎ while (where you carry out an operation as long as some Boolean expression remains true)

The "for" Loop

The most basic type of loop operation in JavaScript is the "for" loop. Its basic syntax looks like this:

```
for ([initial expression]; [end condition]; [update expression]) {
    statements }
```

You'll see this loop used most often when the programmer knows how many times some statement will be executed. For example, to carry out an operation ten times, you could write a statement like this:

```
for (i = 1; i <= 10; i++) {
    //do something }
```

This loop first initializes the variable "i" (which we call the "counter") to a value of 1. Each time through the loop, it updates the value of "i" by adding 1 to it with the "++" postfix operator. Each time through the loop, it also checks to see if the value of "i" is still less than or equal to 10. As long as it is, the statements in the body are executed.

If the initial expression portion of a "for" statement results in the end condition failing the first time through the loop, it doesn't execute. For example, this code results in the statement body never running:

```
for (i = 100; i <= 10; i++) {
    //do something }
```

The counter variable "i" is already greater than 10 when the loop starts, so nothing happens.

All three elements of the parameter list in a "for" loop are optional. Leaving all of them out creates an "infinite loop" that runs forever, which is probably not what you want! (You may, however, use the "break" statement discussed later in this section to terminate even this kind of loop.)

The "for...in" Loop

To perform some operation on all of the properties of an object, you can use the JavaScript "for...in" statement. Its basic syntax looks like this:

```
for (var in obj) {
    //do something }
```

The most obvious use for this statement would be to print all the properties of an object and their values. You might define a function called "dump_properties" that looks like this example adapted from Netscape's online JavaScript documentation:

```
function dump_properties(obj, obj_name) {
    var result = "", i = ""
    for (i in obj)
        result += obj_name + "." + i + " = " + obj[i] + "\n"
    return result
}
```

You could then call this function in a script later in the document and use it to print any object's properties to the document in the current window:

```
document.write (dump_properties (clothing, "blouse1ForTrip"))
```

You could also use the "for...in" statement to test whether a given object has a specific property. (You might want to do this, for example, if you have a script that creates instances of a particular type of object but adds a property to selected instances of that object.) The following loop would do what you want (we'll discuss the "break" statement shortly):

```
found = false
for (i in clothing) {
    if (i != "store") {
        continue}
    else
        document.write (clothing.store + "<P>")
        found = true
        break }
if (! found) alert ("No store property!")
```

The "while" Loop

The last type of loop statement in JavaScript is the "while" statement. Its basic syntax looks like this:

```
while (condition) {
```

The "condition" must evaluate to a Boolean value (true or false). As long as the condition remains true, the statement body executes. As soon as it becomes false, the loop terminates. Notice that the condition is checked before the loop executes so that if it is false the first time it is encountered, the loop never executes.

Unlike the "for" loop, the parameters to the "while" loop do not perform any operations that will result in the loop terminating. You must therefore be careful to write the "while" loop so that it includes some way to stop executing. You could do this by:

◎ defining the condition to involve a variable whose value you alter inside the loop

◎ including a "break" statement at a strategic point in the loop

The example I used in the discussion of the "for" loop, which carries out a task tentimes, could be written as a "while" loop like this:

```
i = 1
while (i <= 10) {
    //do something
    i++
```

Notice that I had to initialize the variable "i" outside the loop. Also notice that I incremented the value of "i" inside the loop so that after ten iterations, the loop will conclude when the condition "i <= 10" becomes false.

Loop Control with "break" and "continue"

The "break" statement immediately terminates the current loop and resumes execution with the first statement following the end of the loop, if there is one. It applies to all three types of loops and behaves the same in all of them.

You often use the "break" statement when you are testing for a condition that can occur only once in a loop or when you are interested only in the first occurrence of that condition. When the desired condition is encountered, further processing is unnecessary and perhaps even erroneous. We saw an example of this statement in the example of a "for...in" loop earlier. There, once I encountered a property for which I was looking, I wanted to stop looking at additional properties and just process the one I'd found.

If you want to do some processing but not all of it when a particular condition is met, you will use the "continue" statement inside a block of statements within the loop.

The "continue" statement behaves slightly differently depending on the type of loop. In a "for" loop, the "continue" statement jumps back to the beginning of the loop and executes the update expression. In a "for...in" loop, it looks at the next property in the object. In a "while" loop, it jumps back to the condition and performs the test to see if execution should continue.

You will frequently find a need to combine "break" and "continue" statements in JavaScripts. Now you can understand my earlier example. Here it is again:

```
found = false
for (i in clothing) {
    if (i != "store") {
        continue}
```

```
        else
            document.write (clothing.store + "<P>")
            found = true
            break }
if (! found) alert ("No store property!")
```

The "continue" statement on the fourth line returns to the top the loop and checks the next property of the clothing object, if more properties need to be checked. The "break" statement acts to stop the loop when it finds a property called "store," so that it won't keep processing after one such property is found.

Using Frames in JavaScripts

In Chapter 3, we looked at the newly introduced concept of frames in Netscape 2.0. There, my emphasis was on creating frames, getting content into them, and planning a window layout for their use. You may have wondered at the time how you were going to coordinate activities among the contents of all those frames. What if, for example, you wanted a user's click on a link in one frame of a window to cause the contents of another frame to change? This advantage is, after all, clearly the real power of frames.

In this section, I'll describe how to work with frames in your JavaScripts. As you'll see, it is hardly mysterious.

The Key Idea: Target

A frame, you'll recall, is just a type of window object from JavaScript's perspective. Frames have all the same properties and built-in methods that windows have. And, like windows, they can serve as the destination object for links and form output, the two most common uses for changing the contents of a frame once it's been opened and initialized.

You already know that the standard form for a hypertext link in a Web document looks like this:

```
<A HREF="url to go to">text to link</A>
```

Netscape 2.0 adds a new property to links called "target." The target property of a link includes the name of the window in which to display the URL. This property expands the basic link syntax so it looks like this:

```
<A HREF="url to go to" TARGET="window name">text to link</A>
```

When the user clicks on the text "text to link," the URL is displayed in a window called "window name." If such a window doesn't exist, it will be created and opened.

Because a frame is exactly like a window, you can probably figure out that you will use the "target" keyword to control interaction between frames in a window.

Sample Scripting

In this brief example, I'll create a two-frame window with a Table of Contents in the left frame and the contents of the chapters displayed in the right frame. Here is the HTML that will create the window with the frames:

```
<FRAMESET COLS="40%,60%">
<FRAME SRC="myTOC.html" NAME="toc">
<FRAME  SRC="doc1.html" NAME="pages">
</FRAMESET>
```

(For this example, the first frame, named "toc" in the HTML above, does not need a name at all. But I've adopted the convention of naming frames when they're created. Then, if I do need to refer to them later, I won't have to go back and edit the markup code to give them a name.)

Now is a good time to bring up what has rapidly become one of the most common scripting errors among JavaScripters using frames. If you put the <FRAMESET> tag after a <BODY> tag has already appeared, your frames will not display. Remember, frames **replace** body elements in an HTML document. You should delete the <BODY> and </BODY> tags if you're working with a page-creation tool that automatically generates a skeletal HTML for you.

The initial document that loads into the right frame (which isn't necessary; you could leave this frame with no source document and fill it only on demand) looks like this:

```
<HTML>
<HEAD><TITLE>doc1</TITLE></HEAD>
<BODY>
<H4>This is document #1, which opens the right-hand frame when the window
opens and before the user has selected anything from the Table of Contents
in the left-hand frame.</H4>

</BODY>
</HTML>
```

I've given the window a title even though its contents will be displayed in a frame that has no title. If, during testing, something goes wrong and a new window opens, it will betray itself by its title!

The contents of "myTOC.html" are shown here:

```
<HTML>
<HEAD><TITLE>Dan's TOC</TITLE></HEAD>
<BODY>
<H2>Table of Contents</H2>
<H3>Section 1</H3>
<UL>
<LI><A HREF="Text11.html" TARGET="pages">Chapter 1</A><BR>

<LI><A HREF="Text12.html" TARGET="pages">Chapter 2</A><BR>

<LI><A HREF="Text13.html" TARGET="pages">Chapter 3</A><BR>

</UL>
<P>
<H3>Section 2</H3>
<UL>
<LI><A HREF="Text21.html" TARGET="pages">Chapter 1</A><BR>
<LI>
<LI><A HREF="Text22.html" TARGET="pages">Chapter 2</A><BR>
<LI>
<LI><A HREF="Text23.html" TARGET="pages">Chapter 3</A><BR>
</UL></BODY>
</HTML>
```

This section is obviously where the key frame scripting activity takes place. Each link in the Table of Contents (the Section headings are not links) specifies a TARGET in addition to the source URL. The target is the name of the right-hand frame, assigned when I created it in the script above. When the user clicks on one of these links, the contents of the right-hand pane change to show the selected material.

Figure 8.4 shows the window as it looks when it opens. Notice that the default document, "doc1.html," appears in the right-hand frame.

When the user clicks on the "Chapter 1" link under "Section 1" in the Table of Contents, the window changes so that it looks like Figure 8.5.

Events and Event Handlers

The last topic of this chapter is events. The concept should not be new to you. You've probably worked with events in other scripting or programming environments, and I introduced the notion in Chapter 7. In this section, we'll look at:

- events as a concept
- creating event handlers
- built-in event handlers for JavaScript objects

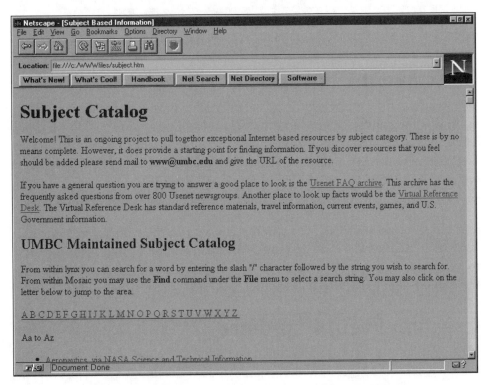

Figure 8.4   This demo window illustrates the scripted frame at startup.

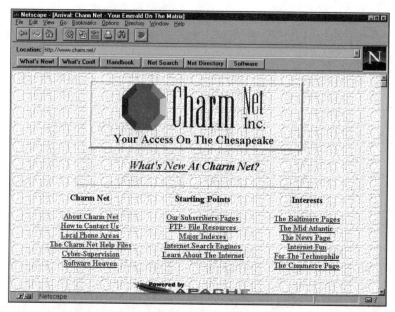

Figure 8.5   This window illustrates the scripted frame in use.

Basic Event Concepts

Users generate most of the events that are interesting to you as a JavaScripter. They do this by moving the mouse, clicking the mouse, opening or closing windows, activating frames, and engaging in a number of other user behaviors. When they take these actions, events are generated by the system. You can "trap" these events and take some action in response to them. If you don't trap them in your scripts, they are simply ignored (except, of course, that they carry out the user's intent).

You can think of events as messages that are sent to the whole Navigator universe (as it exists on the local desktop). Any object in the active page can choose to respond to an event. All it needs to do is define a handler of the same name as the event, assign a script to that handler, and then wait for the event to occur.

Creating Event Handlers

When you create a Netscape object that is capable of dealing with events, you can cause it to react to an event by adding some text to its definition. This text consists of the name of the event, followed by an equal sign, followed by a function call or a complete JavaScript without the <SCRIPT> and </SCRIPT> tags. (I'll describe these objects and the events they can handle in the next section.)

Here's a simple example. Suppose you have a "Submit" button on a form on your page, and you want to confirm that the user really wants to submit the form when he or she clicks the button. You could define the "Submit" button like this:

```
<INPUT TYPE = "submit" VALUE="Send It!" onClick="confirmIntent()">
```

You'd have to define the function "confirmIntent" before this point on the page, of course.

Remember earlier in this chapter when I described how the "this" keyword could be used to create generic functions? In that example, I used an "onChange" event for text objects to trigger the validation. We're applying the same principle here. I created an event handler when I added the text object to the form, and then when the event occurred, the script or function supplied as a parameter to the event name was triggered.

All JavaScript events have names that begin with the word "on" to signal that they are event names to be triggered and reacted to "on" the occurrence of some action.

Built-In Events

Most, but not all, Netscape objects define one or more events for which a valid handler can be created. If you create an event handler for an object that doesn't react to such events, no harm is done, but nothing happens, either.

The nine built-in events in JavaScript can be divided into four categories, as follows:

- mouse events
- focus events (which are in some ways a subset of form events)
- form events
- window events

MOUSE EVENTS

The first mouse event is onClick, which occurs when the user clicks on any mouse button and releases it without moving it away from the object on which it was first clicked. The second mouse event is onMouseOver, which occurs when the user moves the mouse, without holding down a button, inside the boundaries of a link object.

The onClick event handler applies to the following types of object:

@ button
@ checkbox
@ radio
@ link
@ reset
@ submit

The onMouseOver event only applies to links.

FOCUS EVENTS

At any one time on a Web page, only one interactive object can have the focus at a time. The object with the focus is the one to which mouse clicks and keyboard entries will be sent by the system. When an object gains the focus (typically by the user clicking into its boundaries or tabbing into it), an onFocus event is generated. When an object loses the focus (typically by the user clicking on another object or tabbing out of it), an onBlur event is generated. These two events apply to select, text, and textarea objects only.

FORM EVENTS

Three events relate to data completion and form submission. These events are:

@ onChange, which occurs when a text, textarea, or select object loses the focus after its value changes
@ onSelect, which occurs when the user selects some or all of the text in a text or textarea object
@ onSubmit, which occurs when the user clicks the "submit" button on a form

Notice that the onChange event isn't sent until the focus is changed. A user who changes the value in a text object but doesn't tab out of it, can change it again and again without triggering this event.

WINDOW EVENTS

Two events relate to windows: onLoad and onUnload. The onLoad event occurs when the Navigator finishes loading a window (or all of the frames in a window containing frames). The onUnload event occurs when you exit a document.

Event handlers for both of these events are defined in either the <BODY> or the <FRAMESET> tags, although they are actually applicable to the window as a whole.

JAVASCRIPT
IN ACTION
IX

Let's put JavaScript through its paces. In this chapter, I'll describe and explain four applications of increasing complexity. For each example, I outline the problem I'm trying to solve and explain why HTML without JavaScript won't meet that need. Then I'll discuss how I designed the solution. Next, I'll walk you through the JavaScript code as well as any other pertinent design considerations.

The examples in this chapter focus almost exclusively on JavaScript. In Chapter 12, I'll broaden the focus to encompass frames, and other features of Netscape.

The four examples in this chapter are:

- Today's Cafeteria Menu, which demonstrates JavaScript's conditional processing and HTML generation capabilities
- Kiosk Window Display, which uses JavaScript's ability to change certain attributes of new windows as they open; this feature enables you to create a browser experience over which you can have more direct controlStatus
- Scroller, which shows you how to use the status bar in a Netscape Navigator window to display scrolling messages that grab people's attention
- Dynamic Form Emailer, which shows off JavaScript's ability by creating a form "on the fly," validating user input to that form, and emailing the user's entries without using a CGI application

Today's Cafeteria Menu

The Human Resources Department recently inaugurated a company cafeteria program and just hired a new manager, Ms. Brimley. She is a real fan of technology. She has decided that the cafeteria should have its own Web presence on the company's internal network. (Some Web newcomers call an internal network an "intranet" even though internal networks pre-date the Internet by a number of years.)

Ms. Brimley has outlined a fairly ambitious plan for the cafeteria's Web site. Like a good Webmaster, you are starting with a small, manageable task to get her accustomed to the power and limitations of the Web. You decide to start with a page that simply displays the week's menu. This is a piece of cake. (Not the menu, the task of creating this page.) Unfortunately, Ms. Brimley finds the result something less than compelling. She wants the page to display only the menu for the day on which the employee checks the menu.

The Problem

HTML, of course, does not support conditional processing. All of the HTML on a given page displays; you can't hide information selectively. (Some third-party tools such as NetCloak from Maxum allow more flexibility in this regard, but we'll ignore them for the moment in the interest of seeing how JavaScript could help us reach our goal.)

Ms. Brimley wants it to be easy for people to look up today's cafeteria menu. She'd rather not require the user, for example, to select a day from a list box or click a button to tell us which day's menu they want. "Surely the computer knows what day it is?" she half-asks, half-demands.

Well, the computer may know, but the Web page doesn't, at least not without a little help from JavaScript.

Designing a Solution

I could have approached this project a number of ways. I chose a method that simplifies the programming and explanation of my design, but I know other solutions may have been easier for the person maintaining the menus on the Web pages.

I went with a single-page solution and one medium-sized JavaScript. I assumed that the person who had to enter each week's menus would know HTML and be comfortable editing Web documents. If either of those assumptions had been invalid, of course, my design approach would be different.

This page will simply check today's date when it is opened. It will then use a built-in JavaScript function to determine the day of the week and display the menu for that day. Nothing very complicated.

The Code

Here's the main JavaScript skeleton. It doesn't include the menu information but it provides placeholders indicating where that data will be placed in the finished routine. I'll show you the completed routine shortly.

```
<HTML>
<SCRIPT LANGUAGE="JavaScript">
var theDate = new Date()
<HEAD><TITLE>Today's Cafeteria Menu</TITLE>
<--!hiding script from non-JavaScript browsers
var theDay = theDate.getDay ()
newWin = window.open("","newWin")
newWin.document.open ()
newWin.document.write ("<title>Cafeteria Menu for Today</title><p>")
if ((theDay == 0) || (theDay == 6)) {
    newWin.document.write("<h2>No company lunch on the weekends!</h2><p>")
newWin.document.close() }
if (theDay == 1) {
    newWin.document.write("<h2><center>Menu for Monday:</h2></center>")
}
if (theDay == 2) {
    newWin.document.write("<h2><center>Menu for Tuesday:</h2></center>")
}
 if (theDay == 3) {
    newWin.document.write("<h2><center>Menu for Wednesday:</h2></center>")
}
if (theDay == 4) {
    newWin.document.write("<h2><center>Menu for Thursday:</h2></center>")
}
if (theDay == 5) {
    newWin.document.write("<h2><center>Menu for Friday:</h2></center>")
}
newWin.document.close()
close()
-->
</SCRIPT>

</HEAD>
<BODY>
</BODY>
</HTML>
```

The first two lines after the <SCRIPT> tag generate a new date (which will be today's date in a JavaScript-specific format). Then we use a built-in method, Date.getDay (), to get the number of the current day of the week. JavaScript treats the days as if the week begins on Sunday, giving Sunday a value of 0.

Next, we just have to determine what menu to display. The rest of the script, then, is a series of "if" statements that simply determine if the number of the day of the week matches some value. If so, certain information is displayed; if not, the checking continues. We ultimately check for every legal value for the day of the week, so we know that, sooner or later, something will be printed.

We need to review the last two lines before the </SCRIPT> tag, also. The first one forces the document in the newly generated window to close. This step flushes the buffer of any text that has not displayed yet in the document. The problem of undisplayed text doesn't occur often, but when it does, it can cause crashes. You want to close the document when you finish writing information to it.

The other line closes the current window (the one from which the script was invoked and the new window opened). Neatness counts! Clean up after yourself. This window has no further value. If the users close the menu window, they should not have to deal with an essentially dead window.

You can test this script to see that it does what you expect for all seven days of the week. Edit the first line of the script so that it creates a date object for a date whose day of the week you know. For example, March 10, 1996, fell on a Sunday (I know because it's my birthday!), so if you changed the first line of the script to read like this:

```
var theDate = new Date ("March 10, 1996")
```

you would expect the window to display the result shown in Figure 9.1.

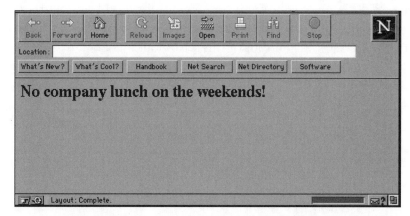

Figure 9.1   After you open a window with the date set to a known Sunday, this menu displays.

You'd expect the result shown in Figure 9.2, but you might not see that result if you're running on a Macintosh. A bug in Netscape 2.x caused dates to be off by one day, so that March 10, 1996, though clearly a Sunday, is reported as a Monday. Netscape expects to have this bug fixed in Netscape 3.0

One final point: I defined this entire function in the <HEAD> portion of the HTML document. Remember that scripts that appear in the <HEAD> are executed when the page is loaded. Those appearing in the <BODY> portion of a document aren't executed until they are called on by a user action or some other event.

Now let's take a look at a fragment of this script to see how it handles displaying a given day's menu when the skeleton is replaced by a fully functional JavaScript. Here's the code for Monday's menu:

```
if (theDay == 1) {
    newWin.document.write("<h2><center>Menu for Monday:</h2></center>")
    newWin.document.write("<ul>"+
"<li>" + "Beef Barley Soup" + "<br>" +
"<li>" + "Green Salad" + "<br>" +
"<li>" + "Penne Pasta With Mild Italian Sausage" + "<br>" +
"<li>" + "Vanilla Bean Gelato" + "<br>" +
"</ul><p>")}
```

I formatted the menu as a bulleted (unordered) list in HTML, with each item on a separate line but not spaced like separate paragraphs (using the <br> instead of the <p> tag). The output of this script looks like Figure 9.2.

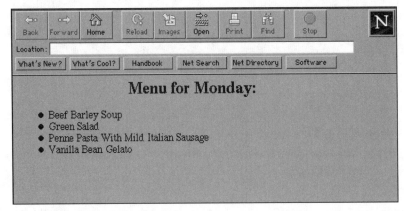

Figure 9.2   This menu window shows Monday's menu as an unordered list.

OK, ready? Here's the whole script, with appropriate menu displays for each day.

```
<HTML>
<HEAD><TITLE>Today's Cafeteria Menu</TITLE>
<-!hiding script from non-JavaScript browsers
<SCRIPT LANGUAGE="JavaScript">
var theDate = new Date( )
var theDay = theDate.getDay ()
newWin = window.open("","newWin")
newWin.document.open ()
newWin.document.write ("<title>Cafeteria Menu for Today</title><p>")
if ((theDay == 0) || (theDay == 6)) {
    newWin.document.write("<h2>No company lunch on the weekends!</h2><p>")
newWin.document.close() }
if (theDay == 1) {
    newWin.document.write("<h2><center>Menu for Monday:</h2></center>")
    newWin.document.write("<ul>"+
"<li>" + "Beef Barley Soup" + "<br>" +
 "<li>" + "Green Salad" + "<br>" +
"<li>" + "Penne Pasta With Mild Italian Sausage" + "<br>" +
"<li>" + "Vanilla Bean Gelato" + "<br>" +
"</ul><p>")}
if (theDay == 2) {
    newWin.document.write("<h2><center>Menu for Tuesday:</h2></center>")
    newWin.document.write("<ul>"+
"<li>" +"Chicken Noodle Soup" + "<br>" +
"<li>" + "Chef's Salad" + "<br>" +
"<li>" + "Seafood Collage" + "<br>" +
"<li>" + "Apple Pie" + "<br>" +
"</ul><p>")}
if (theDay == 3) {
    newWin.document.write("<h2><center>Menu for Wednesday:</h2></center>")
    newWin.document.write("<ul>"+
"<li>" + "Lentil Soup" + "<br>" +
"<li>" + "Garden Salad" + "<br>" +
"<li>" + "Grilled Eggplant Parmesan" + "<br>" +
"<li>" + "Flan" + "<br>" +
"</ul><p>")}
if (theDay == 4) {
    newWin.document.write("<h2><center>Menu for Thursday:</h2></center>")
    newWin.document.write("<ul>"+
"<li>" + "Navy Bean Soup" + "<br>" +
"<li>" + "Spinach Salad" + "<br>" +
"<li>" + "Meatloaf with Mashed Potatoes" + "<br>" +
"<li>" + "Brownie" + "<br>" +
"</ul><p>")}
if (theDay == 5) {
    newWin.document.write("<h2><center>Menu for Friday:</h2></center>")
    newWin.document.write("<ul>"+
"<li>" + "Clam Chowder" + "<br>" +
"<li>" + "English-Style Fish and Chips" + "<br>" +
```

```
"<li>" + "Tapioca Pudding" + "<br>" +
"</ul><p>")}

newWin.document.close()
close()

</SCRIPT>
-->
</HEAD>
<BODY>
</BODY>
</HTML>
```

Ms. Brimley only has to edit the contents of each day's menu and save the HTML file to update the employees on the delectable offerings of the company cafeteria.

Kiosk Window Display

The sample application in this section shows you how to create a Netscape Navigator window with no controls through which the user could either become lost or venture outside boundaries you wish to define.

The Problem

The World Wide Web would be a good choice for an interface for many applications, except that it affords the user too many choices. We call such applications "kiosk" applications, because they tend to resemble information kiosks in which the user's interaction with the content and system is strictly controlled. Each screen permits the user a very limited number of choices.

In an unmodified Navigator browser window, the user can make an almost infinite variety of choices. Most of the choices are unpredictable to the set of pages that make up the user's current application context (the material you want the user to browse). These activities include:

- moving backward and forward in the current list of pages that have been browsed
- returning to whatever the user has defined as "Home"
- providing a specific URL anywhere on the Web to which to navigate
- returning to Netscape's home page (using the animated "N" icon)
- checking out what's new or cool at the Netscape site

@ opening the Netscape documentation

@ conducting a search through Netscape's home site

@ accessing Netscape's software download and upgrade area

The user can choose to hide or show most of the elements of a Navigator window that can alter the navigational experience. The Options menu includes items for hiding the toolbar, the location entry box, and the directory buttons along the bottom of the location entry box. We can't rely on the user to make these choices correctly; after all, we're trying to create a user experience that minimizes the user's need to make choices. Further, even if the user were able and willing to make the appropriate menu choices for a given window, the menu choices remain in effect only for the current window. When a new window is opened, the choices revert to their default condition, which is to show all of these elements.

Designing the Solution

Recall from Chapter 7 that a number of window object properties affect the window's display. These properties can be set when the window is opened, by supplying a string as the third argument to the open() method when sent, or applied to a window object.

To achieve the kiosk look and feel we're after, we'll want to open a window with none of the following:

@ toolbar

@ location

@ directories

@ menubar

The menubar poses a special problem on the Macintosh. While Windows and UNIX typically have window-specific menubars, the Macintosh has a system-wide menubar that doesn't "belong" to a specific window or even completely to a single application. As a result, hiding the menubar on the Macintosh has essentially no effect. Perhaps a subsequent release of Netscape Navigator for the Macintosh will address this need, but for the moment, just know that you can't hide the Macintosh menubar from JavaScript.

In Chapter 7, I did a little soft-shoe shuffle to avoid getting into the complexities of how the various properties of a window interact with one another. In the absence of an example, working through those interactions can be a little time-consuming. But we're ready to take the time to do that now.

You already know from lots of experience that if you open a new window with a statement like this:

```
newWindow = window.open("","")
```

you will get a standard Navigator window with all the usual accouterments.

The missing third argument is a single string that defines properties for the window as it is opened. For example, you can hide the location entry box but show the navigation and other buttons by opening the window with a statement such as this:

```
newWindow = window.open("","","toolbar=yes")
```

This code fragment, properly implemented in an HTML document, produces a window that looks like the one in Figure 9.3.

(If you change the line so that it explicitly does not show the location box, the result is the same. I think there are a significant number of anomalies in the way window properties work in window.open() statements in JavaScript, at least in the release available at press time.)

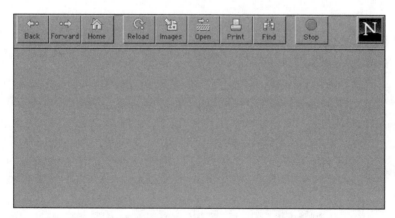

Figure 9.3   We opened this window with a toolbar only.

Fortunately, we don't need to get into too many of the nuances of the list of window attributes to solve our problem. Much experimentation leads to the conclusion that providing a simple empty string as the third argument in the window.open() method call leads to a kiosk-style window. It's not at all clear to me why this is the case, but it is.

Once we've forced a new window to open in kiosk mode, all subsequent windows that we open with a window.open () method call will also open in that mode. This process continues until we supply a third parameter that changes the behavior. We really only need to place and execute the JavaScript in a single window (presumably the first one we open) to achieve the desired effect.

The Code

I decided to define a function in the <HEAD> portion of the first document that I expected the user to answer in my sample application. This function will open a new window in kiosk mode, and close itself, leaving the user viewing all subsequent linked windows in kiosk mode.

Here's the code for the function I called makeKiosk():

```
<SCRIPT LANGUAGE="JAVASCRIPT">
function makeKiosk () {
var isMac = navigator.userAgent.indexOf("Mac") !=-1
kioskWindow = window.open("http://kiosk2.html","kioskWindow","")
if (isMac) {
kioskWindow = window.open ("http://kiosk2.html","kioskWindow","") }
kioskWindow.name="Kiosk Demo Window"
window.close()
}
</SCRIPT>
```

The most interesting aspect of this script has nothing to do with the problem at hand. The first executable line (after the "function" statement) defines a variable called isMac. Netscape 2.x has a bug on the Mac and UNIX versions that prevents a newly created window from displaying a URL unless it is forced to open a second time. But on a Windows platform, opening the window twice is ill-advised.

To test whether the user is running Netscape on a Macintosh, I take advantage of the built-in Navigator property called userAgent. This property contains a string that looks something like this:

```
Mozilla/2.01 (Macintosh; I; PPC)
```

(This result occurs when you use Navigator 2.01 on a PowerPC Macintosh. Your results may be different.) By searching for the string "Mac," I can find out whether that sub-string is contained in the userAgent string. If it is in the string, JavaScript returns the beginning position of the string (in this case, the number 15). If it can't find the string (we're running on a Windows platform), it returns the value -1. I check for that value and set the value of the Boolean (logic) variable isMac to true or false, accordingly.

Now, when I open the new window on the appropriate URL, I open it once and then check the isMac variable. If it's true, I open the window a second time; otherwise, I skip the second window.open() method call.

With the function defined, I just need a way to invoke it. I start the user with a window whose only purpose is to set up the proper kiosk mode. I use an "onload" event for the window to trigger a call to the makeKiosk() function. Such a tag must be embedded in the <BODY> tag, as shown here:

```
<BODY onload="makeKiosk()">
```

(You may, of course, have other properties defined in the <BODY> tag. They can be left in place. The ordering of properties is also unimportant, so you can put this "onload" property anywhere convenient in the <BODY> tag.)

When the user opens this page, the makeKiosk function is invoked. This function opens a new window with the kiosk style, loads a URL document into it, and closes the original calling document. Exactly what we wanted!

Here's the complete HTML for this page, just for the sake of completeness:

```
<HTML>
<HEAD><TITLE>Kiosk Demo</TITLE>
<SCRIPT LANGUAGE="JAVASCRIPT">
function makeKiosk () {
var isMac = navigator.userAgent.indexOf("Mac") !=-1
kioskWindow = window.open ("http://kiosk2.html","kioskWindow","")
if (isMac) {
kioskWindow = window.open ("http://kiosk2.html","kioskWindow","") }
kioskWindow.name="Kiosk Demo Window"
window.close()
}
</SCRIPT>
```

```
</HEAD>
<BODY onload="makeKiosk()">

<A HREF="kiosk3.html">Open another window</A>.
</BODY>
</HTML>
```

As you can see, I added an HREF link to the page. Clicking on this link opens another window, just to prove that we stay in kiosk mode even though the third window doesn't have a single reference to the makeKiosk function.

Status Scroller

Shortly after JavaScript became available in early pre-release copies of Netscape 2, people started writing JavaScripts that displayed text in the status bar at the bottom of the window. Displaying text in that area is easy; getting it to scroll like an animated news banner in Times Square is another matter entirely.

The Problem

By itself, HTML gives you no control over the appearance of anything displayed in a window outside the HTML viewing area. No standard HTML exists to change what appears in the status pane of a Netscape browser window.

The status pane is an obvious place to put information for the user. I showed you in Chapter 7 how to put helpful information into the status pane while the user rolled the mouse over certain objects. The problem with that approach is that on a busy screen, the user might well overlook such a tip. But if we animate the text, we'll get the user's attention.

In fact, you might get too much of the user's attention. Many people have begun to rebel at the inclusion of scrolling text in the status pane of the browser window, suggesting that it is offensive because it screams for extra attention. I think this attitude is a bit of an overreaction, influenced somewhat, no doubt, by the backlash against the <BLINK> text attribute Netscape introduced soon after shipping its first browsers.

Designing the Solution

As I pointed out in Chapter 7, a window object in Netscape has a property called status that defines or returns the contents of the status pane in the browser window. You can change this property by a simple one-line JavaScript:

```
status="This text will display in the status pane."
```

Problems appear when you change the status pane's contents; for example, how transient or permanent will your changes be? As I was writing this chapter, Netscape was working on a solution that would clean up some of this confusion. If you experiment with the material in this section and things don't always seem to work as described, double-check that you are running the latest revision.

Merely changing the status pane's contents can capture the user's attention. This approach works particularly well when the user is expecting the change, as in the case of a tip or hint for which you have prepared the user in documentation or notes. You can, for example, replace the usual URL (which is often a meaningless collection of gibberish characters to an uninitiated reader) with a meaningful description of the link location. To do this task, you can take advantage of a link object's onMouseOver event capability with a script fragment something like this:

```
<A HREF="http://www.news.com" onMouseOver='status="Late-breaking news of
  the company";return(true);'>Check out company news</A>
```

When the user positions the mouse over the text "Check out company news," the status pane changes to reveal that this link takes the user to "Late-breaking news of the company."

You can probably think of lots of other uses for the status pane, some of them undoubtedly more interesting than this example.

The problem with relying on the status pane for messages to which you really want to call attention is that users can become too accustomed to seeing its contents change. They may stop paying attention. So we need something that will attract their eyes when it happens.

Enter the concept of scrolling text. This JavaScript solution takes advantage of the status pane update capability of a Netscape window along with the window.setTimeout method. The setTimeout method causes a one-time delay before an action takes place. For example, you might write something like this:

```
t1 = setTimeout("status='You lack status';return(true);",2000)
```

Recall from Chapter 7 that the setTimeout method takes two parameters. The first parameter is the action to be taken. In this case, it's a two-line JavaScript using semicolons as statement separators. The second argument is the number of milliseconds (thousandths of a second) to delay before carrying out the action. In this case, the script will pause for two seconds, then update the status pane.

As of Version 2.01 of Netscape Navigator, repeated calls to setTimeout were reported to be causing memory leaks and crashes on some systems, particularly, apparently, Macintosh systems. Exercise caution when using setTimeout methods in your JavaScripts.

To cause text to scroll in the status pane, then, we will have to define a function that can be called when the page is loaded. This function will use setTimeout to cause an appropriate delay between updates of the status pane, so that the text doesn't simply race unreadably through the area. Then it will update the status pane at each interval, adding one or more characters to the stream being displayed. It also must be able to detect when it reaches the end of the string being scrolled, to determine its next action. Finally, it would be cool if we could turn off the scrolling after some number of repetitions so it doesn't become annoying.

The Code

Thomas van der Heijden (Thom@bART.nl) originally wrote the script that handles this status pane scrolling. The latest version can be found at http://

www.bart.nl/~thom/index2.html. I have made some slight modifications to van der Heijden's original script, mostly for clarity. His script is one of the cleanest implementations of status pane scrolling I've seen.

The script has two functions: scroll_start and scroll_stop. To invoke the scroll_start function, you use the following syntax:

```
scroll_start(scroll_speed, status_bar_size, scroll_delay, loop_count,
  message)
```

The five arguments to this function are as follows:

- scroll_speed determines the speed with which the text scrolls through the status pane. Experimentation reveals that a speed of 1 is about right.
- status_bar_size determines the number of characters in width that will be used in the status pane. Because the user can resize the window and with it the status pane, we need to know in advance how wide an area you can use for scrolling text. The number is somewhat arbitrary; it defaults to 200.
- scroll_delay is the amount of time to delay before starting scrolling. This delay gives the window a chance to finish updating the status pane to indicate it's read the document. The default value is 60 milliseconds, which seems to work well even on fast machines.
- loop_count is the number of times you want the message to scroll before it stops. A value of -1, which is the default, scrolls endlessly.
- message is, of course, a text string containing the message to be scrolled.

The scroll_stop function requires no arguments.

This script uses a number of variables, five corresponding to the inputs to the scroll_start function and the following control variables used for various purposes:

- scrl_timer_active is a Boolean that the script uses to determine whether there is an active scroller (in which case this variable's value is true) or not (in which case it is false)
- scrl_timer_id, which is used to store the identifier of the timer created by the call to setTimeout. You need this value to later stop the timer.
- scrl_wrap, containing a value that tells the scroller when a message is complete. Its initial value is 100.

Let's look at the scroll_start function's code:

```
function scroll_start(spd, size, time, loop, msg) {
    scroll_stop();
    scrl_speed = spd;
    scrl_status_size = size;
    scrl_time = time;
    scrl_loop = loop;
    scrl_wrap = msg.length;
    diff = (size/msg.length)+1;
    for (x=0; x<diff; x++)
        scrl_msg += msg + " ";
    scroll_status();
    scrl_timer_active = true;
}
```

The first line makes sure that any timers already in effect as a result of calls to this function are terminated. The next five lines simply place inputs to the function into local variables for use during execution. The next line calculates the length of the message string, using the built-in length method, and assigns the result to scrl_wrap.

The seventh line of the script determines how many "buffers" will be needed to accommodate smooth scrolling of the message through the status pane, given the length of the message. It creates a variable called diff that is used in a for loop momentarily. For example, if you have a 40-character message and a 200-character scrolling area, this calculation results in diff having a value of 6.

Using the value in diff for a loop control, the for loop sets up the message to contain a series of concatenated copies of the scrolling text, separated by a space. This process ensures that the scrolling area will eventually fill with message and keep scrolling smoothly.

The next-to-last line of the script calls the function scroll_status. The actual updating of the status pane occurs here. Let's look at the code for the scroll_status function:

```
function scroll_status() {
    window.status = scrl_msg.substring(scrl_idx,
scrl_idx+scrl_status_size);
    scrl_idx += scrl_speed;
    if (scrl_idx >= scrl_wrap) {
        scrl_idx -= scrl_wrap;
if (scrl_loop != -1)
```

```
      if (-scrl_loop <= 0)
   scrl_speed = 0;
      }
      scrl_timer_id = window.setTimeout("scroll_status()",scrl_time);
}
```

The first line of this script grabs a portion of the message text (the multi-copy version created in scroll_start, as described above). It starts at the current value of scrl_idx, and continues for a number of characters equal to the width of the status pane. It then adds the scrolling speed to the starting index of this string. You can see how the scrolling speed controls the rate at which text scrolls; the higher the speed, the more characters are added to the string at one time.

Now we have to perform two boundary checks. The first check, contained in the next two lines, determines if it is time to wrap the text (start a new round of scrolling), based on the fact that we've reached the end of the string. The second check, contained in the next three lines, determines whether we've looped enough times. If the loop value is -1, we skip this processing because the loop should go on indefinitely. If, however, the value is something other than -1, we decrement the loop counter and see if it's time to stop. If so, we set the scroll speed to 0. This setting has the combined effect of stopping the scrolling and leaving our message displayed in the status pane.

Finally, we call the setTimeout function to initiate (or continue) the scrolling.

For the sake of completeness, let's look at the scroll_stop function, even though it's quite simple:

```
function scroll_stop() {
    if (scrl_timer_active)
        window.clearTimeout(scrl_timer_id);
    scrl_timer_active = false;
}
```

First, the function makes sure an active scroller exists. If not, we don't want to try to stop it because that's never a good idea! If a timer is in effect, we use clearTimeout to end the timing loop and set the Boolean scrl_timer_active to false. (Recall that when scroll_start begins its processing, it checks this value.)

That's all there is to it. (Yeah, right!) This script is longer than the other scripts we've looked at so far. I'll reproduce it in its entirety here, including the comments in the original code by van der Heijden, as well as some I added or clarified. You can also find this script on the CD-ROM accompanying this book.

```
/* Status scroll v.1.04
Done too many times already...but this is a bit cleaner than the other ones.

Usage:

   onLoad=scroll_start(scroll_speed, status_bar_size, scroll_delay,
loop_count, message);

   onUnload=scroll_stop();

(c)1996 Thomas van der Heijden (Thom@bART.nl)

*/

var scrl_timer_active = false;
var scrl_timer_id = null;
var scrl_speed = 1;
var scrl_status_size = 200;
var scrl_time = 60;
var scrl_idx = 0;
var scrl_msg = "";
var scrl_wrap = 100;
var scrl_loop = -1; // -1 = loop infinite, otherwise #times to loop

function scroll_start(spd, size, time, loop, msg) {

    scroll_stop();              // stop any previous timer
    scrl_speed = spd;           // save scroll speed
    scrl_status_size = size;    // save status bar size
    scrl_time = time;           // save scroll delay
    scrl_loop = loop;           // save no. of times to loop
    scrl_wrap = msg.length;
    diff = (size/msg.length)+1; // create multiple buffer message
    for (x=0; x<diff; x++)
        scrl_msg += msg + " ";
    scroll_status();            // start scrolling...
    scrl_timer_active = true;
}


function scroll_stop() {
    if (scrl_timer_active)
        window.clearTimeout(scrl_timer_id);
    scrl_timer_active = false;
}

function scroll_status() {
    window.status = scrl_msg.substring(scrl_idx,
scrl_idx+scrl_status_size);
    scrl_idx += scrl_speed;
    if (scrl_idx >= scrl_wrap) {
```

```
        scrl_idx -= scrl_wrap;
if (scrl_loop != -1)
    if (−scrl_loop <= 0)
  scrl_speed = 0;
    status="";
    }

    scrl_timer_id = window.setTimeout("scroll_status()",scrl_time);
}
// −>
</SCRIPT>
```

Dynamic Form Emailer

Forms are one of the most useful features of Netscape and Netscape-compatible browsers. Not part of the original HTML specification, forms are being incorporated into the next version of that document. Most browsers now support HTML forms, which have quickly become entrenched in the Web.

In this section, we'll build a script that:

- generates a form using document.write statements
- modifies the form as it is being generated, based on the user's platform
- validates the entry of information into fields on the form
- submits the final form to an email address without the benefit of a CGI application

The Problem

Krista Simone, product manager for a new software product called Detect-O-Blue, has asked you to create a form for users to order the program. It's a free product that promotes your company's other software. You don't need to deal with payment information. The only requirement is that the user agree to talk to a representative of the company after receiving the package to answer some survey questions.

The form should have places for the user to enter the following information:

- name
- age
- street address
- city
- state
- zip code

- email address
- operating system
- date to make follow-up call

All of these fields must be completed. In addition, the form should handle the following field validation:

- age is a number between 18 and 99
- email address is properly formatted
- operating system is consistent with user's browser
- date is in the future

There's nothing too complicated here, but the overall requirement is a little daunting. Pure HTML clearly cannot handle this requirement; some JavaScript is definitely called for here.

Just to complicate life, I'm going to throw in another condition. Let's say you're a fairly new Webmaster, and you don't know how to write CGIs and aren't eager to learn in view of your 398-item To Do List. You'd like to find a way to handle the emailing of this form without a CGI. (This requirement is not far-fetched, by the way. Many Web site hosts don't permit CGIs and essentially block you from doing much with form processing. I'll show you a neat way around that problem in this section.)

Designing the Solution

Creating and presenting the order form to the user is easy. HTML can handle all of it quite nicely. But, let's do something impressive. Perhaps we could create the selection item (popup menu/list) of operating systems on the fly to coincide with the platform with which the user is browsing the site. That would be really cool. We'll use a JavaScript that takes one of three conditional branches based on whether the user is running a Macintosh, Windows system, or something else (UNIX, presumably). This approach is a great way to ensure that the user doesn't enter a different operating system from the one they're using.

In a real-world situation, of course, you might not want to use this approach. The user could be browsing with a Macintosh today but using a Windows system at the office. In that case, the user might want to order the Windows version of the product. Because my purpose isn't to create a commercially viable program but rather to show off some JavaScript power, I'll stay with this design.

You may be asked more than once to validate data entered into a form. I'm going to show you how to create generic, reusable code solutions to problems that go beyond the scope of our one project. JavaScript and Netscape don't give us a convenient way to use such reusable code, but we can at least shortcut our typing on future projects a bit.

To make the form emailable without the need for a CGI, I'm going to take advantage of a Netscape feature that isn't supported yet in all browsers. To understand this feature, I need to provide a bit of background on forms processing in HTML. This explanation may go a little beyond what you already know.

Form Processing and the ENCTYPE Attribute

Originally, the draft HTML 2.0 specification for a form included an attribute called ENCTYPE, which stands for "ENClosure TYPE." The default value for this attribute is the MIME type "application/x-www-form-urlencoded." This attribute value simply means that the form is being submitted in a form with which the URL parser can deal. Processing the input from a form submitted over the Web involves a fair amount of work, because of the way URL encoding deals with spaces and other special characters such as quotation marks.

A pending specification change, formally known as RFC 1867, adds a new ENCTYPE value called "multipart/form-data" that allows you to upload one or more files along with the FORM data.

If you're interested in RFCs and how the HTML standard evolves, you might find this note interesting. If you're not, feel free to skip this discussion.

When someone wants to add a new capability to HTML, they have to go through a standardization process. Part of that process involves the publication of a Request for Comments (RFC), issued by a standards-setting body of the Internet. This RFC is circulated as widely as possible and is open for input from anyone with an opinion. Only after the RFC has been available for a long enough period (as determined by the people who manage this aspect of the Internet's evolution and growth) can the specification it describes become part of the official HTML standard.

RFC 1867 envisions a new type of FORM data submission process. Netscape 2 supports this file upload extension as described in the RFC.

Defining an ENCTYPE for Form Email

To require that a form's data be uploaded as one or more files, you need to add the ENCTYPE attribute to the ACTION portion of a FORM definition. You also need to define the action as a "mailto:" action. Here's a sample of how you would approach this problem:

```
<FORM NAME="Detect-o-Blue_Order" method=POST ENCTYPE='multipart/form-data'
ACTION='mailto:"orders@thecompany.com"+"?ORDER_FORM||/>
```

The two differences between this FORM definition tag and those with which you have worked before are:

- the ENCTYPE attribute, which you've probably never had to deal with before because you were using the default (and only available) value
- a "mailto:" access method rather than the "HTTP:" access method normally supplied for the ACTION attribute

The Code

I like to break software projects into small, testable modules as often as possible. I'll follow that approach for the first part of this project. It will give us more interaction with JavaScript, and you may find this approach to learning a little easier than downing a big gulp of code all in one swallow.

First, I'll walk through the validation functions we'll use in this application. Then I'll show you the form-generation code, including the conditional processing section where I'll spend most of my time. Finally, I'll explain how we incorporate the email form submission into this project. Finally, I'll end up with a listing of the entire script so you can review portions of it in context.

DATA VALIDATION FUNCTIONS

In this form, we need to be able to validate data the following ways:

- for all fields, confirm that they are not empty
- for the age field, confirm that it is a number between 18 and 99
- for email address, confirm that it is properly formatted
- for the follow-up date, make sure it's a date after today

We'll deal with the validation of the operating system by our dynamic form generation approach, so we don't need to write a validation function for it. The user won't be able to make an invalid choice.

We can take several approaches to validating data. For example, we could avoid the necessity of confirming that the age field contains a valid number in the range by creating the input component as a SELECTION rather than a TEXT field. We could then define the SELECTION object's possible values to be each number between 18 and 99. That method is cumbersome, and the resulting pop-up list would be very long.

Similarly, we could arbitrarily decide that the follow-up date field should be a SELECTION whose options are dynamically generated to be valid dates, starting tomorrow and continuing for some arbitrary number of days. That method would be an interesting exercise.

I'm going to take the most straightforward approach because it's also the way I can best demonstrate how to use JavaScript for this task.

TESTING FOR REQUIRED FIELD

Let's begin with the function that confirms that a particular field is not empty. Here's the code:

```
function requireEntry (theField) {
if (theField.value=="") {
alert ("This field is required!")
theField.focus()
return (false) }
}
```

This approach passes the function a parameter that identifies the form object (theField) that I wish to validate. Then I get the value of that field and check it against the empty string. If the match fails—if the field has some content—nothing happens. If the match succeeds, however, I take three steps:

- post an alert notifying the user of the problem
- after the alert is dismissed, return focus to the field
- return the Boolean "false" to the calling function

(We don't make use of this last step, but a function should always return some value, so I include it here. You could use this function if you wanted to keep track of invalid responses, for example.)

Let's test this function.

Create a page with the following HTML:

```
<HTML>
<HEAD><TITLE>Untitled</TITLE>
<SCRIPT LANGUAGE="JAVASCRIPT">
function requireEntry (theField) {
if (theField.value=="") {
alert ("This field is required!")
theField.focus()
return (false) }
}
</SCRIPT>
</HEAD>
<BODY>
Here's a test field:
<FORM>
<INPUT TYPE=TEXT NAME=age onBlur="requireEntry(age)">
</FORM>
</BODY>
</HTML>
```

The only really new thing here is the "onBlur" method call in the <INPUT> tag. When a user enters data or performs some other task, the object where the input occurs becomes the target, or focus, of the keyboard or mouse events. Then, when the user does something to cause it to lose that focus, the object receives the onBlur event. Some programming languages call this event "loseFocus" or "losingFocus," which would have been a little clearer, but I guess "blur" is a little cuter. I dislike cute myself, but there you are!

Load this page into your Netscape 2 or later browser, click into the only field (if it isn't automatically selected for you), and simply tab out of it without entering anything. The result should look like Figure 9.4.

When you click the "OK" button in the dialog, the cursor should be blinking in the field. Enter a value (at this point it doesn't matter what you enter) and then tab. Nothing happens, just as we expect.

I use this same Web document for each of the validation functions I want to test. Meanwhile, I copy and paste the working function into a text document or my favorite HTML editor for safekeeping. When I finish, I can simply copy and paste them into my final document.

Confirming Field Values Are within Range

The age field confirmation looks like this:

```
<SCRIPT LANGUAGE="JAVASCRIPT">
function rangeCheck (theField, minValue, maxValue) {
var numValue = parseInt (theField.value,10)
if (numValue< minValue || numValue > maxValue) {
alert ("Please enter a number between" + minValue + " and " + maxValue)
theField.focus()
theField.select()
return(false) }
}
</SCRIPT>
```

Again, rather than create a function that just checks for a number between 18 and 99, I wrote a generic function called rangeCheck. This function takes three input parameters:

- ◎ the name of the form object whose value you wish to validate
- ◎ the minimum acceptable value for the object
- ◎ the maximum acceptable value for the object

Figure 9.4   Failing to enter a value into a required field produces a dialog.

Modify the earlier HTML document for testing this function so it looks like this:

```
<HTML>
<HEAD><TITLE>Untitled</TITLE>
<SCRIPT LANGUAGE="JAVASCRIPT">
function rangeCheck (theField, minValue, maxValue) {
lvar numValue = parseInt (theField.value,10)
if (numValue < minValue || numValue > maxValue) {
alert ("Please enter a number between" + minValue + " and " + maxValue)
theField.focus()
theField.select()
return(false) }
}
</SCRIPT>
</HEAD>
<BODY>
Here's a test field:
<FORM>
Age: <INPUT TYPE=TEXT NAME=age onBlur="rangeCheck(age,18,99)">
</FORM>
</BODY>
</HTML>
```

Notice that I changed the "onBlur" function to call "rangeCheck" instead of "requireField." What are the consequences of this change? Let's test the document and find out.

Load the document into your Netscape browser. Enter a number (like 5) into the field and tab out of it. The result should look like Figure 9.5.

Enter a number like 51. Nothing should happen. So far, so good, But what if you leave the field empty? Try it. Nothing happens. When you enter either text or nothing in this field, the built-in parseInt method doesn't return a value that is out of the range for which we are checking.

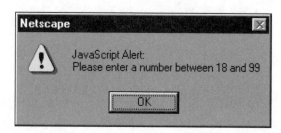

Figure 9.5   Entering a number outside the acceptable range produces a dialog.

CHECKING FOR NON-NUMERIC VALUES

We need to modify this function so that it catches non-numeric entries. We also need to change the way we validate the field to ensure that the field has some value in it. Let's handle the second task first because it's easy. We can use this technique elsewhere in this sample application. Just edit the line where the field is defined so that it carries out the fieldRequired check first, then the rangeCheck:

```
<INPUT TYPE=TEXT NAME=age onBlur="requireEntry(age);
rangeCheck(age,18,99)">
```

Now reload the page and try tabbing out of the field without entering a value. It works!

Next, let's tackle the problem of how we determine if the user has entered a numerical value.

The documentation for the parseInt method tells us that if everyone reading this page used a Windows version of the Netscape browser, this step would be easy. parseInt on a Windows machine returns a value of -1. We could simply check for that value and react accordingly. However, we are not willing to make that assumption.

I wrote a routine that simply scans through the value of the field and ensures that each character is between the character zero ("0") and the character nine ("9"). If they are all within that range, I know we have a numeric value; if any are not, we have an error. Here's the code:

```
function checkNumeric (theField) {
   fldValue = theField.value
   for (var i = 0 ; i < fldValue.length; i++) {
   var ch = fldValue.substring (i, i+1)
   if (ch < "0" || "9" < ch) {
   alert ("This field requires only numbers!")
   theField.focus ()
   theField.select ()
   return (false)
   break
 }
}  return (true)}
```

The only new material here is the "break" statement, which terminates the loop. Without this statement, the alert notifying the user that the field requires numbers only would be issued once for each non-numeric character in the field. That result could get darned annoying!

By now you are comfortable with the testing process. Change the line that has the input field defined so that it reads like this:

```
Age: <INPUT TYPE=TEXT NAME=age onBlur="requireEntry(age);
checkNumeric(age); rangeCheck(age,18,99)">
```

Note that I inserted the checkNumeric function call ahead of the rangeCheck. If the value isn't numeric, we don't need to check the range of values (although, as we've already seen, doing so won't cause a problem on a non-numeric field).

Validating an Email Address

Dealing with invalid email addresses is a Webmaster's nightmare. You know a customer or reader out there somewhere wants something from you, but you can't find them because they typed their email address incorrectly. It's maddening. (Sometimes, of course, such invalid entries are deliberate and malicious. I'm working on a script to slap the hands of those people. For now, let's assume we're dealing with an ideal world where people just make honest mistakes.)

To be valid, an email address must meet the following three criteria:

- @ be at least eight characters long
- @ contain an "@" symbol
- @ contain at least three characters between the "@" sign and the next period (dot)

Writing a function to test a string for these characteristics is fairly straightforward. Here's my cut at this function:

```
<SCRIPT LANGUAGE="JAVASCRIPT">
  function checkEmail (theField) {
  var i = 0
  testString = theField.value
  if (testString.length < 8) {
  alert ("Email address too short to be valid")
  theField.focus ()
  theField.select ()
  return (false)
  }
  if ((i = testString.indexOf ("@",1)) < 1) {
  alert ("Email addresses must include an '@' sign")
  theField.focus ()
  theField.select ()
  return (false)
  }
```

```
   if (testString.indexOf (".",i) <= i+3) {
   alert ("Email addresses must have at least three characters between the
   '@' and the first dot.")
   theField.focus ()
   theField.select ()
   return (false)
    }
   }
</SCRIPT>
```

This function performs the three checks in the logical progression of:

@ first, making sure there are enough characters (because if there aren't, no other test matters)

@ then, ensuring that there is an "@" sign (because if there isn't, we sure can't check to see where the first period following the "@" sign is)

@ finally, ensuring that the first period falls at least three characters after the "@" sign

Build a test page and include an entry field with the following HTML code:

```
Email: <INPUT TYPE=TEXT NAME=email onBlur="checkEmail(email)">
```

Try entering various combinations of letters and see if the script behaves as expected when confronted with correct and incorrect email addresses.

DYNAMIC PAGE GENERATION

We can use document.write function calls to create the content of the page we want to display to the user. This function allows us to craft portions of the form dynamically, which is not possible if we simply load a URL into a new window.

Clearly in this case, where the only thing we're changing is one SELECT object, we could easily have two separate pages and just load the appropriate URL based on the platform the user is running. However, the principle of dynamic page generation is critical; it's one of the most popular uses for JavaScript. So we'll continue on this path even though the solution may not be optimal for this specific circumstance.

I am not going to deal here with the issue of how the user gets to the page from which the order form page is generated. I'm not interested in designing the entire system. Instead, I'll focus on the JavaScript that actually creates the page and the form in a new window.

The finished page will look something like Figure 9.6.

You cannot mix dynamic and pre-built page generation in JavaScript. For example, you can't just put the OS question at the end of the form, load a pre-defined URL for the rest of the form, and then magically add a new SELECT object to the page. Recall that content can be generated on a page only before it is actually opened and updated.

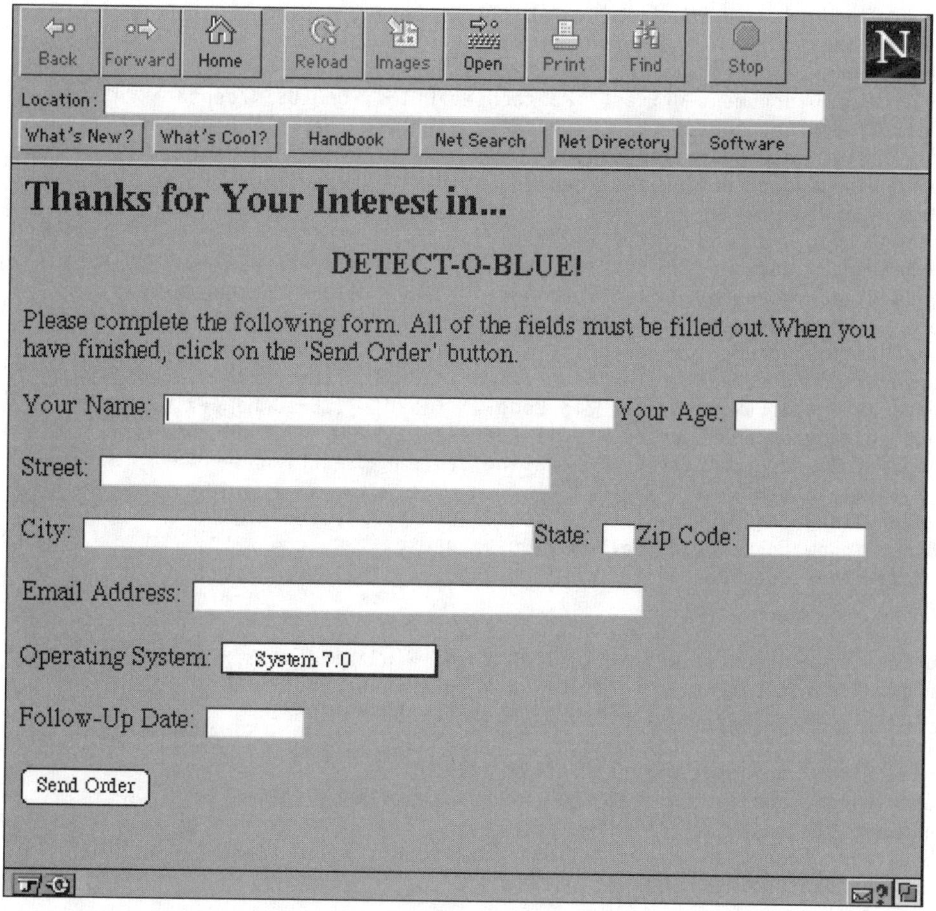

Figure 9.6   The order form page will look like this when we finish.

This page consists almost entirely of a FORM object, which can be tedious in JavaScript. Here's a test HTML document that will create the page shown in Figure 9.6:

```
<HTML>
<HEAD>
<TITLE>Detect-O-Blue Order Form</TITLE>
<SCRIPT LANGUAGE="JAVASCRIPT">
function isMacintosh () {
if (navigator.userAgent.indexOf("Mac") !=-1) {
   return(true) }
else {
   return(false)}
}
orderWindow = window.open ("","orderWindow")
orderWindow.document.write ("<HEAD><TITLE>Detect-O-Blue Order Form</
TITLE></HEAD>")
orderWindow.document.write ("<H2>Thanks for Your Interest in...</H2>")
orderWindow.document.write ("<H3><center>DETECT-O-BLUE!</center></H3>")
orderWindow.document.write ("<P>Please complete the following form. All of
the fields must be filled out.")
orderWindow.document.write("When you have finished, click on the 'Send
Order' button.<P>")
orderWindow.document.write("<FORM>")
orderWindow.document.write("Your Name:   <INPUT SIZE=40 name=custName>")
orderWindow.document.write("Your Age:    <INPUT SIZE=3 name=age><P>")
orderWindow.document.write("Street:      <INPUT SIZE=40 name=street><P>")
orderWindow.document.write("City:        <INPUT SIZE=40 name=city>")
orderWindow.document.write("State:       <INPUT SIZE=2 name=state>")
orderWindow.document.write("Zip Code:    <INPUT SIZE=10 name=zip><P>")
orderWindow.document.write("Email Address:  <INPUT SIZE=40 name=email><P>")
orderWindow.document.write("Operating System: <SELECT name=OS>")
if (isMacintosh()) {
orderWindow.document.write("<OPTION VALUE=Sys7>System 7.0")
orderWindow.document.write("<OPTION VALUE=Sys71>System 7.1")
orderWindow.document.write("<OPTION VALUE=Sys75>System 7.5")
}
else {
orderWindow.document.write("<OPTION VALUE=Win3>Windows 3.x")
orderWindow.document.write("<OPTION VALUE=Win95>Windows 95")
orderWindow.document.write("<OPTION VALUE=DOS>MS-DOS")
}
orderWindow.document.write("</SELECT><P>")
orderWindow.document.write("Follow-Up Date: <INPUT SIZE=8
name=foloDate><P>")
orderWindow.document.write("<INPUT TYPE=submit value='Send Order'><P>")
orderWindow.document.write("</FORM>")
</SCRIPT>
</HEAD>
<BODY>
```

```
</BODY>
</HTML>
```

Our approach is simply to create a new window, give it a name, and then use a bunch of document.write method calls to lay out the form.

Notice the conditional block near the end of the script where I call the function isMacintosh to determine whether the user's system is a Macintosh. If it is, I display the three possible Mac operating systems we recognize; if not, I display three possible Wintel-based operating systems. In a real-world application, of course, we'd have other choices, and, we'd probably do some double-checking (such as a choice of "None of these" for users running weird combinations of operating systems, such as Windows 95 on a Macintosh).

This form does not yet have any method to call when the user clicks the "Send Order" button. It needs one, because when the user clicks on a button you define as having a type of "SUBMIT," JavaScript tries to execute the appropriate method. Adding this capability is our last operation before we put it all together with the validation functions.

SUBMIT ACTION

Remember what I said earlier about the use of the "mailto:" action and the ENCTYPE of "multipart/form-data?" You shouldn't be surprised to find that the coding of this part of the form is quite straightforward. Here's what the code for the form's action should look like:

```
<FORM NAME="Detect-o-Blue_Order" method=POST ENCTYPE='multipart/form-data'
ACTION='mailto:"orders@thecompany.com"+"?ORDER_FORM'>
```

(If this code looks vaguely familiar, it should. It's the same as the sample code I provided earlier. If this doesn't look familiar, maybe you were asleep for that part of the chapter?)

When the user clicks on the SUBMIT button, JavaScript will carry out this command (assuming the Web site is running on a server that supports this new syntax). Then it will mail the order form to orders@thecompany.com.

THE TOTAL PICTURE

We've built all of the pieces. It might seem that now we can copy and paste all of the pieces we've put together into a single script.

I wish it were that simple!

The problem arises with the dynamic order form document we've created. When the script that generates that page finishes executing, the order form window is the front, active window. However, the functions we need to call for data validation are in the window from which the form was generated. Netscape provides no means for calling scripts in a different window. So what do we do?

We have to expand the dynamic document creation process begun in the previous section so that it also writes all of the script functions to the newly created document. In other words, we have to create the new document so that it includes the scripts we expect it to be able to execute.

To go through the entire process of creating these script-storage lines would be a tedious exercise for you and me. I'm leaving most of this process as an exercise for the reader if you want to pursue this project to its conclusion. Essentially, you end up modifying the first part of the script that generates the new order form page so that it looks like this:

```
orderWindow = window.open ("","orderWindow")
orderWindow.document.write ("<HEAD><TITLE>Detect-O-Blue Order Form</
TITLE>")
orderWindow.document.write ("<SCRIPT LANGUAGE='JAVASCRIPT'><P>")
orderWindow.document.write("function requireEntry (theField) { <P>")
orderWindow.document.write("if (theField.value=='') {<P>")
orderWindow.document.write("alert ('This field is required!')<P>")
orderWindow.document.write("theField.focus()<P>")
orderWindow.document.write("return (false) }<P>")
orderWindow.document.write("}")
```

You have to write a last line, too:

```
orderWindow.document.write("</HEAD>")
```

Notice how I handled the quotation marks in the script fragment above. You must be very careful to alternate single and double quotation marks. Failure to do so is a common source of errors and is not always easy to find!

If you use a good text editor to create your HTML, you can combine the copy-paste-move operations to simplify the process of generating JavaScript on the fly, as shown in the above partial example.

An alternative approach to dynamic code crreation is to take advantage of a special feature of frames (see Chapter 12).

USING JAVA APPLETS

One of the most exciting developments in the release of Netscape Navigator 2.0, at least to the programming community, was the ability to include small programs called applets. We write these applets in an entirely new programming language called Java, directly in HTML documents. This chapter focuses on Java applets and how to include them in your Web pages.

A discussion of the Java programming language is well beyond the scope of this book, but, if you find yourself terminally intrigued by the language (based on what little I tell you about it here), you will want to check out the book *Java Programming EXplorer*, also from the Coriolis Group. Fair warning, though: Java is a real programming language, and you'll need some programming experience—or at least some serious scripting background—before you try to learn it.

In this chapter, I'll describe the following:

- @ Some background about Java
- @ The difference between an applet and an application
- @ Why you'd want to accommodate applets in your Web pages
- @ How to incorporate Java applets once you've decided to use them
- @ An example of interesting Java applets that are on the CD-ROM accompanying this book, so you can try out the ideas in the privacy of your own server

What Is Java, Anyway?

It is easy to confuse Java with JavaScript. They are almost incidentally similar. JavaScript is the language that is built right into Netscape Navigator 2. We just spent the last four chapters talking about it, so you know very well what it is and what it can do. It has a limited purpose of providing you with capabilities you can build into your Web pages without knowing much about programming or having to write separate programs.

Java, on the other hand, is a complete general-purpose programming language. Based largely on C and C++—with liberal doses of Smalltalk, Ada, and other object-oriented programming languages—Java is best understood as an attempt to tame the wildness that entered the programming world when C++ was introduced.

Java and C++

C++ has quickly become a dominant programming language, for a number of reasons. One reason is that Bell Labs, where the language originated, gave away the language to universities and others for quite some time. This largesse led to a large, trained cadre of C++ programmers, who then ventured into the software industry. C++ has many advantages over its predecessor, C (which is still probably the most widely used language in modern programming for desktop computers), as well as over other, less recent languages.

But C++ was not without its drawbacks. A discussion of these drawbacks would necessarily become more technical than I want to get here. Let's just summarize by saying that Java's designers at Sun Microsystems decided early that they would fix some of the problems in C++ when creating the Java language. That they did so cleanly and elegantly says a lot about their engineering talent, which was and is substantial.

Java's Origins and Introduction

Java started life as an attempt to write a language and operating system for interactive television and cable TV set-top boxes. (This information may not be particularly useful to you here, but it may make you the hit of your next cocktail party. Of course, if you live someplace like Silicon Valley, everyone not only already knows this but probably claims to have participated in it.) When that market failed to materialize, Sun decided the language was bigger and better than the market for which it had originally been intended. In a clever move, Sun introduced it in the broad context of the Internet.

The real genius of Java may lie not so much in its design as a language (which is quite excellent), but in Sun's market plan for Java. The market was not avidly seeking a new programming language. To the contrary, it was catching its breath from the introduction of Borland's Delphi and Visual Basic and a number of other languages and tools that appeared in rapid-fire succession. Many programmers, when they heard about Java, asked, "Why do we need another programming language?"

Sun's answer was brilliant. It said Java had some specific features that made it perfectly suited to building applications and applets for use and distribution over the Internet. At the time they made these statements (which, by the way, are not entirely true or untrue, as is the case with most marketing hype), the

Internet was the hottest topic in the software universe. Sun stated these claims loudly and clearly, while providing the language and basic tools free of charge on a wide range of desktop platforms. They also ensured that software written on one platform would run on all the others. Sun established a clear and firm niche for Java with this strategy. Some people believe Java will ultimately supplant C++ as the dominant programming language of the last years of this decade. I'm not quite so optimistic, but Java has founded a major beachhead in a very short time.

Java's Characteristics

Java has been described, even by its developers, as "buzzword friendly." Java uses just about every computer programming term that was popular when it was introduced. For our purposes, the most important buzzwords are "secure" and "network-aware."

From the beginning, Java's designers worried about allowing programs written in the new language to become bearers of viruses. The designers anticipated that Java applications typically would be transferred over networks, rather than residing directly on users' desktop machines. In fact, network delivery is one of the main attractions of Java applications and applets. The risk of destructive computer code was a legitimate concern.

Several levels of security are built into Java. For example, the user can control such factors as whether a Java application is permitted to read or write any files on the local system's hard disk. In addition, Java programs, when they are executed on the local user's desktop, double-check their code before running. If Java finds any attempt to tamper with the program code, it simply prevents the application from doing anything, intended or unintended.

The network awareness of Java is harder to describe or understand. Java programs "know" about things like network protocols and transfers, interactions among objects residing on networks, and other, similar elements of a networked computer system. They can take advantage of these objects when appropriate, and they are designed to deal inherently with the network's idiosyncrasies.

Java has many other characteristics, including object orientation, extensibility, and cross-platform portability, which we won't discuss here. These characteristics make it an excellent choice for a primary programming language for networked applications, at least for the next few years.

Applications and Applets

Since Java was introduced, widespread confusion has existed over the difference between applications and applets written in this new language. The confusion is understandable: The two differ very little. But, we can define one fundamental distinction.

An applet requires a host environment such as a Java-aware browser (which, at this writing, means Netscape Navigator version 2.0 or later for most systems, 2.1 or later for the Macintosh). Without such a browser, an applet is useless. An application runs whether or not the user is running Netscape, or, for that matter, any browser (or whether the user's system even has a browser). An application is a stand-alone entity that runs like all other programs on the user's system, while an applet runs and exists only within the context and confines of a browser.

Other than this fundamental distinction, the only other differences between applications and applets are deeply technical. These issues deal with how the program code is packaged and delivered, what it expects of the Virtual Machine (VM) on the receiving machine, and other such technical issues. You can safely ignore these niceties until you start writing applications or applets and need to understand them.

Theoretically, at least, no difference exists between the kinds of programs that can be written in Java and delivered either as applications or applets. However, the limitations of the browser environment make it unlikely that you would write a new word processor as a Java applet, but you might well create a new word processor application in Java.

Incorporating Java Applets

As Webmasters, then, we are concerned primarily with Java applets. These programs need Netscape Navigator as a place to run, so it follows that we need to know how to incorporate them into our HTML pages. Doing so is quite simple.

The basic HTML code to invoke a Java applet has this form:

```
<APPLET CODE = "Java class name" WIDTH=num HEIGHT=num>
</APPLET>
```

Notice that quotation marks enclose the name of the class.

The applet tag tells Netscape that you are about to instruct it to download a Java applet. All Java applets are stored as Java classes with names like:

- Demonstration.class
- JackhammerDuke.class
- LiveImageDemo.class

You must supply both width and height values that define the area of the browser window within which the results of the Java applet's execution will display. Leaving out either or both of these arguments almost guarantees that Navigator (and perhaps your system) will crash.

The </applet> code is also required; applet is a non-empty container HTML tag.

On the CD-ROM accompanying this disk is a demonstration HTML page called "Live Under Construction" (or LIVECNST.HTML) that calls a Java applet. The applet itself is also on the CD-ROM; its name is JackhammerDuke.class. It is one of the many demonstration Java applets created by Sun engineers to show off the power and potential of Java. The code that invokes the Java applet called JackhammerDuke looks like this:

```
<APPLET code="JackhammerDuke.class" WIDTH=300 HEIGHT=100>
</APPLET>
```

A corresponding compiled Java class must reside on the server in an appropriate file path (depending on the security and access settings in effect when the file is transferred). The compiled class must be called JackhammerDuke.class for this applet to work in the context of our page.

When Netscape encounters this tag, it looks for the applet involved, sets aside the required rectangular region, and then tells the server to go ahead and send the applet. The applet is then transferred to your system, where it begins to run as soon as it arrives.

Java applets, as part of their security design, are not cached on your system. As long as the page on which they are called remains displayed, the applet continues to execute. But the moment you switch windows, the applet becomes unavailable and will have to be downloaded again to be reused.

Other Attributes

Besides the mandatory tags identified in the preceding section, you may also add several other attributes to an HTML line designed to invoke a Java applet. These attributes include:

- ALIGN attributes nearly identical to those used for the IMG tag, which you've undoubtedly used many times
- HSPACE and VSPACE to add margins around the graphic regions occupied by applets
- CODEBASE to define a base directory in which Java code can be located PARAM attributes to pass arguments from the browser to the applet

ALIGN Attributes

As with images incorporated into your Web pages with the IMG tag, you can cause text to align with the area allocated to a Java applet in various ways. Table 10.1 summarizes the possible values and their meanings.

HSPACE and VSPACE Attributes

The HSPACE and VSPACE attributes, used when incorporating an applet into your Web page, provide a way to place a region of blank space between the

Table 10.1   ALIGN Attribute Values

ALIGN= Attribute	Alignment Result
TEXTTOP	Top of applet region aligns with the top of the tallest piece of text on the line
TOP	Top of applet region aligns with the top of the tallest object of any kind on the line
ABSMIDDLE	Middle of applet region aligns with middle of largest item on the line
MIDDLE	Middle of applet region aligns with middle of baseline of text
BASELINE or BOTTOM	Bottom of applet region aligns with baseline of text on the line
ABSBOTTOM	Bottom of applet region aligns with bottom of lowest item of any kind on the line

applet's display region and its surrounding text. You set their values equal to the number of pixels of extra space that you want to provide, as in this example:

```
<APPLET CODE="test.class" WIDTH=300 HEIGHT=200 VSPACE=10 HSPACE=50>
```

CODEBASE Attribute

You may wish to store Java applets in a directory other than the one in which the HTML files that invoke them are stored, But, the CODE attribute will accept only the name of the class as its argument. You can use the CODEBASE attribute to define a path other than the default path in which you wish Netscape to search for the applet's code.

For example, suppose you stored all of your Java code in the path "D:/JAVASDK/ CLASSES" and you wanted to invoke the class "test.class" in an HTML tag. You would code this example as shown here:

```
<APPLET CODE="test.class" CODEBASE="D:/JAVASDK/CLASSES/" WIDTH=200
  HEIGHT=150>
</APPLET>
```

Passing Parameters with the PARAM Attribute

Many Java applets need to receive input while they run. To do this, you must supply them with parameters. You handle this task by using the <PARAM> tag in HTML. Parameters are not, of course, mandatory. When they are included, however, they must appear after the opening line that defines the applet (beginning with <APPLET...) and the applet's closing tag (</APPLET>).

After the class of the applet is identified and the graphical region is defined, each line starts with the word "param," which is shorthand for "parameter." Each parameter is associated with a name-value pair. The name provides an identifier by which the Java applet can refer to the parameter in its own code. The value is the content of that parameter.

The basic syntax looks like this:

```
<APPLET CODE="test1.class" WIDTH=300 HEIGHT=180>
<PARAM NAME=paramName1 VALUE="UserName">
```

Multiple Parameters

One of my early favorite Java demos was created by Sun engineer, Jim Graham. It's called LiveImage. Figure 10.1 shows its screen.

Figure 10.1 LiveImage Java applet page.

As you can see from the text at the top of the page in Figure 10.1, seven active areas are in the image on the page. Each area triggers one or more actions. The Java applet that handles this activity needs to know where the user clicks with the mouse to be able to react differently to clicks at various locations. The applet uses <PARAM> tags to accomplish this task.

Here is the HTML code incorporating this applet and its parameters:

```
<applet code="ImageMap.class" width=522 height=486>
<param name=img value="images/jim.graham.gif">
<param name=highlight value="brighter30">
<param name=area1 value="SoundArea,260,180,120,60,audio/hi.au">
<param name=area2 value="NameArea,260,180,120,60,Hi!">
<param name=area3 value="HighlightArea,260,180,120,60">
<param name=area4 value="NameArea,265,125,45,20,That is my right eye">
<param name=area5 value="HighlightArea,265,125,45,20">
<param name=area6 value="NameArea,335,130,45,20,That is my left eye">
<param name=area7 value="HighlightArea,335,130,45,20">
<param name=area8 value="HrefButtonArea,200,7,210,300,../../../people/flar/">
<param name=area9 value="RoundHrefButtonArea,60,0,100,120,example2.html">
<param name=area10 value="SoundArea,425,98,27,27,audio/chirp1.au">
<param name=area11 value="NameArea,425,98,27,27,Chirp!">
<param name=area12 value="HighlightArea,425,98,27,27">
<param name=area13 value="ClickArea,0,0,522,486">
</applet>
```

In some cases, the value of a parameter consists only of an identifier-sounding string and four numbers in a comma-separated list, like this:

```
<param name=area3 value="HighlightArea,260,180,120,60">
```

When the user clicks or moves the mouse within the region bounded by the rectangle whose coordinates are the four locations shown, the Java applet's HighlightArea method is called.

Other parameters include not only what we can now deduce is a method name, but also a file name or other sixth parameter, as in this line:

```
<param name=area10 value="SoundArea,425,98,27,27,audio/chirp1.au">
```

In this example, the user clicking in the area bounded by the indicated rectangle will call the method SoundArea in the Java applet, passing along a request to do something with a file called "audio/chirp1.au." (You probably figured out that this method plays an audio file.)

MULTIPLE APPLETS ON A PAGE

No rule limits you to one Java applet per Web page. You can include as many <APPLET></APPLET> tags as you'd like. (Of course, you will encounter memory and performance barriers that place a practical limit on the number of applets to use on a page.)

If the applets refer to one another while they are running on the page, you need a way to identify them to each other. To do so, add a NAME attribute to the applet tag, as in this example:

```
<APPLET NAME="timer" CODE=timer3.class WIDTH=300 HEIGHT=150>
</APPLET>
```

The value supplied for the NAME attribute can be used elsewhere on the same page to allow Java applets to refer to and call other Java applets.

Some Sample Applets

The rest of this chapter shows a few sample Java applets and examines how they are incorporated into Web pages. I have two main purposes in this section:

- To give you an idea of what things Java does well (for which you might wish to obtain applets)
- To familiarize you with invoking applets in your HTML

The CD-ROM accompanying this book contains all of the applet examples in this section.

Hangman, Java Style

Hangman has always been a favorite game of programmers who are learning to do interactive software. It has the virtue of simplicity (the user can press only a single key at a time, and the program must respond in only one of four ways: right, wrong, you guessed it, or you're dead). Yet it is interesting enough not to become boring for the programmer or the user, at least not too quickly.

Figure 10.2 shows a page in the Netscape browser with the applet running. This page shows how things look at the beginning of a game of Hang Duke (named for the funny-looking little character who is Java's mascot and symbol).

The user types individual letters. As each one is registered, the applet either places the letter in the word space in all appropriate locations, to the accompaniment of Duke's sigh of relief, or puts the letter near the hangman's noose, causing Duke to scream. Another part of Duke is drawn and the program waits for the next letter.

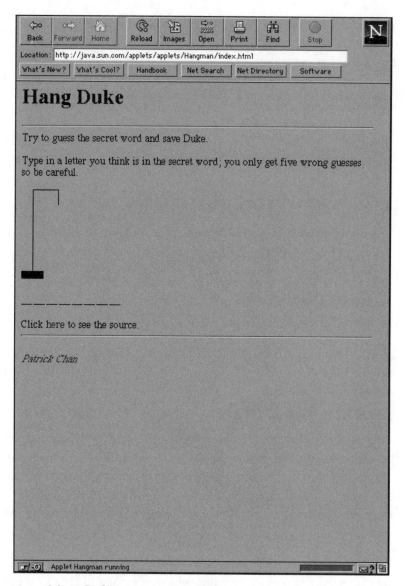

Figure 10.2   Hang Duke page at start of game.

If you don't guess the word before you've made five wrong guesses, the program spells the word for you and draws the completed Duke, who screams agonizingly as he meets his demise (see Figure 10.3).

Here's the portion of the HTML code that does the work and displays the text in the window:

Figure 10.3   Hang Duke at end of game.

```
<title>Hang Duke Demo</title>
<body>
<h1>Hang Duke</h1>
<hr>
Try to guess the secret word and save Duke.
<p>
Type in a letter you think is in the secret word;
```

```
you only get five wrong guesses so be careful.
<p>
<applet code="Hangman.class" width=300 height=150>
</applet>
<p>
```

Watch 'Em Sort!

Figure 10.4 shows the opening screen of one of my favorite Java applets. This applet shows you how three different sort algorithms work by visually sorting a pile of lines of varying length.

You click on the algorithm you want to understand and then watch as the lines sort in real time before your eyes. It's pretty cool; you quickly understand why one sorting algorithm works better than another. This applet demonstrates using Java for educational purposes. Figure 10.5 shows the screen after one of the piles of lines has been sorted.

Here is the HTML code that calls the applet used on thAT page. Notice that a parameter is associated with each applet call.

```
<pre>
<strong>Bi-Directional</strong>
<strong>Bubble Sort</strong>
<strong>Bubble Sort</strong>
<strong>Quick Sort</strong>
<applet code="SortItem.class" width=100 height=100><param name="alg"
value="BubbleSort">
</applet>
<applet code="SortItem.class" width=100 height=100><param name="alg"
value="BidirectionalBubbleSort">
</applet>

<applet code="SortItem.class" width=100 height=100><param name="alg"
  value="QSort">
</applet>
</pre>
```

When the user clicks on one of the groups of lines, the applet decodes the click location and determines what value to pass as the "alg" parameter to the SortItem.class applet. (The identifier "alg" is shorthand for "algorithm," in case that wasn't clear.)

Slick Stock Quotation Page

Figure 10.6 shows one of the more robust Java applet demonstrations available at the Sun Java site at this writing. It displays a moving ticker of quotations

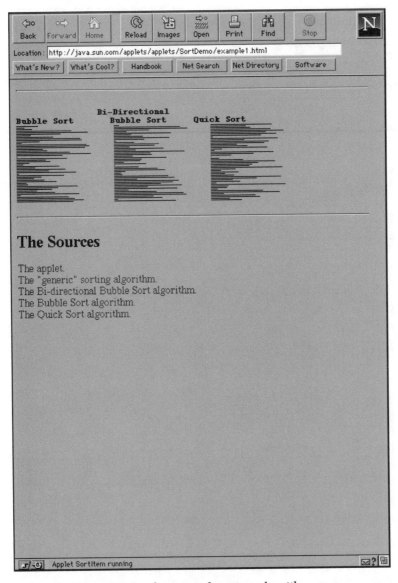

Location: http://java.sun.com/applets/applets/SortDemo/example1.html

What's New?   What's Cool?   Handbook   Net Search   Net Directory   Software

Bi-Directional
Bubble Sort   **Bubble Sort**   **Quick Sort**

The Sources

The applet.
The "generic" sorting algorithm.
The Bi-directional Bubble Sort algorithm.
The Bubble Sort algorithm.
The Quick Sort algorithm.

Applet SortItem running

Figure 10.4   Opening screen of animated sorting algorithm page.

across the middle of the page and three graphs of stocks that are updated every five seconds.

This page also has a region where you can check on news events that might have affected a particular stock's price change. Figure 10.7 shows that portion of the page.

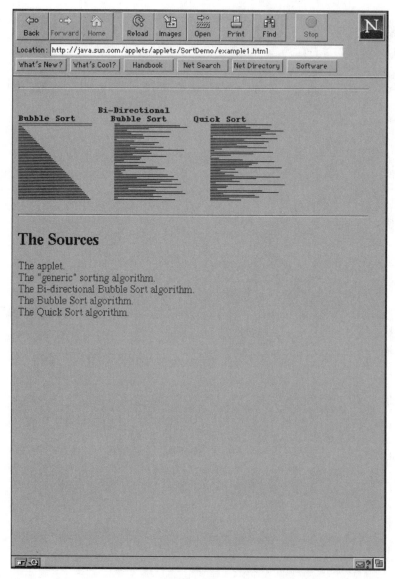

Figure 10.5   Animated sorting algorithm page after sort of one pile.

This page includes several applet calls. Here's the first one, which deals with the real-time ticker that repeats across the center of the original display:

```
<applet codebase=classes code="StockTicker.class" width=500 height=20>
    <param name=stocks value=
      "SUNW|HWP|SGI|MSFT|INTC|IBM|DEC|CY|ADBE|AAPL|SPX|ZRA|NSCP|NEATO">
    <param name=staticdata value=tickerdata>
```

```
    <param name=fudge value=true>
</applet>
```

This snippet uses three parameters, called "stocks," "staticdata," and "fudge." The first has a value that contains the stock symbols of a number of companies whose stocks might be watched in this application, if it were connected to a source of stock prices in real time.

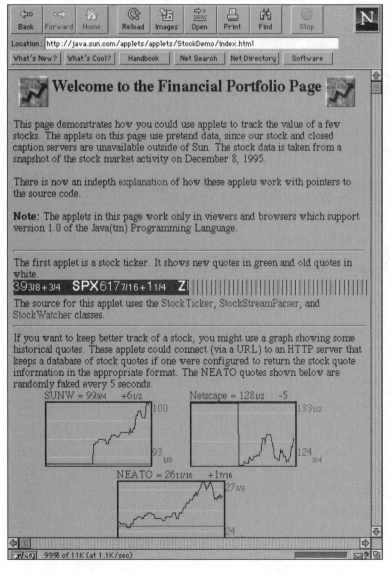

Figure 10.6   Live stock quotation page.

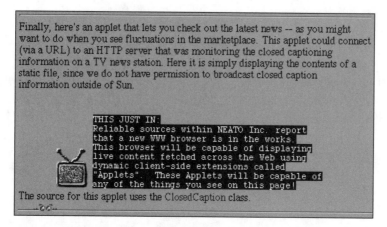

Figure 10.7   Live stock quotation page news section.

The following HTML fragment deals with the graphs of the charts displayed near the bottom of Figure 10.6.

```
<applet codebase=classes code=QuoteChart.class" width=190 height=100>
    <param name=staticdata value=chartdata%>
    <param name=stock value=SUNW>
    <param name=history value="8h">
    <param name=fudge value=true>
</applet>
<applet codebase=classes code="QuoteChart.class" width=190 height=100>
    <param name=staticdata value=chartdata%>
    <param name=stock value=NSCP>
    <param name=label value=Netscape>
    <param name=history value="8h">
    <param name=fudge value=true>
</applet>
<applet codebase=classes code="QuoteChart.class" width=190 height=100>
    <param name=staticdata value=chartdata%>
    <param name=stock value=NEATO>
    <param name=history value="10m">
    <param name=fudge value=true>
</applet>
```

Here, developer Jim Graham used three calls to the QuoteChart.class applet, passing different values each time for the named parameters (staticdata, stock, history, and fudge).

You should by now see a pattern emerging in which your pages will call the same applet several times using parameters to change the behavior of that applet on the fly. This is a common usage of Java applets. The person who writes the applet tries to write a generic program that you can control by supplying appropriate parameters.

Cool Dynamic Graph

The last example of a Java applet I'll show you in this chapter is one of the first I ever saw. This graph is still one of the most impressive examples, when you consider what it's doing. It has the deceptively simple name "Graph Layout," so it's easy to pass over when you're surfing the Web looking for cool applets.

Figure 10.8 shows this applet in action. The user has just clicked the "Scramble" button to start this graph system in a state of randomness.

Each of the little rectangles is labeled with an object that is more or less strongly, or directly, related to the central object, a rectangular dude named "joe." Each of these objects has a connection to one or more other objects. You can't see it, but each of these connections has a strength factor that determines how closely objects "want" to be together. For example, the "joe" object wants to be very close to the "dog" object, but the "mouse" object wants to be far away from the "cat" object. (If you want more detail, you can turn on the display of these values by checking the "Stress" checkbox.)

As this applet runs, the objects gradually settle into a state of stability where all of the objects are as close to or as far from other objects as they can get without breaking other relationship requirements. Figure 10.9 shows this state.

Here is the HTML that invokes this whole process and manages the user interaction. (The user can, in addition to clicking on any of the four buttons, actually grab an object in the graph and move it somewhere. The rest of the objects follow and gradually settle back into a stable pattern.)

```
<applet code="Graph.class" width=400 height=400>
<param name=edges value="joe-food,joe-dog,joe-tea,joe-cat,joe-table,table-
```

```
plate/50,plate-food/30,food-mouse/100,food-dog/100,mouse-cat/150,table-cup/
30,cup-tea/30,dog-cat/80,cup-spoon/50,plate-fork,dog-flea1,dog-flea2,flea1-
flea2/20,plate-kniFe">
<param name=center value="joe">
</applet>
```

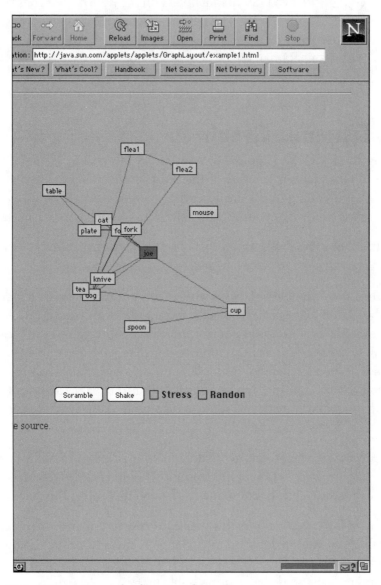

Figure 10.8 Dynamic graph after scrambling.

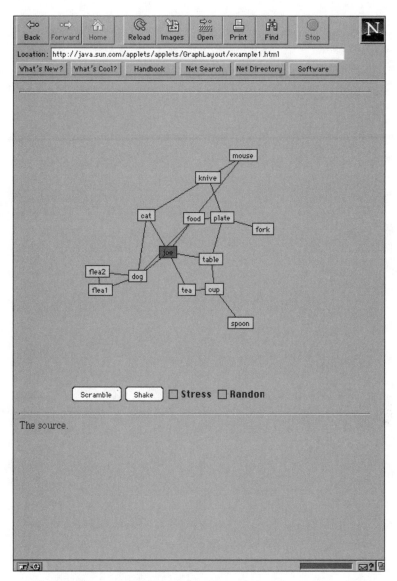

Figure 10.9 Dynamic graph after stabilizing.

You might wonder whether you, without access to the source code of the Java applet, could change the behavior of the graph just by changing the parameters of the call to the applet. The answer is that you could. You must load the HTML page you created rather than the one in the demo. You could not only change the relationships, you could also change the contents of the graph itself.

CALLING CGIS AND EXTERNAL APPLICATIONS

XI

Now that you've learned how to incorporate Java applets into your Web pages, it should come as no surprise that you can also include other kinds of external applications as part of your HTML work. In this chapter, I'll discuss these other techniques.

Essentially, you can incorporate two types of applications directly into your Netscape-based Web pages: CGI applications and OLE objects. (At this writing, OLE is only supported in Netscape for Windows, but Microsoft has been evangelizing the use of OLE on the Macintosh. It is just a matter of time before Netscape and other browsers for the Macintosh support OLE objects as well.)

Some time soon, you will be able to add OpenDoc objects to the list of external applications and objects you can invoke from within HTML coding on your Web page. OpenDoc, which Apple Computer originated, is a superset of OLE 2.0 from Microsoft, which is gaining slowly but steadily in industry-wide acceptance.

Calling CGI Applications

From the beginning of the Web, Common Gateway Interface (CGI) scripts and applications have played a key role in helping Webmasters create applications that act as if they were integrated into the user's browser. The CGI standard was implemented in numerous programming and scripting languages during the few years the Web has existed.

You can write CGIs in such diverse tools and languages as:

- C and C++ (on Macintosh and Windows)
- Visual Basic (on Windows)
- AppleScript (on Macintosh)
- UserTalk scripting language in UserLand Frontier (on Macintosh)
- various versions and dialects of Perl (on Macintosh and Windows)

(You could use many other tools and languages as well; this list is just a sample of the most popular and widely used languages for CGI development.)

You need more knowledge to create CGIs than to simply use them in your HTML documents. I can't go into detail in this book about how to write CGI applications and scripts; our focus here is to avoid programming activities. If you want to learn how to write CGIs, you can pick up any of several good books on the subject. Netscape and HTML Explorer 2nd Edition and Serving the Web (both Coriolis Group Books).

To execute a CGI script or application from within your Web pages, you generally use a URL that calls the program (whose file extension is usually but not always either .cgi or .acgi). The URL probably passes along some information that the program needs as parameters before it can carry out its assignment.

For example, you might call a database CGI application to retrieve information about a product in which the user has an interest. The request might invoke the CGI and pass along a product ID in a URL that looks something like this:

```
http://www.server.com/cgi/db2get.cgi?Product_ID=CPUP4-1123
```

Here, the text following the question mark makes up the query to be submitted to the database. Information that follows a question mark in a URL is called a "query string." The CGI application behind the scenes must have been designed to parse this information into understandable "database-ese," so the program can ultimately return to the user the information sought by the query.

The CGI application you are using—or the "glue" between HTML and that application—is documented so that you know what information it needs passed along to do its job.

Netscape and OLE

The new Netscape supports Microsoft's industry-standard Object Linking and Embedding (OLE) protocol, Version 2 (also known as OLE 2.0). OLE plays a major role in the world of Windows platforms. It is also available for Macintosh, though it is less widely supported there for historical reasons.

The two types of OLE object types are clients and servers. Netscape supports both types of use.

Netscape as OLE Client

Netscape Navigator 2.0 or later for Windows can be used as an OLE container object, or client. In this role, Netscape becomes the host for another Windows application capable of playing the role of a server. This other application (for example, Microsoft Word) is inserted directly within the Netscape Navigator's window.

Once a word application (actually, a document created by Word) is embedded in Netscape Navigator, the user can click on that document, and all of the capabilities of Word become immediately available from within the Navigator.

You place an OLE server document inside a Web document viewed with Netscape using the EMBED tag, as shown here:

```
<EMBED SRC="booklist.doc">
```

The result looks like Figure 11.1. Notice that the Word table worksheet appears in-line with HTML portions of the Web document.

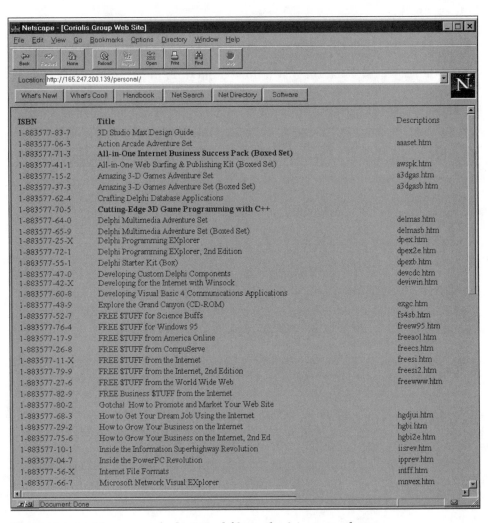

Figure 11.1 You can embed a Word file in the Navigator browser.

When the user clicks on any portion of the Word file in the Navigator browser, the menu bar and other capabilities of Word replace those of the Navigator. The user can manipulate the file exactly as if he or she were working directly from Word.

Navigator as Server

Netscape Navigator can also be used as an OLE server. You can create powerful and seamless application environments. For example, you could embed a reference to your company's home page in a Microsoft Word for Windows document. When the user clicks on this reference, the Navigator browser actually embeds itself in the Word document, with the company's home page open. When the user clicks on any portion of that Web page, all of the capabilities of the Netscape Navigator browser become available exactly as if the user were running the Navigator as a stand-alone application.

OLE documents can inter-operate with other OLE documents in several "modes." A discussion of OLE and its intricacies is beyond the scope of this book. Netscape Navigator for Windows is designed to play any available role in the world of OLE, including those involved in OLE automation. The Navigator defines a complete Application Programming Interface (API) through which it can be called from other OLE automation applications and controlled from those programs.

JAVASCRIPT ON THE WEB

XII

In this chapter, I return to JavaScript. When the new Netscape release became available, many people began jumping on the Java bandwagon, brushing JavaScript aside as a kind of inferior relative. But as a few keen observers began to do intriguing things with JavaScript and others began hearing about these things, the JavaScript scene heated up and became a place of its own.

There are, by now, almost certainly tens of thousands of Web sites using JavaScript and perhaps hundreds of sites providing information, sample programs, tutorials, advice, and general support. In this chapter, I'll take a look at some of the more intriguing JavaScript sites and activities on the World Wide Web.

As with any such undertaking, there is a clear danger here: by the time I've written this and the wonderful people at the Coriolis Group have produced it in book form and the trucks of books have made their way to distributors, who have in turn put the books on still other trucks and routed them to your local bookstore, there will be hundreds or thousands of new places I should have mentioned.

Because of this, I begin this chapter with a look at five of the sites that seem to be most interested in keeping up with the expanding JavaScript activity on the Web. By using one or the other (or both) of these as starting points for your JavaScript adventure, you'll be able to stay as current as possible with this fast-moving technology.

After I discuss these five Web launch pads, I'll bring you a semi-random sample of other sites that are doing cool stuff with JavaScript. In some cases, I'll give you a peek at source code; in some of those cases, I'll comment on the code. There's a lot to learn from some of these people and I've tried to pick some of the very best JavaScripters out there, though I'm equally certain I've missed a bunch of them in the process.

I divide the last portion of the chapter into two major segments:

- cool sites
- script source

The first category contains notes and references about sites where the source code was either unavailable, protected by copyright, or for some other reason inappropriate to include in the chapter (e.g., it was too long). The second contains sites from which I include JavaScript source code. They are also cool sites. In fact, the fact that they have usable source available makes them perhaps even cooler!

(Incidentally, the URLs for all of the sites mentioned in this chapter are on the CD-ROM accompanying this book. In addition, the source code listed in this chapter is also available on the CD.)

JavaScript Jump Stations

One of the most interesting phenomena engendered by the emergence of the World Wide Web has, for me, been the proliferation of sites that provide free access points to information about all kinds of topics. These sites, which I call "jump stations" because they provide us a launching pad for focused Web exploration, are labors of love for the most part, provided by people who just enjoy doing this sort of thing.

Sometimes, these sites are part of a larger site complex with a commercial purpose; that's fine, too. They still provide a great deal of helpful information. With so much content on the Web—and with the size and scope of it all growing by enormous leaps and bounds hourly—it would be impossible to have a pleasurable, focused experience without the assistance of these Jump Station Operators.

There are quite a number of JavaScript sites that provide this service. The five I'll focus on in this section are:

- Andy Augustine's Frequency Graphics JavaScript 411 site (http://www.freqgrafx.com/411/)
- Andrew Wooldrige's JavaScript Index (http://www.c2.org/~andreww/javascript/)
- Ryan Peters' Unofficial JavaScript Resource Center (http:/www.intercom.net/user/mecha/java.html)
- Netscape's own home site area devoted to JavaScript (http:/home.netscape.com/comprod/products/navigator/version_2.0/script/script_info/index.html)
- Gamelan's JavaScript page (reached via a frame window at http://www.gamelan.com/

Each of these sites has features to recommend it but each is unique as well. I'll try to point out the real strengths of each site along the way but my primary purpose in this section is to give you some idea what you can find at each of these places rather than my opinion of them.

JavaScript 411

The JavaScript 411 site (see Figure 12.1) is billed as "your complete source for JavaScript information." While it falls short of that promise, it does have some very useful content.

This site is divided into the following areas:

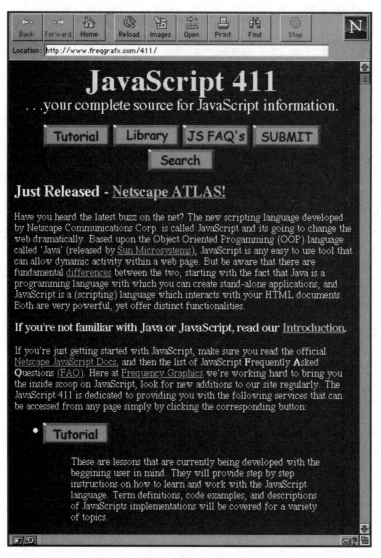

Figure 12.1   JavaScript 411 home page.

◎ Tutorial, where the beginnings of an on-line tutorial are taking shape (see Figure 12.2 for the opening portion of the "Hello World" tutorial, which I found to be quite complete)

◎ Library, containing code snippets

◎ JS FAQs, home for an unofficial but growing FAQ (Frequently Asked Questions, for the uninitiated) that lists some known bugs and workarounds that can be very helpful in the early JavaScript going

Figure 12.2   Opening screen of JavaScript Tutorial.

The site also has an easy way for you to submit code snippets for consideration for inclusion in the library and a simple search engine for finding information on the site.

Andy recently added a new section of his FAQ (in fact, it is really a separate FAQ) to cover the then-forthcoming release of Netscape codenamed Atlas. He seems to try really hard to stay on top of all the latest developments in JavaScript and his site has a newsy flavor that is refreshing.

JavaScript Index

This site, which JavaScript aficionados have already taken to referring to as "JSI," is more a classical Jump Station than JavaScript 411. It consists almost entirely of links to other sites, although the author, Andrew Wooldridge, does have a collection of articles and his own musings as well.

Figure 12.3 shows the opening page of the JavaScript Index site.

Andrew makes good use of JavaScript on the site itself, too. As you can see from Figure 12.3, there is a clock which is updated every second. The stars that highlight new items rotate just after you load the page to call attention to themselves but then, in a nicely tasteful acknowledgment that not all of us are so lucky as to have an ISDN line, they don't keep moving.

He divides the site's contents into three broad categories:

- JavaScript In Action
- Learn About JavaScript
- Talk About JavaScript

Under the first heading, the most interesting thing I found was his list of "Widgets," which contained some of the lesser-known and helpful or intriguing JavaScripts on the Web. He seems not only to keep this up to date but also to provide short and sometimes witty comments on the sites so you can get some idea whether they might appeal to you.

Unofficial JavaScript Resource Guide

Ryan Peters' JavaScript site (see Figure 12.4) has one of the most unusual and interesting looks of any Web site I've seen. It's open, airy, makes use of monospaced type and colors, and is interesting enough that if you stumble in by accident, you'll probably stay at least for a while.

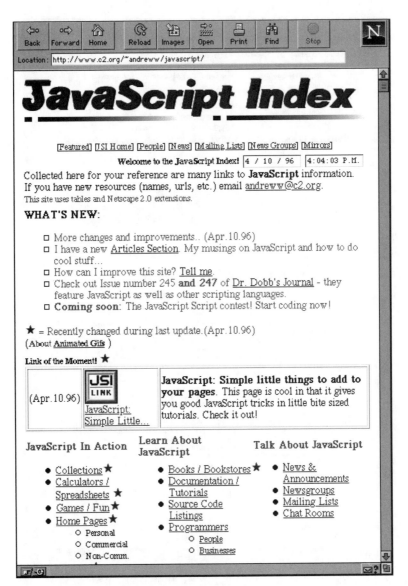

Figure 12.3   JavaScript Index site main page.

The heart of this site is in the easy-to-use and easy-to-follow JavaScript source examples he provides (see Figure 12.5). These scripts are aimed at the pure JavaScript beginner looking for a starting point and they are pretty well done.

Ryan also provides links to other JavaScript sites, both of the jump station variety and those containing examples and other kinds of information.

Figure 12.4 Unofficial JavaScript Resource Guide home page.

Netscape's JavaScript Resources Page

Figure 12.6 shows Netscape's own JavaScript Resources page. Don't let its sparse design and content fool you; behind each of the links here lies depth, in some cases serious depth!

Apart from the examples, some of which are quite good, the most useful thing on this site is the link to the official Netscape on-line documentation for

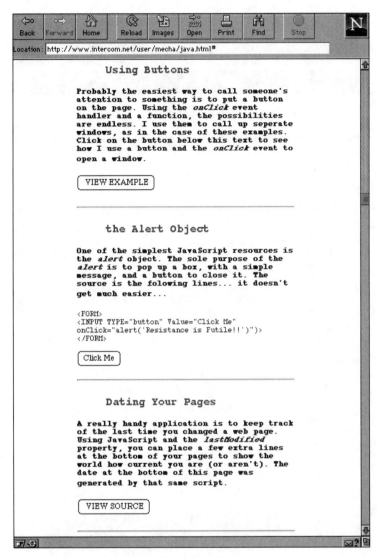

Figure 12.5 Examples on Ryan Peters' JavaScript page

JavaScript. The direct URL for this page is http://home.netscape.com/eng/mozilla/Gold/handbook/javascript/index.html.

In the documentation area itself, you can find a great example of the combined use of frames and JavaScript. With the click of a button (see Figure 12.7), you can decide whether the left frame of the documentation window should contain a Table of Contents for the documents or an index of all their content.

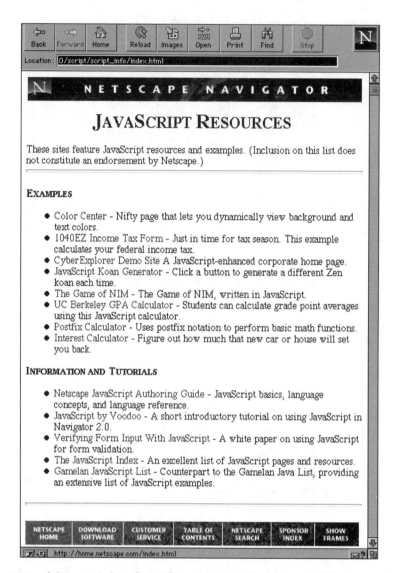

Figure 12.6   Netscape's JavaScript Resources page.

Gamelan's JavaScript Site

The folks at EarthWeb maintain some serious JavaScript and Java index content. In fact, this site is probably the granddaddy of all the JavaScript jump stations. Virtually any example I found mentioned on another site was not only included here (see Figure 12.8) but also featured a description of the example with some useful information.

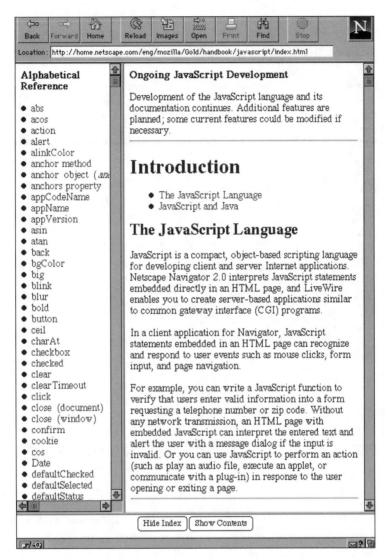

Figure 12.7   Switching between Contents and Index in Netscape JavaScript documentation

By the time you read this, the number of JavaScript entries in their index of examples will undoubtedly be more than 100 and probably soaring its way toward or past the 200 mark. These people really stay on top of JavaScript example development.

Their alphabetical listing of things JavaScript lets you know whether the particular entry represents an application or a site (though the distinctions among

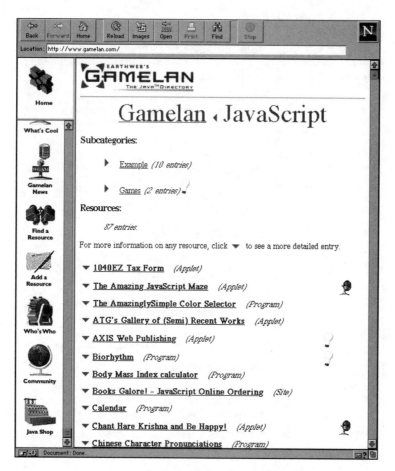

Figure 12.8   Gamelan JavaScript page.

applets, applications, and programs are sometimes a little unclear). If an entry points to a site, it's probably a jump station in its own right.

(Incidentally, the name of this site is not pronounced as you might think, as if this were a local area network containing computer games. It is pronounced, according to its owners, GAH-meh-lonn; they even have a link to an audio file demonstrating the correct pronunciation.)

JavaScript is just one part of this incredibly rich site. Also covered here are Java, multimedia, programming utilities, news, and a host of other topics. Gamelan's site is sponsored and is clearly a serious commercial undertaking.

Cool Sites

In this section, I'll take you on a tour of sites that are making good use of JavaScript or where JavaScript-specific examples are presented but where I have not been able to include in this book the source code. There are a number of reasons I couldn't include source:

- It may have been copyrighted and time did not permit me to seek appropriate permission from the author to include it in my book.
- It may have been difficult to access. In frame pages, particularly, the source code sometimes lives in a page that you don't actually see referenced in your browser. In that case, some digging is required to find the source and I didn't always have the time or inclination to do so.
- The code may have been available but either too long or too complex to reproduce in this book.

In any case, I always provide the URL for these sites (and the URLs are in the bookmark file on the CD-ROM accompanying this book) so if you are particularly intrigued by one or more of these applications, you can simply connect to the site yourself.

This category was the hardest one for me to cull to a reasonable size. Not only are there hundreds of cool JavaScript-enhanced sites out there, but every day dozens or hundreds of new ones are added. I distinctly recall one late night when I was gathering material for this chapter, I went to the Gamelan site (see previous section) and found one that sounded intriguing. I linked to it and then back to Gamelan. In the time I was gone, three new cool sites had been added!

Please consider these sites, then, to be representative of some of the best stuff I could find in a relatively limited time several weeks or months ago, depending on when you're reading these words. I'm sure there are tons of great sites I missed or that didn't exist when I wrote this. I would, of course, always enjoy hearing about them (dan@gui.com).

With the caveats out of the way, let me give you a quick overview of the cool sites I'll be showing you in this section:

- Tertius the Scribe, an interactive story that invites you as a reader to add to the plot (http://vanbc.wimsey.com/~grantm/tertius/)

- Charles Goodin's "Simple Little Things to Add to Your Pages" site (http://tanega.com/java/java.html)

- an amazing neural network page done entirely in HTML and JavaScript (http://www.neosoft.com/~hav/nnhtml.htm)

- an HTML editor written entirely in JavaScript that you can embed in your own pages (http://www.cirs.com/~raydaly/hjdemo.shtml)

Tertius the Scribe

One of the most creative uses to which I've seen JavaScript put is the interactive story called "Tertius the Scribe." Figure 12.9 shows the opening scene of this story and the controls available to readers.

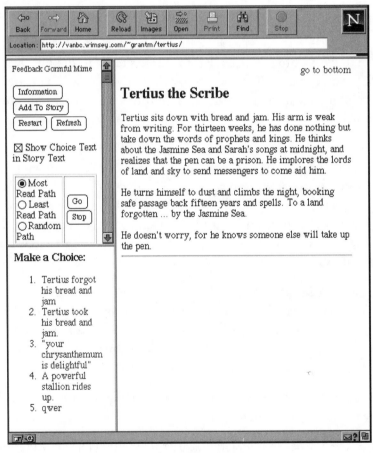

Figure 12.9   Opening scene of 'Tertius the Scribe' story.

In the upper left pane, you can follow one of several paths in the story: the one that has, to date, been most frequently followed; the one that has been least frequently followed or one chosen at random by the JavaScript. You can also add your own path to the story using the "Add to Story" button.

The lower left pane offers you choices among the paths that have been added so that if you don't want to pursue paths based on frequency of travel or a random one, you can click on a specific path continuation line and be taken to that part of the ever-evolving story.

When I wrote about this site, not everything was yet working (what site isn't under construction?) but there was enough richness here to be intriguing. I plan to drop back from time to time to see what progress is being made.

Charles Goodin's Collection

The author of this site denies he's a programmer, but he's certainly provided an interesting array of JavaScript "canned" solutions for someone who doesn't do this for a living! This site has a nice informality about its presentation and organization. Essentially, it's a collection of quite useful JavaScripts, including the following:

- several approaches to generating alert dialogs
- updating the status bar
- history and location buttons
- email buttons
- how to open windows
- changing the background color of a document or frame

A Neural Network in JavaScript?

I was pretty skeptical when I read about Horace Vallas' Web page containing neural network examples carried out in JavaScript. I know just enough about neural networks to know that they are incredibly complicated and that they have an array of intriguing uses.

So I linked to his site and did some exploring. Guess what? This stuff is real, or at least *seems* to be. The site (see Figure 12.10) features a couple of simple but nonetheless helpful explorations of neural net algorithms. It turns out the author is a neural network consultant.

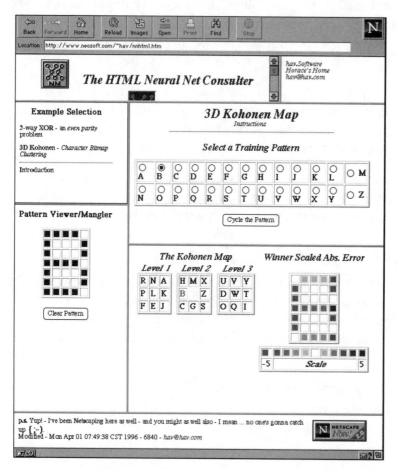

Figure 12.10   A neural network done in JavaScript does character recognition before your eyes!

In Figure 12.10, Valls' neural network is engaging in one of the most demonstrable of the tasks for which the technology is suited: character recognition. You could spend hours trying different letter patterns and cycling through the results and in the process learn a lot about how neural networks work.

The site is nicely designed and very useful and every once in a while, I find myself pausing to think, "Gee, and all of this is done in JavaScript!" Wow.

An HTML Editor in JavaScript

I am a confessed computer language junkie. I've probably written books about a broader array of programming languages than any other author. One of the things I find most intriguing is the development of language tools that are written in the language they support. This was one of my fascinations with Smalltalk.

The HTMLjive editor shown in Figure 12.11 isn't exactly in that niche, but it's close enough to be interesting. This page provides a JavaScript-created HTML editor that has the promise of being a really useful product as it matures.

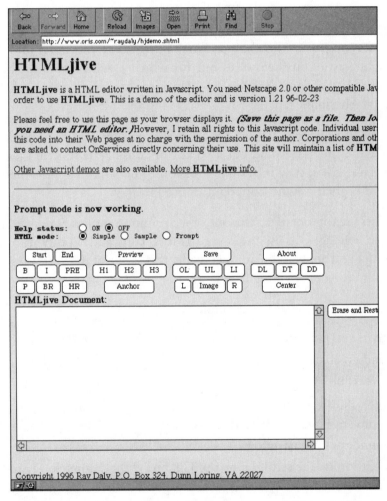

Figure 12.11   A beginning HTML editor is written entirely in JavaScript.

The buttons arrayed above the editing area place HTML commands into the window. You can then add your text and other elements to create the HTML for a Web page.

Ray Daly, the author of HTMLjive, allows you to download the page as a file and load it on your local system to use as an HTML editor. It won't scare off HoT MeTaL or Microsoft's Front Page, but as a freebie, it's a pretty interesting tool that I'm sure Daly will improve over time.

Source Code Examples

Now for the fun part of this chapter. I'm going to show you seven sites that are not only interesting in themselves but for which I will be able to show you JavaScript source code so that you can appreciate how much can be done with this deceptively simple language.

The seven source-code example sites I'll show you represent hard work on the part of their authors. It would not be polite or considerate to steal their source code. In some cases, they include permission to do so, often with the proviso that you leave their original copyright notice intact.

Each of these scripts demonstrates one or more important JavaScript techniques, though, so whether you use the source as it is, copy and modify it, or simply learn from it and apply it to your own code, this is one of the best ways to learn any programming or scripting language.

Briefly, these eight source code examples are:

- fade-in and fade-out of page backgrounds
- a random color generator
- an "invisible" maze
- a more "visible" maze
- a complete game of five-card stud poker
- a Soundex code generator
- a variation on the scrolling text of Chapter 9 that more closely resembles ticker tape and plays directly in the window rather than in the status bar

Fading Backgrounds

Have you ever visited a Web site which seemed to dissolve into view as you opened it? The color might start out black and fade in stages to gray or even white. Or it might start out blue and gradually lighten until it's a very light blue or white. This effect can be quite a dramatic way to call attention to your page.

There are a number of ways of accomplishing this task, but the one I want to show you is done completely in JavaScript. Figure 12.12 shows you the site where the technique is demonstrated. The URL for this page is http://eto.com/JavaScript/. It is an extremely well-done tutorial that walks you step by step through the process of learning not only what the JavaScript does but how it does it.

Here is the source code for this background fading technique. Note that it is not a complete HTML page, but rather a JavaScript text file only. It is stored on the CD-ROM as fade.txt.

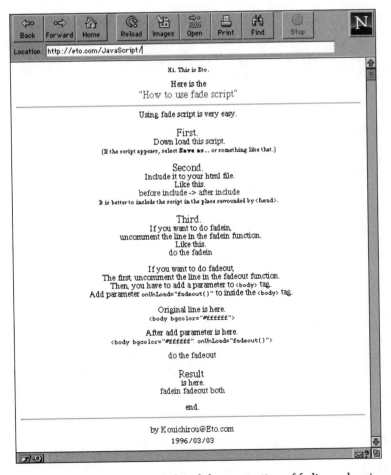

Figure 12.12   Page contains a tutorial and demonstration of fading colors in and out.

```
<script language="JavaScript">
<!--
/****************************************************************
 * fade script ver0.1 by Kouichirou@Eto.com 1996/02/20
 * Copyright (c) 1996 Kouichirou Eto. All Rights Reserved.
 * You can freely copy, use, modify this script,
 * if the credit is given in the source.
 * If you would like to get information for this script,
 * please access <http://eto.com/JavaScript/>
 */

function makearray(n) {
    this.length = n;
    for(var i = 1; i <= n; i++)
        this[i] = 0;
    return this;
}

hexa = new makearray(16);
for(var i = 0; i < 10; i++)
    hexa[i] = i;
hexa[10]="a"; hexa[11]="b"; hexa[12]="c";
hexa[13]="d"; hexa[14]="e"; hexa[15]="f";

function hex(i) {
    if (i < 0)
        return "00";
    else if (i > 255)
        return "ff";
    else
        return "" + hexa[Math.floor(i/16)] + hexa[i%16];
}

function setbgColor(r, g, b) {
    var hr = hex(r); var hg = hex(g); var hb = hex(b);
    document.bgColor = "#"+hr+hg+hb;
}

function fade(sr, sg, sb, er, eg, eb, step) {
    for(var i = 0; i <= step; i++) {
        setbgColor(
        Math.floor(sr * ((step-i)/step) + er * (i/step)),
        Math.floor(sg * ((step-i)/step) + eg * (i/step)),
        Math.floor(sb * ((step-i)/step) + eb * (i/step)));
    }
}

/* Usage:
 *    fade(inr,ing,inb, outr,outg,outb, step);
 * example.
 *    fade(0,0,0, 255,255,255, 255);
 * fade from black to white with very slow speed.
 *    fade(255,0,0, 0,0,255, 50);
```

```
 *    fade(0xff,0x00,0x00, 0x00,0x00,0xff, 50); // same as above
 * fade from red to blue with fast speed.
 * step 2 is very fast and step 255 is very slow.
 */

function fadein() {
/*    fade(0,0,0, 255,255,255, 64);*/
}

function fadeout() {
/*    fade(255,255,255, 0,0,0, 64);*/
}

/* do fadein */
fadein();

/***** end fade script *****/
/**********************************************************/

// -->
</script>
```

This script demonstrates a couple of fairly interesting techniques.

Notice the first function, makearray(), which creates an array of a length provided as the argument to the function and initializes all of its elements to 0. This is a reusable function; you could build it into any script you are writing that needs to create one or more arrays and provide a nicely generic way of accomplishing a common programming task.

The other noteworthy scripting technique demonstrated by the author, Kouichirou Eto, is the use of parameters to provide all information needed by a script. This parameter-driven approach to function creation is an excellent approach and is much more readable than providing information in the form of variables that store information outside the function call itself.

As you can see from the author's comments, you cause colors to fade in and out with calls to the functions fadein() and fadeout(), providing seven parameters:

- a comma-separated list of three decimal values representing the RGB color to start the fade process
- a second comma-separated list of three decimal values representing the RGB color with which to end the fade process
- a single decimal value indicating the speed with which you wish the fade to occur, with 255 being slowest

Eto's script then converts the decimal values to hexadecimal values as required by the document.bgColor property, and assigns them as appropriate. It sets up a loop and cycles through the colors.

Random Color Generator

Jason Bloomberg, who has done some of the best-crafted JavaScripts I've seen (in fact, he's the author of two of the seven I'm featuring in this discussion), has written a random background color generator that produces some very nice results.

At his site's home page (see Figure 12.13), he points out that if you don't like the color combination on the page, just click on the "Reload" button (or the text in the page that corresponds to that button) and get a whole new look.

Like Eto in the previous section, Bloomberg needs to generate hexadecimal values to deal with the way RGB colors are handled in JavaScript. He takes an entirely different approach from Eto's, as you can see in the source code for the main routine here:

```
<HTML>
<HEAD>
<TITLE>Jason Bloomberg's Home Page</TITLE>
<script language = "JavaScript">
<!-- hide

newstr= true;
var theseed3=1;

function tostr(num)
    {
    str="error";
    if (0 <= num && num < 10)
        str = "" + num;
    if (num == 10)
        str = "A";
    if (num == 11)
        str = "B";
    if (num == 12)
        str = "C";
    if (num == 13)
        str = "D";
    if (num == 14)
        str = "E";
    if (num == 15)
        str = "F";
    return str;
    }
```

```
function hex(num)
    {
    if (newstr)
        thestr = "";
    if (num < 16)
        {
        thestr = tostr(num) + thestr;
        newstr = true;
        }
    else
        {
        quotient = num >> 4;
        remainder = num % 16;
        thestr = tostr (remainder) + thestr;
        newstr = false;
        hex(quotient);
        }
    }

function random(maxnum)
    {
    var theseed2 = 0;
    thedate=new Date();
    theseed = Math.sqrt(theseed3 *
(47.3457373545383+thedate.getSeconds()))*(91.7808957845674+thedate.getMinutes());
    theseed3 = 3495937*(1000000*theseed-Math.floor(1000000*theseed))
    theseed2 = Math.floor(theseed3) % maxnum;
    return theseed2;
    }

// unhide -->
</script>
</head>
<FRAMESET ROWS="40, *">
  <FRAME SRC="jason/head.html" NAME="head"  noresize marginheight="4"
SCROLLING="no">
<FRAMESET COLS="128, *">
  <FRAME SRC="jason/images.html" NAME="images" noresize  SCROLLING="no">
<FRAMESET ROWS="*,40">
  <FRAME SRC="jason/text.html" NAME="text" marginwidth=32 marginheight=16
noresize>
  <FRAME SRC="jason/buttons.html" NAME="buttons" noresize marginheight="4"
SCROLLING="no">
    </FRAMESET>
  </FRAMESET>
</FRAMESET>

<noframe>
<body>
<center>
<B><FONT SIZE="+3">J</FONT><FONT SIZE="+1">ASON </FONT> <FONT SIZE="+3">B</
```

```
FONT><FONT SIZE="+1">LOOMBERG'S </FONT> <FONT SIZE="+3">H</FONT><FONT
SIZE="+1">OME </FONT> <FONT SIZE="+3">P</FONT><FONT SIZE="+1">AGE </FONT></
B>
<p>
<h2>This page requires Netscape 2.0!</h2>
</center>
</body>
</noframe>
</html>
```

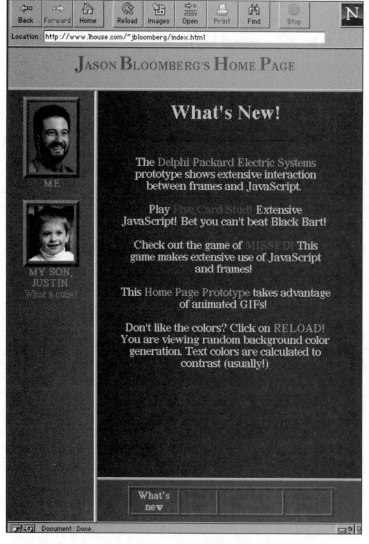

Figure 12.13   Jason Bloomberg generates page colors randomly.

As you can see, Bloomberg goes to some lengths to ensure that the numbers he is using as random color value bases are as random as possible. (There's a whole science to this random stuff that I won't go into because: (a) I don't have space and time; and (b) I don't begin to understand it!)

Note, too, that Bloomberg uses frames here. Hardly surprising, given that we've already looked at the page and know that it uses frames. But the bewildering thing that might strike you if you read the code closely is that there don't seem to be any calls to the functions hex and random anywhere on this page. So where does the background color get changed?

Each document that is loaded into a frame in this window has code that deals with the background, text and link colors for itself. Here, for example, is part of the code for one of the pages that loads into a frame in this window:

```
bgrandom = top.random(0XFFFFFF);
textrandom = 0XFFFFFF ^ bgrandom;
vlinkrandom = 0XBBBBBB ^ bgrandom;
linkrandom = 0X444444 ^ bgrandom;

top.hex(bgrandom);
bghex = top.thestr;

top.hex(textrandom);
texthex = top.thestr;

top.hex(vlinkrandom);
vlinkhex = top.thestr;

top.hex(linkrandom);
linkhex = top.thestr;

document.write("<body bgcolor='", bghex, "' text='", texthex, "' vlink='",
vlinkhex, "' link = '", linkhex,"'>");
```

It all culminates in the last line in the above code fragment. The document.write method sends a <body> tag to the document with randomly generated values assigned to the four types of objects that can take a color property.

This illustrates another important point that I glossed over in Chapter 9 in the interest of focusing on JavaScript itself. If you have a multi-framed window in Netscape, you can define functions in one document displayed in one frame and call those functions from another document displayed in another frame. This suggests that a way to create a pseudo-library of reusable code would be to create a document where all of the functions are defined. You could then include this document in a tiny frame in any window where you want to use it.

An "Invisible" Maze

Give the world a programming or scripting language and people will immediately start trying to figure out how to have fun with it by creating games. Go figure. JavaScript has been used to create a wide variety of games already, including Nim, poker, adventure games, a "talking magic 8-ball" for decision-making and who knows what else.

Two of the first game programs created with JavaScript are both mazes (see Figure 12.14) In this section, I'm going to explore one by Jim Tipton that has to

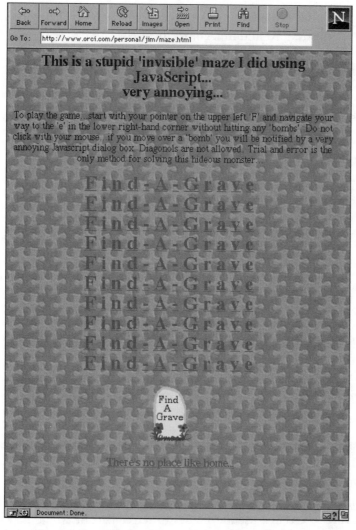

Figure 12.14   Seemingly innocent page hides diabolical maze game in JavaScript.

be one of the most diabolical puzzle designs I've stumbled across. The page looks harmless enough at first glance.

The large letters that make up the bulk of the page are, in reality, a maze. Without clicking your mouse, you move your pointer slowly over the letters beginning with the "F" in the upper left corner, trying to find a safe path through the maze of letters to the grave at the bottom of the screen. At each step, you'll either be given some encouragement in the status bar (some of these messages are hilarious, by the way) or you'll see a JavaScript dialog box pop up and let you know that you have failed...again!

Tipton makes good use of the onMouseEnter event for the letters to create the maze's uncanny psychic effect. ("How does it *know* where the mouse is?" an uninitiated observer might well wonder.)

Here's the source code for this intriguing little ditty, stored on the CD-ROM as gravmaze.htm. (No fair studying it to figure out how to beat the maze, though! Remember, it's a grave maze.)

```
<html>
<head>
<script language="LiveScript">
<!-- Hiding
    function hello() {
       alert("KaBooom!   Keep trying!");
    }
    function end(){alert("HEEEEEEHHHAAAAAW!  You made it!");}
// -->
</script>
<title>My extremely annoying maze...</title>

</head>
<body background="puzzle.jpg" TEXT="#00008A" link="#ff0000"
vlink="ff0000"><center>
<h2>This is a stupid 'invisible' maze I did using JavaScript...<br>very
annoying...</h2>
To play the game...start with your pointer on the upper left 'F' and navi-
gate your way to the 'e' in the lower right-hand corner without hitting any
'bombs'.  Do not click with your mouse...if you move over a 'bomb' you will
be notified by a very annoying Javascript dialog box.  Diagonols are not
allowed.  Trial and error is the only method for solving this hideous
monster...
<h1>
<a href="" onMouseOver="window.status='Starting Block'; return true">F</a>
<a href="" onMouseOver="hello()">i</a>
<a href="" onMouseOver="hello()">n</a>
```

```
<a href="" onMouseOver="hello()">d</a>
<a href="" onMouseOver="hello()">-</a>
<a href="" onMouseOver="hello()">A</a>
<a href="" onMouseOver="hello()">-</a>
<a href="" onMouseOver="hello()">G</a>
<a href="" onMouseOver="hello()">r</a>
<a href="" onMouseOver="hello()">a</a>
<a href="" onMouseOver="hello()">v</a>
<a href="" onMouseOver="hello()">e</a>
<br>

<a href="" onMouseOver="window.status='Good...your first steps'; return
true">F</a>
<a href="" onMouseOver="window.status='Still alive...'; return true">i</a>
<a href="" onMouseOver="window.status='Continue onwards...'; return
true">n</a>
<a href="" onMouseOver="hello()">d</a>
<a href="" onMouseOver="hello()">-</a>
<a href="" onMouseOver="hello()">A</a>
<a href="" onMouseOver="hello()">-</a>
<a href="" onMouseOver="hello()">G</a>
<a href="" onMouseOver="hello()">r</a>
<a href="" onMouseOver="hello()">a</a>
<a href="" onMouseOver="hello()">v</a>
<a href="" onMouseOver="hello()">e</a>
<br>

<a href="" onMouseOver="hello()">F</a>
<a href="" onMouseOver="hello()">i</a>
<a href="" onMouseOver="window.status='You are the lizard king...'; return
true">n</a>
<a href="" onMouseOver="hello()">d</a>
<a href="" onMouseOver="hello()">-</a>
<a href="" onMouseOver="hello()">A</a>
<a href="" onMouseOver="hello()">-</a>
<a href="" onMouseOver="hello()">G</a>
<a href="" onMouseOver="hello()">r</a>
<a href="" onMouseOver="hello()">a</a>
<a href="" onMouseOver="hello()">v</a>
<a href="" onMouseOver="hello()">e</a>
<br>

<a href="" onMouseOver="hello()">F</a>
<a href="" onMouseOver="hello()">i</a>
<a href="" onMouseOver="window.status='You can do anything...'; return
true">n</a>
<a href="" onMouseOver="window.status='Go East, young man (or woman)...';
return true">d</a>
<a href="" onMouseOver="window.status='You are master of all you sur-
vey...'; return true">-</a>
<a href="" onMouseOver="window.status='Go, go, go...'; return true">A</a>
<a href="" onMouseOver="window.status='Push him away...'; return true">-</
```

```
a>
<a href="" `onMouseOver="window.status='Heeehaw!!!   About half way
there...'; return true">G</a>
<a href="" onMouseOver="hello()">r</a>
<a href="" onMouseOver="hello()">a</a>
<a href="" onMouseOver="hello()">v</a>
<a href="" onMouseOver="hello()">e</a>
<br>

<a href="" onMouseOver="hello()">F</a>
<a href="" onMouseOver="hello()">i</a>
<a href="" onMouseOver="hello()">n</a>
<a href="" onMouseOver="hello()">d</a>
<a href="" onMouseOver="hello()">-</a>
<a href="" onMouseOver="hello()">A</a>
<a href="" onMouseOver="hello()">-</a>
<a href="" onMouseOver="window.status='Dont eat the clues...'; return
true">G</a>
<a href="" onMouseOver="hello()">r</a>
<a href="" onMouseOver="hello()">a</a>
<a href="" onMouseOver="hello()">v</a>
<a href="" onMouseOver="hello()">e</a>
<br>

<a href="" onMouseOver="hello()">F</a>
<a href="" onMouseOver="hello()">i</a>
<a href="" onMouseOver="hello()">n</a>
<a href="" onMouseOver="hello()">d</a>
<a href="" onMouseOver="window.status='Annoyed yet?...'; return true">-</a>
<a href="" onMouseOver="window.status='Almost there...'; return true">A</a>
<a href="" onMouseOver="window.status='Even paranoids have real enemies.  -
Delmore Schwartz'; return true">-</a>
<a href="" onMouseOver="window.status='Hell is...other people.  -Sartre';
return true">G</a>
<a href="" onMouseOver="hello()">r</a>
<a href="" onMouseOver="hello()">a</a>
<a href="" onMouseOver="hello()">v</a>
<a href="" onMouseOver="hello()">e</a>
<br>

<a href="" onMouseOver="hello()">F</a>
<a href="" onMouseOver="hello()">i</a>
<a href="" onMouseOver="hello()">n</a>
<a href="" onMouseOver="hello()">d</a>
<a href="" onMouseOver="window.status='Keep going...'; return true">-</a>
<a href="" onMouseOver="hello()">A</a>
<a href="" onMouseOver="hello()">-</a>
<a href="" onMouseOver="hello()">G</a>
<a href="" onMouseOver="hello()">r</a>
<a href="" onMouseOver="hello()">a</a>
<a href="" onMouseOver="hello()">v</a>
<a href="" onMouseOver="hello()">e</a>
```

```
<br>

<a href="" onMouseOver="hello()">F</a>
<a href="" onMouseOver="hello()">i</a>
<a href="" onMouseOver="hello()">n</a>
<a href="" onMouseOver="hello()">d</a>
<a href="" onMouseOver="window.status='Almost there...'; return true">-</a>
<a href="" onMouseOver="window.status='Use the force...'; return true">A</a>
<a href="" onMouseOver="window.status='Closer...'; return true">-</a>
<a href="" onMouseOver="window.status='Closer!!!'; return true">G</a>
<a href="" onMouseOver="window.status='Continue on your current course...';
return true">r</a>
<a href="" onMouseOver="window.status='Rhymes with Beast...'; return true">a</a>
<a href="" onMouseOver="window.status='Change Direction...'; return true">v</a>
<a href="" onMouseOver="hello()">e</a>
<br>

<a href="" onMouseOver="hello()">F</a>
<a href="" onMouseOver="hello()">i</a>
<a href="" onMouseOver="hello()">n</a>
<a href="" onMouseOver="hello()">d</a>
<a href="" onMouseOver="hello()">-</a>
<a href="" onMouseOver="hello()">A</a>
<a href="" onMouseOver="hello()">-</a>
<a href="" onMouseOver="hello()">G</a>
<a href="" onMouseOver="hello()">r</a>
<a href="" onMouseOver="hello()">a</a>
<a href="" onMouseOver="window.status='You are special...'; return true">v</a>
<a href="" onMouseOver="hello()">e</a>
<br>

<a href="" onMouseOver="hello()">F</a>
<a href="" onMouseOver="hello()">i</a>
<a href="" onMouseOver="hello()">n</a>
<a href="" onMouseOver="hello()">d</a>
<a href="" onMouseOver="hello()">-</a>
<a href="" onMouseOver="hello()">A</a>
<a href="" onMouseOver="hello()">-</a>
<a href="" onMouseOver="hello()">G</a>
<a href="" onMouseOver="hello()">r</a>
<a href="" onMouseOver="window.status='Very, very close!!!'; return true">a</a>
<a href="" onMouseOver="window.status='One last step!!!'; return true">v</a>
<a href="" onMouseOver="end()">e</a>
<br> </h1>
<a href="index.html"><img src="home.gif" border=0><h3>There's no place like
home...</h3></a></center>
</body>
</html>
```

Encountering a call to the function "hello" is not a good thing, as you can see.

Clever stuff in a very simple JavaScript approach that shows some ingenuity for Tipton having thought of it.

A Different Maze

Here's another kind of maze. In this one, you actually have a character (represented by the * symbol) to move around inside the maze using the four buttons

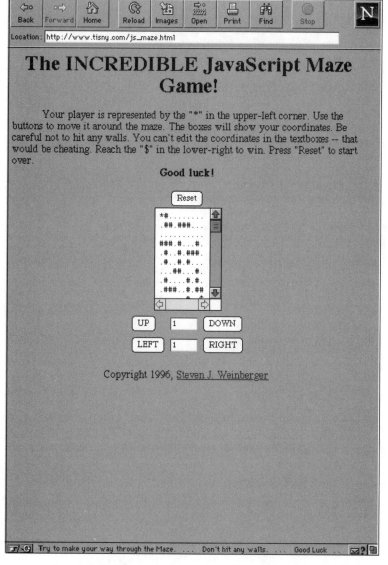

Figure 12.15 A more visible maze game lets you move your piece with buttons.

on the screen ("UP," "DOWN," "LEFT," and "RIGHT"). Figure 12.15 shows you the screen containing this piece of work.

As you click the buttons, the values showing the row and column at which your character is located update and the editing textarea object's contents change accordingly as well. I was really impressed at the speed with which this maze executed, thinking that author Steven Weinberger had found a way to make array manipulation fast. It turns out that Weinberger outsmarted me by not using an array for the maze at all. The secret to his approach is embedded in a comment in the source code below (found on the CD-ROM as jsmaze.htm):

```
<html>
<head>
<title>The Amazing JavaScript Maze</title>

<!-- begin Script here

    Copyright 1996 by Steven Weinberger of Transaction Information
    Systems. All rights reserved.

    I can be reached at: steve@garcia.tisny.com, weinberg@yu1.yu.edu,
    vidkid@inch.com for comments, suggestions, etc.

    Free permission is given to re-use or modify this code,
    if and only if this copyright notice is kept in.

    This program/page illustrates the ability to create a grid on-screen,
    and plot and animate in it.  The main parts can be used to build a
    variety of useful programs (mostly games). -->

<script>
var line = "";
var x = 0;
var y = 0;
var full="*";
var blank = ".";
var wall = "#";
var goal = "$";

var fill = "";


// Functions to create the board

function makeboard() {
    for (var i=1; i<= 10; i++)
        this[i] = new makeRow();
    return this;
}
```

```
function makeRow() {
    for (var i=1; i<= 10; i++)
        this[i]=blank;
    return this;
}


// Functions to fill & clear the board.

function clearBoard (form) {
// Clears & resets the board
    x = 0;
    y = 0;
    form.xval.value = 1;
    form.yval.value = 1;
    for (var i=1; i<= 10; i++)
        for (var j=1; j<= 10; j++)
            theBoard[i][j]=blank;
    drawMaze();
    fillBoard(form);
    return;
}

function fillBoard (form) {
    // Clear board buffer
    line = "";
    form.grid.value = "";
    // Fill board buffer
    for (var i=1; i<= 10; i++)
        for (var j=1; j<= 10; j++)
            line += theBoard[i][j];
    // Move buffer contents to board
    form.grid.value=line;
}

function plot (v, h) {
    theBoard[v][h] = fill;
}

function drawMaze() {
// Plots the walls of the maze
//
// Ideally, a function should do this automatically,
// or maybe I should write a maze generating function in JS!
// Note: This program operates in Y,X co-ordinates (not standard X,Y).

    theBoard[10][10] = goal;
    theBoard[1][2] = wall;
    theBoard[2][2] = wall;
    theBoard[4][1] = wall;
    theBoard[4][2] = wall;
    theBoard[4][3] = wall;
```

```
        theBoard[2][3] = wall;
        theBoard[5][2] = wall;
        theBoard[6][2] = wall;
        theBoard[2][5] = wall;
        theBoard[4][5] = wall;
        theBoard[5][5] = wall;
        theBoard[2][6] = wall;
        theBoard[2][7] = wall;
        theBoard[9][10] = wall;
        theBoard[9][9] = wall;
        theBoard[8][9] = wall;
        theBoard[7][9] = wall;
        theBoard[10][7] = wall;
        theBoard[9][7] = wall;
        theBoard[8][7] = wall;
        theBoard[6][7] = wall;
        theBoard[9][2] = wall;
        theBoard[9][3] = wall;
        theBoard[9][4] = wall;
        theBoard[8][2] = wall;
        theBoard[7][4] = wall;
        theBoard[7][5] = wall;
        theBoard[6][5] = wall;
        theBoard[5][7] = wall;
        theBoard[5][8] = wall;
        theBoard[5][9] = wall;
        theBoard[4][9] = wall;
}

function update(form) {
    var horiz = eval(form.xval.value);
    var vert = eval(form.yval.value);
    plot(vert,horiz);
    fillBoard(form);
    return;
}

function initBoard() {
    theBoard = new makeboard();
    fill = full;
    clearBoard(document.board);
    update(document.board);
}

// Functions to handle the player piece
//
// I suppose I could have written one function to handle this,
// but it was getting too complex.  Feel free to try.
//

function decx(form) {
    fill = blank;
```

```
        update(form);
        checkx = eval(form.xval.value - 1);
        checky = form.yval.value;
        if (form.xval.value > 1) {
            if (theBoard[checky][checkx] != wall) {
                form.xval.value=eval(form.xval.value - 1);
            }
            else {
                alert("THUD!\nYou hit a wall.");
            }
            if (theBoard[checky][checkx] == goal) {
                alert("YOU WIN!");
                location.href="http://www.tisny.com/js_demo.html";
            }
        }
        fill = full;
        update(form);
    }

    function incx(form) {
        fill = blank;
        update(form);
        checkx = eval(1 * form.xval.value + 1);
        checky = form.yval.value;
        if (form.xval.value < 10) {
            if (theBoard[checky][checkx] != wall) {
                form.xval.value=eval(1 * form.xval.value + 1);
            }
            else {
                alert("THUD!\nYou hit a wall.");
            }
            if (theBoard[checky][checkx] == goal) {
                alert("YOU WIN!");
                location.href="http://www.tisny.com/js_demo.html";
            }
        }
        fill = full;
        update(form);
    }

    function decy(form) {
        fill = blank;
        update(form);
        checkx = form.xval.value;
        checky = eval(form.yval.value - 1);
        if (form.yval.value > 1) {
            if (theBoard[checky][checkx] != wall) {
                form.yval.value=eval(form.yval.value - 1);
            }
            else {
                alert("THUD!\nYou hit a wall.");
            }
```

```
            if (theBoard[checky][checkx] == goal) {
                alert("YOU WIN!");
                location.href="http://www.tisny.com/js_demo.html";
            }
        }
    fill = full;
    update(form);
}

function incy(form) {
    fill = blank;
    update(form);
    checkx = form.xval.value;
    checky = eval(1 * form.yval.value + 1);
    if (form.yval.value < 10) {
        if (theBoard[checky][checkx] != wall) {
            form.yval.value=eval(1 * form.yval.value + 1);
        }
        else {
            alert("THUD!\nYou hit a wall.");
        }
        if (theBoard[checky][checkx] == goal) {
            alert("YOU WIN!");
            //Change to location of your choice.
            //location.href="http://www.tisny.com/js_demo.html";
        }
    }
    fill = full;
    update(form);
}


// Various Functions

function cheater (form) {
// Refuse to change values manually, and start over. CHEATER!
    alert("You can't change this value manually.\nPlease use the buttons.");
    clearBoard(form);
    update(form);
}



// Scrolling Status Bar
// This scrolling status bar was taken from shareware
// I make no claims on it, and placed it here as an enhancement to my page

function scrollit_r2l(seed)
{
    var m1 = "Welcome to the Amazing JavaScript Maze.   . . .    ";
    var m2 = "Try to make your way through the Maze.   . . .    ";
    var m3 = "Don't hit any walls.   . . .    ";
    var m4 = "Good Luck  . . . ";
```

```
            var msg=m1+m2+m3+m4;
            var out = " ";
            var c    = 1;

            if (seed > 100) {
                seed-;
                var cmd="scrollit_r21(" + seed + ")";
                timerTwo=window.setTimeout(cmd,100);
            }
            else if (seed <= 100 && seed > 0) {
                for (c=0 ; c < seed ; c++) {
                    out+=" ";
                }
                out+=msg;
                seed-;
                var cmd="scrollit_r21(" + seed + ")";
                window.status=out;
                timerTwo=window.setTimeout(cmd,100);
            }
            else if (seed <= 0) {
                if (-seed < msg.length) {
                    out+=msg.substring(-seed,msg.length);
                    seed-;
                    var cmd="scrollit_r21(" + seed + ")";
                    window.status=out;
                    timerTwo=window.setTimeout(cmd,100);
                }
                else {
                    window.status=" ";
                    timerTwo=window.setTimeout("scrollit_r21(100)",75);
                }
            }
        }
    }


// End of functions
</script>

<body onLoad="timerONE=window.setTimeout('scrollit_r21(100)',500);initBoard();">
<center>
<h1>The INCREDIBLE JavaScript Maze Game!</h1>
</center>
<dd>Your player is represented by the "*" in the upper-left corner.
Use the buttons to move it around the maze.  The boxes will show your
coordinates. Be careful not to hit any walls. You can't edit the coordi-
nates
in the textboxes — that would be cheating. Reach the "$" in the lower-right
to win.
Press "Reset" to start over.<br>
<center>
<b>Good luck!</b>
<p>
```

```
<form method="post" name="board">
<input type='button' value='Reset'
onClick='clearBoard(this.form);update(document.board);'>
<br>
<textarea name="grid" rows="9" cols="10" wrap=virtual></textarea><br>
<!-- virtual-wrap is the key! Now one text line becomes a grid! -->
<table>
<tr>
  <td><input type='button' value='UP' onClick='decy(this.form)'></td>
  <td><input type='text' value='1' size=5 name='yval'
onChange='cheater(this.form);'></td>
  <td><input type='button' value='DOWN' onClick='incy(this.form)'></td>
<tr>
  <td><input type='button' value='LEFT' onClick='decx(this.form)'></td>
  <td><input type='text' value='1' size=5 name='xval'
onChange='cheater(this.form);'></td>
  <td><input type='button' value='RIGHT' onClick='incx(this.form)'></td>
</table>
</form>
<p>
Copyright 1996, <a href="mailto:steve@garcia.tisny.com">Steven J.
Weinberger</a>
</center>
</body>
</html>
```

The code is quite well-commented and probably doesn't benefit very much from a long-winded textual explanation. Still, I *am* a writer, so I couldn't resist adding one or two notes.

Notice that he does use an array for the layout but he uses a textarea with its draw attribute set to "virtual" to handle the updating. Very clever move that results in speedy results on the screen.

I also found his use of the onChange event for the two text boxes that he doesn't want you to edit to be quite intuitive and smart. Try editing one of those boxes directly and see how Weinberger slaps your hand!

Five-Card Stud Poker

We're back with Jason Bloomberg again. The same guy who wrote the random color background example I discussed earlier created, in an amazingly small amount of space, a five-card stud poker game that is astonishing in its speed, realism, and pure enjoyment.

Figure 12.16 shows you the window containing this game, after the cards are dealt. (But I'd encourage you to visit his site at http://www.lhouse.com/

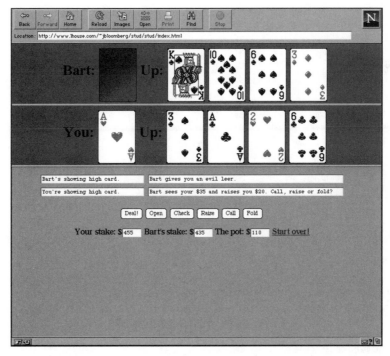

Figure 12.16 Five-card stud poker game in progress at Jason Bloomberg's site.

~jbloomberg/stud/index.html. He opens with a saloon scenario that is as funny as a lot of stuff you'll see on TV.)

You will need to visit his site or load the page off the CD-ROM (poker.html) to see the good use of color. The card faces were a public domain set of graphics he found on the Web.

The buttons all work as you'd expect and Bart does a lot of kibitzing while he tries to beat you. (Which he does with annoying regularity, by the way.)

Bloomberg has two variations of stud poker on his site. One has wild cards and the other doesn't. Here's the source code for the version without wild cards (used with Bloomberg's kind permission for your instruction):

```
<html>
<head>
<title>Five Card Stud</title>

<!--COPYRIGHT (C) 1996 BY JASON BLOOMBERG. -->
<!--ALL RIGHTS RESERVED. -->
```

```
<!--YOU MAY NOT USE ANY OF THIS CODE WITHOUT PERMISSION. -->
<!--EMAIL ME AT JBLOOMBERG@LHOUSE.COM IF YOU WANT PERMISSION!-->

<script language="JavaScript">
<!-- hide

var theseed3 = 1;

var clubs = 0;
var diamonds = 1;
var hearts = 2;
var spades = 3;

var decksize = 52;
var handsize = 5;

var keycard = 0;
var otherkeycard = 0;

var winner = "";
var status = "start";
var newstatus = "open";
var switchstatus = true;

var showholecard = false;

function random(maxnum)
    {
    var theseed2 = 0;
    thedate=new Date();
    theseed = Math.sqrt(theseed3 *
(47.3457373545383+thedate.getSeconds())*(91.7808957845674+thedate.getMinutes()));
    theseed3 = 3495937*(1000000*theseed-Math.floor(1000000*theseed))
    theseed2 = Math.floor(theseed3) % maxnum;
    return theseed2;
    }

function initarray(thisnum)
    {
    this.length=thisnum;
    for (var i = 0; i < thisnum; i++)
        this[i]=0;
    return this
    }

function cleararray(that)
    {
    for (var i = 0; i < that.length; i++)
        that[i]=0;
    }

deck = new initarray(decksize);
```

```
you = new initarray(handsize);
bart = new initarray(handsize);
thekey = new initarray(handsize);
bartkey = new initarray(handsize);
yourkey = new initarray(handsize);

function drawcard(which)
    {
    okay = false;
    while (okay == false)
        {
        okay = true;
        test = random(decksize);
        for (var i = 0; i < which; i++)
            {
            if (deck[i] == test)
                okay = false;
            }
        if (okay)
            deck[which] = test;
        }
    }

function dealcards()
    {
    for (var i = 0; i < handsize; i++)
        for (var j = 0; j < 2; j++)
            {
            drawcard(2 * i + j);
            if (j == 0)
                you[i] = deck[2 * i + j]
            else
                bart[i] = deck[2 * i + j]
            }
    }

function stackdeck()
    {
    you[0] = 0;
    you[1] = 1;
    you[2] = 50;
    you[3] = 40;
    you[4] = 8;
    bart[0] = 43;
    bart[1] = 5;
    bart[2] = 51;
    bart[3] = 3;
    bart[4] = 2;
    }

function suit(card)
```

```
    {
    var that = "";
    val = card % 4;
    if (val == 0)
        that = "c";
    if (val == 1)
        that = "d";
    if (val == 2)
        that = "h";
    if (val == 3)
        that = "s";
    return that;
    }

function face(card)
    {
    var val = 0;
    val = Math.floor(card / 4) + 2;
    return val;
    }

function teststraight(onebelow, player, startcard)
    {
    var isstraight1 = true;
    for (var i = onebelow; i >= onebelow - 3 + startcard; i--)
// start at top card, count down four
        {
        var testvalue = false;
        for (var j = startcard; j <= 4; j++)
            if (face(player[j]) == i)
                testvalue = true;        // card required for a straight is
                                         //in hand
            if (testvalue == false)
                isstraight1 = false;     // one failed card means no straight
        }
    return isstraight1;
    }

function playerhas(player, startcard, guess)    //startcard == 0 means all
                                                //five; startcard == 1 means
                                                four showing

    {
    var ct = new initarray(15);
    for (var i = 2; i <= 14; i++)
        for (var j = startcard; j < 5; j++)
            if (face(player[j]) == i)
                ct[i]++;

    var isstraight = false;
    var isflush = false;
```

```
var thishand = "high card";
cleararray(thekey);
var keyflag = 0;
for (var i = 2; i <= 14; i++)
    {
    if (ct[i] == 4)
        {
        thishand = "four of a kind";
        thekey[0] = i;
        ct[i] = 0;
        keyflag = 1;
        }
    if (ct[i] == 3)
        {
        if (thishand == "a pair")
            thishand = "a full house"
        else
            thishand = (guess) ? "four of a kind" :   "three of a kind";
        thekey[0] = i;
        ct[i] = 0;
        keyflag = 1;
        }
    if (ct[i] == 2)
        {
        if (thishand == "three of a kind")
            thishand = "a full house";
        if (thishand == "a pair")
            {
            thishand = (guess) ? "a full house" : "two pair";
            thekey[1] = (i < thekey[0]) ? i : thekey[0];
            // set to the lesser
            thekey[0] = (i < thekey[0]) ? thekey[0] : i;
            // set to the greater
            keyflag = 2;
            }
        if (thishand == "high card")
            {
            thishand = (guess) ? "three of a kind" : "a pair";
            thekey[0] = i;
            keyflag = 1;
            }
        ct[i] = 0;
        }
        for (var i = 14; i >= 2; i-)
            if (ct[i] > 0)
                {
                thekey[keyflag] = i;
                keyflag++;
                }
        if (thishand == "high card")
            {
```

```
                            isflush = true;
                            var testsuit = suit(player[startcard]);
                            for (var i = startcard + 1; i <= 4; i++)
                                if (suit(player[i]) != testsuit)
                                    isflush = false;
                                if (isflush)
                                    thishand = "a flush";

                            isstraight = false;
                            if (thekey[0] == 14)
                                {
                                var test = teststraight(5, player, startcard);
                                if (test)
                                    thekey[0] = 5;
                                isstraight = test || teststraight(13, player,
                                startcard);
                                }
                            else
                                isstraight = teststraight(thekey[0] - 1, player,
                                startcard);
                            if (isstraight)
                                if (isflush)
                                    thishand = "a straight flush"
                                else
                                    thishand = "a straight";
                        if (startcard != 0  && !guess)
                            thishand = "high card";
                        if (guess && (thishand == "high card"))
                            thishand = "a pair";
                }
        return thishand;
        }


function betterhand(bartstart, youstart, bartguess, youguess)
    {
    var winner = "";
    var barthas = playerhas(bart, bartstart, bartguess);
    for (i = 0; i < handsize; i++)
        bartkey[i] = thekey[i];
    var youhave = playerhas(you, youstart, youguess);
    for (i = 0; i < handsize; i++)
        yourkey[i] = thekey[i];
    alert(bartkey == yourkey);
    if (barthas == youhave)
        {
        winner = "push";
        for (i = 0; i < handsize; i++)
            {
            alert(winner + "B:" + bartkey[i] + "Y:" + yourkey[i]);
            if (winner == "push")
                {
```

```
                        if (bartkey[i] > yourkey[i])
                            winner =  "bart";
                        if (bartkey[i] < yourkey[i])
                            winner =  "you";
                    }
                }
            }
    else
        if (barthas == "a straight flush")
            winner = "bart"
        else
            if (youhave == "a straight flush")
                winner = "you"
            else
                if (barthas == "four of a kind")
                    winner = "bart"
                    else
                    if (youhave == "four of a kind")
                        winner = "you"
                    else
                        if (barthas == "a full house")
                            winner = "bart"
                        else
                            if (youhave == "a full house")
                                winner = "you"
                            else
                                if (barthas == "a flush")
                                    winner = "bart"
                                else
                                    if (youhave == "a flush")
                                        winner = "you"
                                    else
                                        if (barthas == "a straight")
                                            winner = "bart"
                                        else
                                            if (youhave == "a straight")
                                                winner = "you"
                                            else
                                                if (barthas == "three of a
                                                    kind")
                                                    winner = "bart"
                                                else
                                                    if (youhave == "three
                                                        of a kind")
                                                        winner = "you"
                                                    else
                                                        if (barthas == "two
                                                            pair")
                                                            winner = "bart"
                                                        else
```

```
                                    if (youhave == "two pair")
                                       winner = "you"
                                    else
                                    if (barthas == "a pair")
                                       winner = "bart"
                                    else
                                       winner = "you";
                    alert("betterhand: " + winner + " B: " + barthas + " Y: "
+ youhave);
                    return winner;
       }

// unhide ->
</script>
</head>

<frameset rows="120,120,*">
    <frame src="thetop.html" name="thetop" noresize scrolling=no>
    <frame src="middle.html" name="middle" noresize scrolling=no>
    <frame src="bottom.html" name="bottom" noresize>
</frameset>
</html>
```

As you can see, Bloomberg reuses code; the random number generator here is the same as he used in his random background color generator.

Most of this code is readable and self-explanatory. After using some random numbers to decide which cards to give each player, the script draws the layout and waits for the user to tell it what he wants to do.

Since it's stud poker, the process is pretty simple. A round of betting takes place after which Bart's card is revealed. The decision about who wins the hand is made in a deeply nested but straightforward series of "if-then-else" statements.

Soundex Generator

I've always been intrigued by the Soundex concept. Essentially, this algorithm, developed for the Census Bureau, lets you index or sort items (typically peoples' surnames) by the way they sound rather than by how they're spelled. For example, all of the various ways of spelling my last name (and there are apparently at least 3 million judging by the relative scarcity of a correct one emerging) sort together when the Soundex code algorithm is applied to them.

This JavaScript version of the Soundex generator was written by Stephen Heise. It is clean and straight-forward. (Find it on the CD-ROM as soundex.htm.)

```html
<html>
<head>
<!-- SOUNDEX Code Generator in Java Script
-->
<!-- by Stephen Heise
-->
<!-- mailto:heise@alumni.caltech.edu
-->
<!-- January 15, 1996
-->
<!-- Version 1.0
-->
<title>SOUNDEX Code Generator in Java Script</title>
<script language="JavaScript">
<!-- hide this code from non-scriptable browsers

// create object listing the SOUNDEX values for each letter
// -1 indicates that the letter is not coded, but is used for coding
function makesoundex() {
  this.a = -1
  this.b =  1
  this.c =  2
  this.d =  3
  this.e = -1
  this.f =  1
  this.g =  2
  this.h = -1
  this.i = -1
  this.j =  2
  this.k =  2
  this.l =  4
  this.m =  5
  this.n =  5
  this.o = -1
  this.p =  1
  this.q =  2
  this.r =  6
  this.s =  2
  this.t =  3
  this.u = -1
  this.v =  1
  this.w = -1
  this.x =  2
  this.y = -1
  this.z =  2
}
```

```
var sndx=new makesoundex()

// check to see that the input is valid
function isSurname(name) {
  if (name=="" || name==null) {
    alert("Please enter surname for which to generate SOUNDEX code.")
    return false
  } else {
    for (var i=0; i<name.length; i++) {
      var letter=name.charAt(i)
      if (!(letter>='a' && letter<='z' || letter>='A' && letter<='Z')) {
        alert("Please enter only letters in the surname.")
        return false
      }
    }
  }
  return true
}


// Collapse out directly adjacent sounds
// 1. Assume that surname.length>=1
// 2. Assume that surname contains only lowercase letters
function collapse(surname) {
  if (surname.length==1) {
    return surname
  }
  var right=collapse(surname.substring(1,surname.length))
  if (sndx[surname.charAt(0)]==sndx[right.charAt(0)]) {
    return surname.charAt(0)+right.substring(1,right.length)
  }
  return surname.charAt(0)+right
}


// Compute the SOUNDEX code for the surname
function soundex(form) {
  form.result.value=""
  if (!isSurname(form.surname.value)) {
    return
  }
  var stage1=collapse(form.surname.value.toLowerCase())
  form.result.value+=stage1.charAt(0).toUpperCase() // Retain first letter
  form.result.value+="-" // Separate letter with a dash
  var stage2=stage1.substring(1,stage1.length)
  var count=0
  for (var i=0; i<stage2.length && count<3; i++) {
      if (sndx[stage2.charAt(i)]>0) {
          form.result.value+=sndx[stage2.charAt(i)]
          count++
      }
  }
```

```
        for (; count<3; count++) {
            form.result.value+="0"
        }

        form.surname.select()
        form.surname.focus()
}
//end code hiding -->
</script>
</head>

<body>

<center>
<h1>SOUNDEX Code Generator in Java Script</h1>
<h2>(Requires Netscape 2.0)</h2>
</center>

<p>
SOUNDEX is a phonetic code utililized to index various U.S. Census data
since 1880.
</p>

<p>
Instructions:
<ol>
<li>Enter the surname for which to generate SOUNDEX code.</li>
<li>Click on the SOUNDEX button.</li>
<li>See the corresponding SOUNDEX code in the field.</li>
</ol>
</p>

<hr>

<p>
<form method=post>
Enter the surname for which to generate SOUNDEX code:
<input type=text name=surname size=30 onchange="soundex(this.form)">
<input type=button value=SOUNDEX  onclick="soundex(this.form)">
</p>

<p>
The SOUNDEX code for this surname is:
<input type=text name=result size=15>
</p>
</form>

<hr>
```

```
<i><a href="mailto:heise@alumni.caltech.edu">Stephen Heise</a></i>
check out my <a href="/~teaser/">home page</a>
</body>
</html>
```

Each letter of the alphabet is given a numeric value between 1 and 6 with the exception of a few letters that are assigned a value of -1 because their presence has a different effect on the way a word is pronounced. (These exceptions are vowels and letters that have a quasi-silent sound like "w" and "h".) Heise makes extensive use of the "this" keyword to make the use of the main function as generic as possible.

The JavaScript first validates that the surname isn't blank and that it contains only letters. Then it parses the surname a character at a time, building the Soundex code based on the algorithm developed by the Census Bureau.

Notice that Heise uses a form object to transfer the information entered by the user to the soundex function. He could, of course, us an onClick event to trigger this action just as well, but particularly in a small entry area like this one, a form is just as valid a design and may be argued to make for slightly more understandable code.

Ticker Tape

In Chapter 9, I showed you how to create a scrolling text message in the status bar of your window. Cameron Gregory goes this one better by creating a ticker-tape JavaScript that allows you to put horizontally scrolling messages anywhere on your Web page.

The source code for this script is stored on the CD-ROM as ticker.htm and is provided here for your perusal and study:

```
<html>
<head>
<title>
TickerTape in Java Script
</title>
<script language="javascript">
<!- Ticker Tape in Java Script .. Cameron Gregory cameron@corona.att.com
var tickertapeform
speed=100
len=75
space="
```

```
"
tid = 0;
message="TickerTape in JavaScript .. by Cameron Gregory ..
cameron@corona.att.com .. You are welcome to my home anytime, I live at:
http://www.att.com/homes/cameron/ and http://www.cs.jcu.edu.au/~cameron/"
c= -len;

function move() {
    cend=Math.min(c+len,message.length)
    if (c <0)
        cstart=0
    else
        cstart=c
    if (c < 0)
        f.scroll.value=space.substring(0,-c) +
          message.substring(cstart,cend)
    else
        f.scroll.value=message.substring(cstart,cend)
    c = c +1;
    if (c == message.length ) c = -len;
    tid=window.setTimeout("move()",speed);
}

function start(x) {
    f=x
    tid=window.setTimeout("move()",speed);
}

function cleartid() {
    window.clearTimeout(tid);
}

// for some reason on some pages this crashes netscape
function ticker(m,l,s)
    {
    message=m
    len=l
    speed=s
    document.write('<FORM name=tickertapeform><inputname=scroll size=')
    document.write(len)
    document.write(' value=""></FORM>')
    start(document.tickertapeform);
}

// end-->
</script>


</head>
```

```
<body>

<h3>Ticker Tape</h3>
This page written with Java Script implements a Ticker Tape.
The interface is a single function that takes three arguements:
<p>
<b>ticker(mesg,len,speed)</b>
<ul>
<li> <b>mesg</b> The message!
<li> <b>len</b> The size of the form to create the ticker tape (<i>size=</
i> in a FORM input field), and
<li> <b>speed</b> how fast (in milli seconds?) to scroll.
</ul>


<script language="javascript">
// You need a javascript compatible browser to view the following <br>
ticker("Welcome to my Ticker Tape in Java Script.  Simply add one line to
your HTML and include the script and you are off and running.  You are
welcome at my home aytime, I live at:  .... http://www.att.com/homes/
cameron/ ...  Things that interest me ... Volleyball ... Java Programming
... JavaScript ... CGI ... HTML ... Netscape ... Proxy cachers ...
",75,100)
// end javascipt section <br>
</script>
</center>
<h3>Warning</h3>
I have found Java Script to be quite unstable, when playing with it,
Netscape
2.0 crashed <i>many</i> times.  And consistently too..
<p>
<h3>How To</h3>
<ul>
<li> Include <a href=ticker.txt><b>ticker.txt</b></a> in the <b>HEAD</b>
section of your document.
<li> Add a function call inside your document:
<pre>
&lt;script language="javascript"&gt;
ticker("This is my ticker tape",75,100)
&lt;/script&gt;
</pre>
<li> View the source of this document for an example.
</ul>
Of course you really should comment out the JavaScript to other browsers.

<hr size=4>
<b><a href=/homes/cameron/>Cameron Gregory</a> - <a
href=mailto:cameron@corona.att.com>cameron@corona.att.com</a></b>
</BODY>
</HTML>
```

The ticker function does all the hard work in this script. You pass it three arguments:

- the message to scroll (which can be arbitrarily long)
- the width of the text field to create to display the message
- the speed at which you want to scroll (higher numbers lead to faster scrolling)

Note that Gregory has a comment line in his code that looks like this:

```
// for some reason on some pages this crashes netscape
```

This problem is related to a known bug in Netscape that causes memory to disappear with repeated calls to setTimeout. Netscape is aware of this bug and is fixing it at this writing. It is not, however, fixed in the alpha version of the Atlas (Netscape 3.0) product that was in beta distribution at the time of this writing.

JAVASCRIPT REFERENCE GUIDE

This reference guide is designed to give you an overview of the key features of JavaScript and how JavaScript code is added to your HTML documents. You can refer to it whenever you need to look up a built-in object, property, event, and so on. You'll also find reference material on the syntax of JavaScript and techniques for using the basic components like functions, variables, data types, control statements, and so on.

Writing JavaScript Code

You can embed JavaScript into your HTML document using this simple HTML tag:

```
<SCRIPT>...</SCRIPT>
```

This tag tells a JavaScript-supported browser like the new Netscape that the text between **<SCRIPT>** and **</SCRIPT>** should be processed as script code. When the Web browser encounters this code, it tries to run it line by line. An optional attribute can be included with this tag to specify the language that is used:

```
<SCRIPT LANGUAGE="JavaScript">...</SCRIPT>
```

This is perhaps the best way to open up a JavaScript section of any HTML document, because in the future there may be other new languages (for example Microsoft's upcoming Visual Basic Script) that might require you to mix and match different scripting languages. Therefore, you should get into the habit of identifying the scripting language you're using.

Hiding Your Code from Old Browsers

You can't expect everyone to be using the latest version of Netscape, or even Netscape for that matter. That's why it makes a lot of sense to hide your

JavaScript code so that it doesn't merely display its content in incompatible browsers. JavaScript code placed inside comment fields doesn't display in old browsers, but is still executed by JavaScript-compatible browsers. Here's a quick example:

```
<HTML>
<HEAD>

   <SCRIPT LANGUAGE="JavaScript">
<!-- Begin Javascript -- Using <! tag to hide code
     document.write("Testing Hidden Javascript Code.")
// End of Code. -->
   </SCRIPT>

</HEAD>
<BODY>
<P>
Did you see any code?
</BODY>
</HTML>
```

Notice that you must use the two slash symbols (//) at the beginning of the last comment line. This is one of the comment indicators for JavaScript. If these symbols are omitted, Netscape will treat the comment line as if it were a line of JavaScript code. Notice, too, that the HTML comments appear inside the <SCRIPT> tag; if you placed the line starting with the double-slash outside the script, the browser would see it as a line of text and display it.

General Rules to Follow in Writing JavaScript Statements

As you write the basic JavaScript statements there are some general rules that you must follow so your statements won't be rejected by Netscape:

JavaScript is case sensitive. When you refer to built-in objects, properties, and methods (or those you define), you must use the proper case. For example, to reference the **document** object, you must use a statement like **document.write**("hello") and not **Document.write**("hello").

Grouping statements. JavaScript statements should be placed one per line. If you put multiple statements on a single line, each statement must be separated by a semicolon as shown here:

```
document.write("hello"); document.write("<P>")
```

Some statements are grouped together as part of a *block of statements*; in this case, curly braces are used to specify the beginning of a block ({) and the end (}). Here's an example:

```
If (i < min || i > max) {
  document.write("The variable is out of range")
  document.write("the value of i is" + i)
}
```

If you have statements that won't fit on a single line, you must use the underscore character (_) as a continuation indicator:

```
if (i < min || i > max _
   i <100) document.write("The variable is out of range")
```

Proper comment syntax. JavaScript supports two types of comments: single-line comments that begin with the // characters and multi-line comments that begin with the characters /* and end with the characters */. Here's an example of each style:

```
// This is a single line comment

/* this is a very very very very very very long comment that
   takes up multiple lines */
```

In each case, text after the first comment symbol is ignored.

Using dot notation. JavaScript uses *dot notation* to separate objects and identifiers from properties and function (method) names. For example, in the following statement the dot notation is used to assign a value to the background color property (**bgColor**) of the **document** object:

```
document.bgColor="yellow"
```

Dealing with Quotation Marks in Code

Sometimes you may need to reference strings inside an element. This is to make sure Netscape doesn't abruptly close out an attribute. To do this, you need to use a single quotation mark ('). Here's an example:

```
onClick="myfunc('<INPUT TYPE="button" VALUE="Press Me" astring')">
```

Be sure to alternate double quotation marks with single quotation marks. Since event handlers in HTML must be enclosed in quotation marks, you must use single quotation marks to delimit arguments. For example:

```
<FORM NAME="myform">
<INPUT TYPE="button" NAME="Button1" VALUE="Open Sesame!"
onClick="window.open('stmtsov.html', 'newWin',
'toolbar=no,directories=no')">
</FORM>
```

You can insert quotation marks inside of strings by preceding them with a backslash. For example,

```
Myquote = "The other day I said \"Hello World!\""
document.write(Myquote)
```

When this code is executed, it would output the following:

```
The other day I said "Hello World!"
```

Executing JavaScript Code

When NetScape loads a page, it doesn't evaluate the code until after the page is loaded. Code contained in the <BODY> portion of a document is executed line by line as it is encountered. However, a lot of JavaScript code is executed through functions that are executed when a certain "event" happens, such as a user clicking on a button or within a listbox. Such deferred-execution scripts must be defined in the <HEAD> portion of a document. The following code shows an example of this.

```
<HEAD>
<SCRIPT LANGUAGE="JavaScript">
<!--  to hide script contents from old browsers

function square(i)
{
   document.write("The call passed ", i ," to the function.","<BR>")
   return i * i
}

document.write("The function returned ",square(5),".")
// end hiding contents from old browsers   -->
```

```
</SCRIPT>
</HEAD>
<BODY>
<BR>
All done.
</BODY>
```

This is how the above will appear on the screen.

```
The call passed 5 to the function.
The function returned 25.
All done.
```

Placement of JavaScript Code Is Important!

It's important where you place the JavaScript code in your document. Why? Well not everyone waits for a page to load completely before doing something with it. It's entirely possible that a user might click on a button that executes the code, but because the user hit ESC, the code hasn't loaded to tell Netscape what to do with it. Ouch!

This is easily overcome by placing your JavaScript code in the **<HEAD>**...**</HEAD>** tag section of your HTML code. This way, the JavaScript code is loaded before the user has a chance to do anything that might need a JavaScript response. Of course, not all code can be placed in the **<HEAD>** of the document because you want some code to execute independently of an event.

Updating Pages

You can't dynamically update pages very easily with JavaScript in Navigator. Once the page has been loaded and formatted, you can't change it without reloading the page. Currently, you cannot update a particular part of a page without updating the entire page. The way to work around this is to use frames and target updates directly into frames. You also can't currently print output created with JavaScript. For example, if you had the following in a page:

```
<P>This is some text.
<SCRIPT>document.write("<P>And some generated text")</SCRIPT>
```

And you printed the resulting page from the browser, you would get only "This is some text," even though you would see both lines on your screen.

Langauge Essentials

Key components in any programming language are values, variables, data types, statements, and expressions. In the next section of this Appendix we'll review these basic components.

The Basic JavaScript Language Statements

JavaScript's syntax borrows a bit from the C/C++ languages.

The basic elements of all programming languages are statements. These are the instructions you write to perform actions, make decisions, declare variables, assign values to variables, and so on. The basic statements you can write in JavaScript include:

Variable Declaration Statements—These types of statements are used to declare variables you use in your scripts. You can think of a variable as a simple container that holds values that will later be used in a calculation. Here is an example of how a variable is declared:

```
var i = 10
```

In this case, **i** is declared as a variable and then it is assigned a value of 10. The variable can then be used in other JavaScript statements. Because JavaScript is a "loosely typed" language, you don't have to declare the type of data that will be assigned to a variable. You can assign a numeric value, logical value (True or False), a string, or a null value.

Assignment Statements—These types of statements are used to assign values to variables or properties. A property is a variable predefined by JavaScript or in your scripts and belonging to an object. Here is an example of a simple variable assignment:

```
i = i * 20
```

In this case, **i** is assigned the results of the expression **i * 20**. Since we previously defined **i** as a variable and assigned it an initial value of 10, the results of this expression would be 200. This is the new value that is assigned to **i** in this assignment statement.

Assigning values to properties involves use of the dot notation (see above), as in this example:

```
document.bgColor="blue"
```

Conditional Statements—These are statements that are used to choose among two or more courses of action. Conditional statements allow programs to make logical decisions and then branch depending on the outcome of the decision. The basic conditional statement used in JavaScript is the if-then statement, as shown in this example:

```
if (i < min || i > max) document.write("the variable is out of range")
```

Here, the variable **i** is compared with the variables **min** and **max** to see if it is less than or greater than, respectively. If it is, the statement **document. write("the variable is out of range")** is executed. If the statement is false, nothing happens.

The alternate form of the if-then statement is the if-then-else statement, as shown in this example:

```
if (i < min || i > max) document.write("the variable is out of range")
else document.write("You did it right!")
```

You can combine if-then and if-then-else to produce fairly complex nested conditional statements.

Note that if more than one statement is to be executed as a result of a conditional, the statement block must be enclosed in curly braces.

Looping Statements—These are statements used to repeat actions. They are great for doing things like performing mathematical operations, reading and processing data from forms and so on. Here's an example:

```
for (var i = 0; i < max; i++ {
 document.write("the value of i is " + i + "<BR>")
}
```

In this case, the loop repeats until the variable **i** is equal to the value stored in **max**. Each time the loop repeats, the value of **i** is displayed.

Function Definitions—As I demonstrated in our first script, JavaScript allows us to define our own functions for performing specialized tasks. Usually, you create functions for operations that you plan on performing over and over. Here's a function that multiplies two values:

```
function compute(i,j)
{
    document.writeln
    document.write("The total is " + i*j)
    document.writeln
}
```

When a function like this is defined, it is not actually executed; that comes later when the function is "called." In a sense, a function definition serves as a place-holder for instructions you wish to use later.

Function Calls—Function calls tell JavaScript to execute the instructions listed. For example, when a statement like this is encountered:

```
compute(10,5)
```

Each line of instruction in the **compute**() is executed one at a time.

Values (Data Types)

A programming language has to have the ability to set, store, and manipulate data via named variables. JavaScript works with several key types of values:

- ◎ Numbers: Any type of number like 21 or 1.314
- ◎ Logical (Boolean): These are True (-1) or False (0) values.
- ◎ Strings: Strings are any type of variable treated as text for example "Hello" or "12/31/95" or "123456" would all be valid strings.
- ◎ Null: A null value is a special type of value which is used in certain situations.

Datatype Conversions

Javascript is known as a loosely typed language. This means that you don't have to declare what type of value a variable is going to work with up front. This is both helpful and confusing. On the one hand this makes writing JavaScript programs easier. You can casually declare variables and stuff values in them as you code. On the other hand, you can easily get lost remembering which variables are which. This also means that at some point, say in the beginning of the script, variable R might be equal to the integer 12 and at the end it could be equal to "Eat at Joe's...."

My recommendation is that you watch your variables like a hawk and try to use some self control—JavaScript's flexibility could be a nightmare if you're not careful.

In expressions involving the combination of a string and a numeric value, the resulting value will always be a string. Here's an example:

```
Length=9
Width=9
Area=length*width
Answer="The Area is..."+Area
```

will result in the variable answer being a string equal to: "The Area is 81."

Naming Variables

Javascript has the following rules when it comes to naming a variable:

1. A JavaScript identifier or name must start with either a letter or an underscore ("_"). After that the variable name can be constructed from both numbers (0-9) and letters like "A" or "a".
2. JavaScript is case sensitive! This means that the variable "TEST" is not the same as the variable "test" or "TeSt".

Integers

Integers can be expressed in decimal (base 10), hexadecimal (base 16), or octal (base 8) format. A decimal integer literal consists of a sequence of digits (optionally suffixed as described below) without a leading 0 (zero).

An integer can be expressed in octal or hexadecimal rather than decimal. A leading 0 (zero) on an integer literal means it is in octal; a leading 0x (or 0X) means hexadecimal. Hexadecimal integers can include digits (0-9) and the letters a-f and A-F. Octal integers can include only the digits 0-7.

Floating Point Values

A floating point value is any decimal number or fraction. JavaScript works with floating points easily and uses scientific notation as shown in the following examples:

```
2.1564563
-2.5E10
.9e12
3E-16
```

Boolean Values

The boolean type has two literal values: true and false.

String Values

A string value is any set of characters enclosed in quotation marks, either double or single. Strings can be composed entirely of characters, such as "Hello World!", or even entirely of numbers, such as "124", or both, such "Hello 124". Note, though, that if you have a string of just numbers, say "12" the string will not have the mathematical value of 12. Using the **eval**(), **parseInt**(), and **parseFloat**() functions you can turn a string of numbers into a numerical value for computational purposes.

Special Characters

You can use the following special characters in JavaScript string literals:

\b indicates a backspace

\f indicates a form feed

\n indicates a new line character

\r indicates a carriage return

\t indicates a tab character

Creating Arrays

An array is a series of values assigned to a single variable that all share the same characteristics. For example, assume you wanted to list all the names in a group of 20 people. Instead of creating a separate variable for each one like **NameOne** and **NameTwo** and **NameThree**..., you could create an array called **Names** and assign the first name to **Names**[1], the second name to **Names**[2] ..., until you get to the final name on your list, which would be assigned to **Name**[20].

Understanding Expressions

An expression is basically a formula of some sort. For example A=1, 1+1, Name="Urb" + "LeJeune", and 2>X are all types of expressions. The main types of expressions you can create with JavaScript include:

ARITHMETIC

These are basic numerical expressions, such as 2+2=4 or 81/9+23.

STRING

These expressions deal with text values, be they "Ben" or "3.14344"—anything that is being treated as text is a string (even if it's a number).

LOGICAL

Logical expressions are formulas such as does 2+3=5. All logical expressions result in either a true or false answer.

CONDITIONAL

A conditional expression is somewhat like a logical expression. The difference is that in a logical expression the answer is either true or false, but with a conditional expression you provide the outcome choices, which can be different types of values.

Evaluating Expressions with JavaScript Operators

Tables A.1 and A.2 illustrate how different JavaScript expressions are constructed using the standard JavaScript operators including assignment operators. For the purposes of Table A.1, assume that the variables A and B have been assigned these values: A=8 and B=2.

The % is a special operator called the modulus operator and it takes two values, in the above case, A and B, and divides A by B and returns the value left over. In

Table A.1   Standard JavaScript Assignment Operators

Javascript Expression	Expression Represents	Resulting Value
A+=B	A=A+B	A=10
A-=B	A=A-B	A=6
A*=B	A=A*B	A=16
A/=B	A=A/B	A=4
A%=B	A=A%B	A=0
A=-B	A=-B	A=-2

this example, 8/2 = 4, with no remainder. If the values were 41 and 10, or 41/10, the resulting value would be 1.

For our purposes Table A.2, assume that the variables A and B have been assigned these values: B=0 and A=3.

Comparing Expressions

You can create expressions in JavaScript for comparison purposes. For example you might want to test if "A is greater than B" or if "B does not equal A". In each case you would set up a comparison expression using various comparison operators (==, >, >=, <, <=, !=) to tell JavaScript exactly what it is you want to know.

Many times these expressions are used in conjunction with an if-then statement. For example, the following simple code demonstrates the use of a few comparison expressions:

Table A.2   JavaScript Incrementing Operators

Javascript Expression	Expression Represents	Resulting Value
B=A++	B=A and A=A+1	B=3 and A=4
B=A--	B=A and A=A-1	B=3 and A=2
B=++A	B=A+1 and A=A+1	B=4 and A=4
B=--A	B=B-1 and A=A-1	B=2 and A=2

```html
<HTML>
<HEAD>
<TITLE>Java Function Example</TITLE>
<SCRIPT LANGUAGE="JavaScript">

<!-- Beginning of JavaScript Applet -------

A=5
B=6
C=5

document.write("<H3>Example JavaScript for Comparison Operators<HR><P></
H3>")
document.write("A="+A+" B="+B+" C="+C+"<P><HR>")
if(A==B)
{
    document.write("A does equal B!<P>")
}

if(A!=B)
{
    document.write("A does not equal B!<P>")
}

if(A<B)
{
    document.write("A is less than B!<P>")
}

if(A>=C)
{
    document.write("A is less than or equal to C!")
}

document.write("<HR><P><H3>You Can Also Set A Variable To Return The Result
of a Comparison Expression!</H3><P>")

D=(A>C)

document.write("D equals:"+D+" when it is set to = the expression A>C")
document.write("<HR><P>")

D=(A==C)

document.write("D equals:"+D+" when it is set to = the expression A==C")

   // -- End of JavaScript code -------->

</SCRIPT>
</HEAD>
```

```
<BODY>
</BODY>

</HTML>
```

A comparison operator compares its operands and returns a logical value based on whether the comparison is true or not. While the previous demonstration works with numerical values, comparison expressions may also be used with strings. For example, you could check to see if "Ben"="neB" to see if two strings matched each other. When used on string values, the comparisons are based on the standard lexicographical ordering.

Here's a quick review of the key comparison operators:

- Equal (==): Returns true if the operands are equal.
- Not equal (!=): Returns true if the operands are not equal.
- Greater than (>): Returns true if the left operand is greater than the right operand.
- Greater than or equal to (>=): Returns true if the left operand is greater than or equal to the right operand.
- Less than (<): Returns true if the left operand is less than the right operand.
- Less than or equal to (<=): Returns true if the left operand is less than or equal to the right operand.

String Operators

In addition to the comparison operators, which may be used on string values, you can also add strings together using a simple + operator. For example

```
"The" + "Coriolis" + Group"
```

returns the string:

```
"The Coriolis Group"
```

(The process of combining strings is called "concatenation".)

You can add strings to existing strings by using the shorthand of +=. For example, if you had a string FIRSTPART which was equal to "This Book is", and then you added the following line of JavaScript code:

```
FIRSTPART+=" GREAT!"
```

If you printed out the string, you'd get:

```
"This Book is GREAT!"
```

Defining and Using Functions

Functions are self-contained blocks of code that are called upon either by JavaScript code or by various events triggered by actions in the browser or on forms in the browser. Functions can optionally accept and return values as well. Functions are different from simple JavaScript instructions because they begin with the word **function**. Using this keyword defines a set of scripting instructions that sit in the background until the function name is called by an event, a script, or another function. To define a function in JavaScript is simple. Some functions may take a while to write, but the overall structure of a function is very basic as shown here:

```
function functon-name(arguments)
{
    function-body
}
```

A function in JavaScript is made up of a specific **function** keyword followed by the name of the function and a parameter list in parentheses, which details all the variables that the function requires to work. Here's a simple function that takes a string value, in this case the name of the user, and displays a question asking the user his or her age using the **write**() method:

```
function askuser_age (username)
{
  stringtoprint=username+"What is Your Age?"
  document.write("<B>"+stringtoprint+"</B>")
}
```

This function is a simple one with one parameter. You can actually have lots of parameters, and they can be numbers, strings, Booleans, and even complex objects.

Functions are usually defined within the <HEAD> ... </HEAD> tag pairs of an HTML document. You can define as many functions as you like as long as each function has a different name. By placing your function definitions within the heading section, you can ensure that they can be called by any script, form, or event used in the body section of an HTML document. Since the **<HEAD>** section always is processed before the **<BODY>** section, you'll be certain that Netscape knows about your functions before you try to use them. Even though a function can only be defined once, you can call it as many times as you want.

Here's a simple function that adds up three numbers and returns an answer:

```
<HTML>
<HEAD>
<TITLE>Java Function Example</TITLE>
<SCRIPT LANGUAGE="JavaScript">

<!-- Beginning of JavaScript code ------

   function compute(obj)
   {
   var a=parseFloat(obj.Number1.value)
   var b=parseFloat(obj.Number2.value)
   var c=parseFloat(obj.Number3.value)
   obj.Answer.value=a+b+c
   }

// -- End of JavaScript code ------>

</SCRIPT>
</HEAD>
<BODY>
<FORM NAME="MYFORM">

Number 1:<INPUT TYPE=text NAME="Number1" SIZE=20 ><P>
Number 2:<INPUT TYPE=text NAME="Number2" SIZE=20 ><P>
Number 3:<INPUT TYPE=text NAME="Number3" SIZE=20 ><P>

<INPUT TYPE="button" VALUE="Click Me" onClick="compute(this.form)"><P>
Answer:<INPUT TYPE=text NAME="Answer" SIZE=20 ><P>
</FORM>

</BODY>
</HTML>
```

The Web page created by this example is shown in Figure A.1. Notice how the example combines JavaScript code with an HTML form. The form is used to gather data from the user and the JavaScript code is used to process the data.

Notice also that the function is defined in the heading section of the HTML document, but this time, the body of the document does not contain an explicit

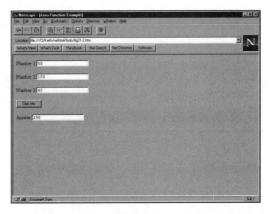

Figure A.1   Using a function to calculate values input from a form.

call to the **compute**() function. The call to this function is hidden in the HTML code that defines the form. Here is the specific line of code:

```
<INPUT TYPE="button" VALUE="Click Me" onClick="compute(this.form)"><P>
```

When the user clicks on the "Click Me" button, the **compute**() function will be called. It will be passed, the information gathered from the form—the three numbers that the user types in. The **compute**() function will then process these numbers, add them together, and return the sum of the numbers. The result is returned using a statement that might look a little unusual to you at the moment:

```
obj.Answer.value=a+b+c
```

Here, the first component, **obj**, is an object that references the form. **Answer** is the component that is used to access **value**, which is the property that stores the result of the function. By placing the result of the function in this property, the HTML code can later access it and display the result:

```
Answer:<INPUT TYPE=text NAME="Answer" SIZE=20 ><P>
```

Returning Values

Functions can be defined to return values to variables and methods as they are called from the body of an HTML document. This is done by using the **return** statement. Here's an example:

```
function compute(a,b,c)
{
   return (a+b+c)
}
```

You could then call this function in the body section of an HTML document by using a statement like this:

```
document.write("The result is " + compute(1,2,3))
```

When you first start to program with JavaScript you'll notice that the terms function and method are used interchangeably quite often. The term method comes from languages like Smalltalk, C++, and Java, which are object-oriented in nature. Because JavaScript is also object-based, functions are often called methods. The basic idea is that methods are used to define the behavior of objects. For example, the **document** object provides a method named **write()** which determines how document objects should display text on the screen.

JavaScript Objects

Objects are the basic JavaScript building blocks. There are two types of objects you will encounter in JavaScript. The first are *built-in* objects provided by Netscape Navigator and the JavaScript language. The second type of objects are *custom objects* you create using JavaScript code. For example, if you were processing strings of text in a script you could create a string object called *personname*.

The built-in objects supported by Netscape are presented in Table A.3.

Objects have *properties* that describe them. For example, the **document** object has a **fontcolor** property that tells Netscape what the color of the document's text is. Objects also have *methods*, which specify the commands they can perform. For example, the **document** object has a method named **write()** which allows you to print text or HTML code to a document. Finally, objects can

Table A.3   The Built-in JavaScript Objects

Object	Description
anchor (anchors array)	Text that serves as the target of a hypertext link.
button	Accesses a pushbutton on an HTML form.
checkbox	Accesses a checkbox on an HTML form.
Date	A special purpose object for processing data and time information.
document	Accesses the current document.
elements array	An array of objects corresponding to form elements such as checkboxes, radion buttons, text object, and so on.
form (forms array)	Accesses forms and objects on forms.
frame (frames array)	The scrollable window used for navigating Web pages.
hidden	Accesses a hidden object on a form.
history	Accesses information on the URLs the user has visited.
link (links array)	Text or image that is used as a hypertext link.
location	Accesses information on the current URL.
Math	A special purpose object designed for performing a variety of mathematical operations.
navigator	Accesses information about the current version of Netscape that is running. Navigator is the top level object.
password	Accesses a text field on an HTML form that is used to obtain a password. When a password is entered, the text is hidden using asterisks (*).
radio	Accesses a radio button on an HTML form.
reset	Accesses a reset button on an HTML form.
select (options array)	Accesses a selection list or scrolling list on an HTML form
string strings.	A special purpose object designed for processing
submit	Processes a submit button on an HTML form.
text	Accesses a text input field on an HTML form.
textarea	Access a multiline input field on an HTML form.
window	The top-level object for each document object.

allows you to print text or HTML code to a document. Finally, objects can trigger *events* that you can write responses for. An event is an action that occurs, such as a mouse click or a window activity like scrolling. As an example, JavaScript provides a built-in **button** object that has an event called **OnClick** which is triggered whenever the user presses the mouse button on a Web page.

JavaScript Properties

Objects can have properties or characteristics that you can set. For instance, when writing a **document** object you might have a property for it like **bgcolor** (background color). When you set this property, the background color of the document in the browser changes. Just as you can create your own objects, you can also create your own properties for those objects. Because of the large assortment of properties that are available, some JavaScript users like to call Java a properties-based language. The complete set of JavaScript properties is listed in Table A.4. This table includes a description of each property along with the name of the object or objects to which the property is assigned.

JavaScript Methods

Methods are a fancy type of function that work specifically with an object. In JavaScript certain objects allow you to do certain things via methods. For example, you can use a statement like this to have the **document** object call the **write**() method to display specified text on the screen:

```
document.write("Here's a test message")
```

Some methods such as **write**() are built into JavaScript, but you can also create your own by using the function notation presented earlier in this reference guide. Tables A.5 through A.14 provide descriptions of the complete set of JavaScript methods. The tables of methods are presented in the order based on Netscape's object hierarchy. Note that some objects, such as **navigator**, **hidden**, **link**, and **location**, do not have methods.

Table A.4 The Set of JavaScript Properties

Properties	Object(s)	Explanation	Sample Code
action	form	You set the form.action property to a string that is the destination URL for data from that form when it is submitted.	MF.action ="String"
alinkColor	document	You set this property to a string that is a hexadecimal or color command that tells the browser what the color of an active link should be in your document.	document.alink Color=""
appCode Name	navigator	By reading this property you can see what the internal codename is for the current version of Navigator that the browser is using.	CN= navigator. appcodename
appName	navigator	By reading this property you can see what the official name is for the current version of Navigator that the browser is using.	AN= navigator.appName
appVersion	navigator	By reading this property you get the exact version number of Navigator that the browser is using.	AV=navigator .appVersion document. bColor=""
bgColor	document	You set this property to a string specifying the color of the document background.	
checked	checkbox, radio	Reading this property returns a Boolean value (true or false) that indicates the current state of a specific checkbox or radio button.	Checkvalue= checkbox.checked

Continued

Table A.4   The Set of JavaScript Properties (Continued)

Properties	Object(s)	Explanation	Sample Code
cookie	document	Reading this property returns the contents of the cookies.	CT=document.cookie
default Checked	checkbox, radio	Reading this property gives you a Boolean value which indicates the default selection state of a checkbox or radio button.	CV=checkbox. defaultChecked
default Selected	options, array	This property indicates the default election state of an option in a select object.	defaultSelected=True
defaultStatus	window	This property controls the default message displayed in the status bar at the bottom of a window in Navigator.	window. defaultStatus= "My Docu ment!"
defaultValue	hidden, password, text, textarea	This property controls a string value which is equal to the default value of a password, text, or textarea object.	Text1.default Value= "Coriolis"
E	Math	Reading this property returns Euler's constant, the base of natural logarithms, which approximately equals 2.718.	EulerConstant =math.E
encoding	form	This property refers to a string that indicates the type of MIME encoding used on a specific form.	Typeof Encoding= form.encoding
fgColor	document	This property controls the color of a document's text. It accepts a string value set to a hexidecimal indicator or a color command.	document.fgColor=""
hash	link, location	Reading this property of a link or a location returns a string which begins with a hash mark (#) that pulls out just the anchor name in the referenced URL.	Anchorname =link.hash
host	link, location,	Reading this property of a link or a location returns a string that gives you the specific hostname:port part of the referenced URL.	NameofHost =link.host

Continued

Table A.4   The Set of JavaScript Properties (Continued)

Properties	Object(s)	Explanation	Sample Code
hostname	link, location	Reading this property of a link or a location returns a string that gives you the specific host and domain name or IP address of the refernced URL's network host.	CN=location .hostname
href	link, location	Reading this property returns a string equal to the entire referenced URL.	Href= link.href
index	options array	This property represents the index value of an option in a select object.	selectName .options[i] .index
lastModified	document	This property consists of a string that represents the date that a document was last modified.	document lastModified
length	frame, radio history, select, forms, arrays, options, anchors, elements, objects, links window,	This property returns an integer equal to the length of the object or array specified.	len=mystring. length
linkColor	document	This property accepts a string value of either a hexadecimal color indicator or specific color command to control the color of a document's hyperlinks.	document.link Color=""
LN2	math	Reading this value returns the natural logarithm of two, equal to about 0.693.	LogofTwo= math.LN2
LN10	math	Reading this value returns the natural logarithm of ten, equal to about 2.302.	LogofTen =math.LN10
location	document	This property returns a string equal to the complete URL of the current document.	Currentlocation =document.location
LOG2E	math	Reading this property returns the base 2 logarithm of e equal to about 1.442	LogofE= math.LOG2E
LOG10E	math	Reading this property returns the base 10 logarithm of e equal to about 0.434	LogofTEN= math.LOG10E
method	form	Use this property to tell Navigator how to send field input from forms to the server.	form.method

Continued

Table A.4	The Set of JavaScript Properties (Continued)		
Properties	**Object(s)**	**Explanation**	**Sample Code**
name	button, frame, checkbox, hidden, radio, password, reset, select, submit, text, textarea, window, options array	Reading this property returns a string specifying the name of the referenced object.	Nameofbutton =button1.name
parent	frame, window	The parent property is a synonym for a window whose frameset contains the current frame.	Parentwindow =frame.parent
pathname	link, location	A string specifying the url-path portion of the URL.	PathofURL =link. pathname
PI	math	The property of this math object returns a value equal to PI or about 3.14159...	Circumference =Diameter *math.PI
port	link, location	This string specifies the communications port used by the server of the referenced link.	portoflink= link.port
protocol	link, location	This string specifies the protocol portion of a URL as specified by the referenced link or location. This is the part of a URL that takes place up to and including the first colon.	Protocoloflink =link.protocol
referrer	document	This property controls the URL of the calling document when a link is chosen by the user.	document.referrer
search	link, location	This property returns a string that begins with a question mark. The string equals the query information in a specified URL.	SearchofURL =link.search
selected	options array	This property controls a Boolean value (true or false) which specifies the current selection state of an option in a select object.	document. form.select =index

Continued

Table A.4   The Set of JavaScript Properties (Continued)

Properties	Object(s)	Explanation	Sample Code
SQRT1_2	math	This math object property reutrns the square root of one-half, roughly 0.707.	math..SQRT1_2
sqrt2	math	This math object property returns the square root of two, which is equal to about 1.414.	math.sqrt2
status	window	The status property of a window controls the message which is displayed on the status bar at the bottom of a window.	window.status ="My Docu ment!"
target	form, link, location	For a form it denotes the name of the window to send responses to when the form is submitted. For a link it tells Navigator which window to display the linked document in.	form.target= "TARGET Frame"
text	options array	This property controls via a string the text which follows an <OPTION> tag in a select object.	document. myform.select listoptions(X). text
title	document	This property controls the title of the document in the browser.	Document.title ="Title is My Document!"
top	window	The top property is a synonym for the top-most Navigator window, which is a "document window" or "Web Browser window."	Topwindow now=window. top
userAgent	navigator	A string representing the value of the user-agent header sent in the HTTP protocol from client to server.	userAgent Header=naviga- tor.userAgent
value	button, radio, checkbox, hidden, password, reset, submit, text, textarea objects, options array	Reading this property returns a string equal to the value of the related object.	Value= document. myform.text1. value

Continued

Table A.4   The Set of JavaScript Properties (Continued)

Properties	Object(s)	Explanation	Sample Code
vlinkColor	document	This property controls the color of visited links. It accepts a hexidecimal string or color command string.	document. vlinkColor=""

Table A.5   The Methods Provided for Processing the window Object

Method	Explanation	Syntax
alert()	Creates an Alert dialog box with the string message.	window.alert("string")
clearTimeout()	This method will clear the current set Timeoutcommand. TimeoutID is a variable that uniquely identifies the setTimeout command you want to stop.	window.cleartime (timeoutID)
close()	Closes the referred to window.	window.close()
confirm()	Creates a Confirm dialog box with OK and Cancel buttons plus the current message.	window.confirm ("string")
open()	Opens new window.	window.open("URL", "windowName", ["windowFeatures"])
prompt()	Creates Prompt dialog box showing message. Gives user a box to reply. InputDefault may be used to give a suggested answer.	window.prompt ("string", [inputDefault])
setTimeout()	This method will execute the JavaScript code contained in the string after the number of milliseconds defined in msec. You should assign the result of this method to a variable for use with clearTimeout (see above).	timerID=window .setTimeout ("string",msec)

Table A.6   The Methods Provided for Processing frame Objects

Method	Explanation	Syntax
clearTimeout()	This method will clear the current set Timeout command. TimeoutID is a variable that uniquely identifies the setTimeout command you want to stop.	frameName.cleartime (timeoutID)
setTimeout()	This method will execute the JavaScript code contained in the string after the number of milliseconds defined in msec.	frameName.setTimeout ("String",msec)

Table A.7   The Methods Provided for Processing history Objects

Method	Explanation	Syntax
back()	Loads the most recently visited URL in the history list. (This is the URL that is accessed when Netscape's Back button is pressed.)	history.back()
forward()	Loads the next URL in the history list.	history.forward()
go()	Loads a URL from the history list.	history.go(delta | "location")

Table A.8   The Methods Provided for Processing document Objects

Method	Explanation	Syntax
clear()	Clears the current document.	document.clear()
close()	Closes the document.	document.close()
open()	Opens the referenced mimeType in the document.	document.open (["mimeType"])
write()	Writes a string or text to the document.	document.write ("string")
writeln()	Writes a string or text to the document, followed by a carriage return, which is ignored by HTML making write() and writeln() exactly equivalent.	document.writeln ("string")

Table A.9   The Method Provided for Processing form Objects

Method	Explanation	Syntax
submit()	Submits the specified form.	formName.submit()

Table A.10   The Methods Provided for Processing password, select, text, and textarea Objects

Method	Explanation	Syntax
blur()	Removes the focus from a specified form element.	passwordName.blur(); textName.blur()
focus()	Assigns the focus to a specified form element.	selectName.focus(); textName.focus()
select()	Selects the input area of the specified password, text, or textarea object.	passwordName.select(); textName.select()

Table A.11   The Method Provided for Processing button, checkbox, radio, reset, and submit Objects

Method	Explanation	Syntax
click()	Simulates a mouse click on the calling from element.	buttonName.click(); radio.Name.click()

Table A.12   The Methods Provided for Processing string Objects

Method	Explanation	Syntax
anchor()	This is used to create an anchor. The text in mystring is the text you want highlighted (the user to see) in the document.	document.write (mystring.anchor ("contents_anchor"())
big()	Causes string to appear as big text.	document.write (mystring.big())
blink()	Causes string to appear as blinking text.	document.write (mystring.blink())
bold()	Causes string to appear as bold text.	document.write (mystring.bold())
charAt()	Retrieves the character at a specified position in a string.	document.write (mystring.charAt(3))
fixed()	Causes a string to be displayed in fixed-pitch font	document.write (mystring.fixed())
fontcolor()	Causes string to appear in the color specified.	document.write (mystring.fontcolor (color))
fontsize()	Causes string to appear as bold text.	document.write (mystring.big())
indexOf()	Looks for the first instance of searchValue (a string) in your current string. The string is searched forwards. FromIndex is a number that denotes where to start from and if omitted the search starts from the first character in the string.	document.write (mystring.IndexOf (searchValue, [fromIndex]())
italics()	Causes string to appear as italic text.	document.write (mystring.italics())

Continued

Table A.12 The Methods Provided for Processing string Objects (Continued)

Method	Explanation	Syntax
lastIndexOf()	Looks for the last instance of searchValue (a string) in the string provided as the first arguement. The string is searched backwards. FromIndex is a number that denotes where to start from and if omitted the search starts from the last character in the string.	document.write (mystring.lastIndexOf (searchValue, [fromIndex]())
link()	Used to create a hypertext link to text you might write to the document. URL is a string denoting the specific URL and the text in mystring is the text you want the user to see in the document.	document.write (mystring.link(URL())
small()	Causes string to appear as small text.	document.write (mystring.small())
strike()	Causes string to appear as striked text.	document.write (mystring.strike())
sub()	Causes string to appear as subscript text.	document.write (mystring.sub())
subString()	This method is used to refer to a portion of a string. indexA and indexB are two numbers 0 to stringlength-1 which denote the specific section of the string to refer to.	Subsetstring=mystring .subString(indexA, indexB)
sup()	Causes string to appear as superscript text.	document.write (mystring.sup())
toLowerCase()	Causes string to be converted to lowercase text.	document.write (mystring.toLower Case())
toUpperCase()	Causes string to be converted to uppercase text.	document.write (mystring.toUpper Case())

JavaScript Events

Events are actions that take place in Netscape. For example, you might click on a button or type in some text, which in turn causes an event to occur. Events are the primary launching pad of JavaScript routines. Learning what the different events are and then thinking up programming responses to them is a key part of learning JavaScript.

Table A.13   The Methods Provided for Processing math Objects

Method	Explanation	Syntax
abs()	Returns the absolute value of a number.	Math.abs(-10)
acos()	Returns the arc cosine (in radians) of a number.	Math.acos(30)
asin()	Returns the arc sine (in radians) of a number.	Math.asin(60)
atan()	Returns the arc tangent (in radians) of a number.	Math.atan(90)
ceil()	Returns the least integer greater than or equal to a number.	Math.ceil(200.546)
cos()	Returns the cosine of a number.	Math.cos(30)
exp()	Returns enumber, where number is the argument, and e is Euler's constant, the base of the natural logarithms.	Math.exp(10)
floor()	Returns the greatest integer less than or equal to a number.	Math.floor(199.345)
log()	Returns the natural logarithm (base e) of a number.	Math.log(10)
max()	Returns the greater of two numbers.	Math.max(100,220)
min()	Returns the lesser of two numbers.	Math.min(100,220)
pow()	Returns base to the exponent power, that is, baseexponent.	Math.pow(base exponent)
random()	Returns a pseudo-random number between zero and one. This method is available on Unix platforms only.	Math.random()
round()	Returns the value of a number rounded to the nearest integer.	Math.round(34.67)
sin()	Returns the sine of a number.	Math.sin(30)
sqrt()	Returns the square root of a number.	Math.sqrt(25)
tan()	Returns the tangent of a number.	Math.tan(60)

Table A.14   The Methods Provided for Processing date Objects

Method	Explanation	Syntax
getDate()	Returns the day of the month for the specified date.	birthday=mybirthday .getDate()

Continued

Table A.14   The Methods Provided for Processing date Objects

Method	Explanation	Syntax
getDay()	Returns a value of 0 (Sunday) through 6 (Saturday) representing the day of the week for the specified date.	Birthweekday= mybirthday.getDay()
getHours()	Returns the hour for the specified date.	birthhour= mybirthday.getHours()
getMinutes()	Returns the minutes for the specified date.	Birthminutes= mybirthday.get Minutes()
getMonth()	Returns the month for the specified date.	birthmonth= mybirthday.getMonth()
getSeconds()	Returns the seconds for the current time.	Birthseconds= mybirthday.get Seconds()
getTime()	Returns the numeric value corresponding to the time for the specified date.	birthtime=my birthday.getTime()
getTimeZone Offset()	Returns the time zone offset in minutes for the current locale.	birthoffset=my birthday.getTimeZone Offset()
getYear()	Returns the year in the specified date.	birthyear=my birthday.getYear()
parse()	Returns the number of milliseconds in a date string since January 1, 1970 00:00:00, local time.	timesince=parse (mybirthday)
setDate()	Sets the day of the month for a specified date.	mybirthday.setDate(25)
setHours()	Sets the hours for a specified date.	mybirthday.set Hours(13)
setMinutes()	Sets the minutes for a specified date.	mybirthday.set Minutes(15)
setMonth()	Sets the month for a specified date.	mybirthday.set Month(6)
setSeconds()	Sets the seconds for a specified date.	mybirthday.set Second(00)
setTime()	Sets the value of a date object by giving it a number representing the milliseconds since January 1, 1970 00:00:00, local time.	mybirthday.set Time(msec)

Continued

Table A.14   The Methods Provided for Processing date Objects (Continued)

Method	Explanation	Syntax
setYear()	Sets the year for a specified date.	mybirthday.set Year(1971)
toGMTString()	Converts a date to a string, using the toGMTString	birthGMT=my birthday.Internet GMT conventions. ()
toLocaleString()	Converts a date to a string, using the current toLocaleString	birthLocale=my birthday. locale's conventions. ()
UTC()	Returns the number of milliseconds in a date object since January 1, 1970 00:00:00, Universal Coordinated Time (GMT).	birthmilliseconds from1970=mybirthday. UTC()

Table A.15   The Events Supported by JavaScript

Event Name	Event Happens When...	Event For...	Actual Syntax	Example Syntax
blur	User removes input focus from form element (e.g., by tabbing out of a control or clicking elsewhere on the form)	text fields, textareas, and selections	onBlur	<INPUT TYPE= INPUT NAME= "TEXT3" SIZE=20 onBlur="blurry (object)">
click	User clicks on form element or link.	buttons, radio buttons, checkboxes, submit buttons, reset buttons, links	onClick	<INPUT TYPE= "button" VALUE= "Test Click Here" onClick="compute (object)">
change	User changes text, text area, or selects element.	text fields, text areas, and selections.	onChange	<INPUT TYPE= INPUTNAME= TEXT2" SIZE=20 onChange= "changed"(object)">
focus	User gives form element input focus by clicking on it or tabbing into it.	text fields, text areas, and selections.	onFocus	<INPUT TYPE= INPUTNAME= "TEXT3" SIZE=20 onFocus= "FocusOn(object)">

Continued

Table A.15   The Events Supported by JavaScript (Continued)

Event Name	Event Happens When...	Event For...	Actual Syntax	Example
load	User loads an HTML document in Netscape.	Documents	onLoad	`<BODY onLoad ="JavaScript Code!">`
mouse over	User moves mouse pointer over a link or anchor.	links	onMouseOver	`<A HREF= "http://home. netscape.com/" onMouseOver= "Javascript Code!">`
select	User selects form element's input field.	text fields, textareas	onSelect	`<INPUT TYPE ="text" VALUE ="" NAME=text1" onSelect="JavaScript Code!">`
submit	User submits a form.	Forms	onSubmit	`form.on Submit= "JavaScript Code!"`
unload	User exits the page.	Documents	onUnload	`<BODY onUnload= "JavaScriptCode!">`

Using Built-in Functions

JavaScript has several "top-level" functions built into the language. They are listed in Table A.16.

Table A.16   The Built-in JavaScript Functions

Function	Description	Example
escape()	Returns the ASCII encoding of a string in the escape("string") set.	ISO Latin-1 character
eval()	Evaluates JavaScript expressions or statements.	eval(string)
isNaN()	Determines if a value passed is a valid number or not.	isNan(value)

Continued

Table A.16 The Built-in JavaScript Functions (Continued)		
Function	**Description** **Example**	
parseFloat()	Converts a floating point number represented as a string to a numeric value.	parseFloat("32.65")
parseInt()	Converts an integer represented as a string to a numeric value. [,rad	parseInt("intstring" ix])
unescape()	Returns the ASCII string for the specified value.	unescape("string")

Creating Custom JavaScript Objects

JavaScript gives us the ability to construct our own objects, called *variable objects*. In addition, we can create our own special functions for those objects which are called custom *methods*. Creating your own object is as simple as defining a variable; you simply think up an object structure and then assign it a value. For example, here is an object named **book**:

```
book.name="Netscape and HTML Explorer"
book.series="Explorer"
book.topic="Internet"
```

In this case properties have been created for this new object and they have been assigned values. Once the properties have been initialized, they can be used in a script. Let's expand on this example and create a script that let's the user enter values into a form and then the values are assigned to our custom object. Once they are assigned they will be displayed back to the user in a text box. This is a useful example because it shows how custom objects are useful for processing Web pages that contain forms:

```
<HTML>
<HEAD>
<TITLE>Java Function Example</TITLE>
<SCRIPT LANGUAGE="JavaScript">

<!-- Beginning of JavaScript code -----
```

```
// Assigns a new book object its values
function assignbook(form)
{
mybook=new book(form.book.value,form.series.value,form.topic.value)
}

// Creates a new book object
function book(name, series, topic)
{
   this.name = name
   this.series = series
   this.topic = topic
}

// Display the values stored in the book object
function showbook(form)
{
form.RESULT.value="Name:"+mybook.name+"   |Series:"+mybook.series+"
|Topic:"+mybook.topic
}

// -- End of JavaScript code ------ -->

</SCRIPT>
</HEAD>

<BODY>
<FORM NAME="MyForm">

Input Book Name:<INPUT TYPE=Text NAME="book" SIZE=20><BR>
Input Book Series:<INPUT TYPE=Text NAME="series" SIZE=20><BR>
Input Book Topic:<INPUT TYPE=Text NAME="topic" SIZE=20><BR>
<HR>
Click Here To Create Object
<INPUT TYPE="button" VALUE="Object Creation"
onClick="assignbook(this.form)"><P>
<INPUT TYPE=TEXT NAME="RESULT" SIZE=50,5>
<INPUT TYPE="button" VALUE="Object Print" onClick="showbook(this.form)"><P>
</FORM>

</BODY>

</HTML>
```

When you load this HTML file, you should see a Web page like the one shown in Figure A.2. Notice the form that is displayed.

The **<HEAD>** section defines three JavaScript functions or methods: **assignbook**(), **book**(), and **showbook**(). These methods are called later when the form is processed. The first method assigns a basic object of book and then

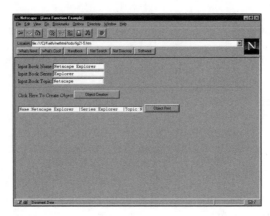

Figure A.2   The JavaScript example that uses a form and a custom object.

creates the properties for it—**name**, **series**, and **topic**. Notice that the **assignbook**() method calls the **book**() method to actually create the new **book** object and assign values to the three properties. The **assignbook**() method assists in moving the values from the input boxes of the form to the new object created named **mybook**.

To actually create a real instance of this object I call the function by assigning a name to the object I'm really creating, in this case the book object **mybook**. I use the "new" keyword before calling the function to denote I am creating a new *instance* of the object. Then I retrieve the object using the **showbook**() method, which displays it in the text at the bottom of the page.

In the <BODY> section of the HTML file, you'll find the instructions for creating the form. Notice that three input fields are defined for the form, which have the same names as the properties defined for the **book** object: **name**, **series**, and **topic**. The actual HTML instruction that causes the **assignbook**() method to be called and thus, get the ball rolling is:

```
<INPUT TYPE="button" VALUE="Object Creation"
  onClick="assignbook(this.form)"><P>
```

Here the **onClick** action is assigned the **assignbook**() method. This causes the method to be called when the user clicks the "Object Creation" button on the form. The parameter that is passed to the method is a reference to the current form. At the moment, the keyword "this" may look a little foreign to you, but I'll explain what it does in a moment.

The method that displays the data that the user enters into the form, **showbook()**, is also triggered by having the user click on a button. In this case, the button defined for this action is "Object Print":

```
<INPUT TYPE="button" VALUE="Object Print" onClick="showbook(this.form)"><P>
```

Again, notice how the method is assigned to the **onClick** action.

Although our script is fairly simple, it illustrates how custom objects can serve as the link between data entered in forms and procedures that can be performed on the data. For example, you could check each data element entered into a form and display a message if the data was not entered correctly. This gives you much more control over the data processing capabilities available with CGI scripts. The more you work with custom objects, the more you'll find that you can create very complex objects which might contain arrays and other objects within them.

Understanding the "this" Keyword

The **this** keyword is essentially used to refer to the current object in play. It's a useful feature because it allows you to create much more general purpose methods, which in turn saves you from having to write a lot of JavaScript code. For example, assume you wanted to check 20 text boxes to see if each text box contained the proper information before executing any more code. With the **this** keyword, you could write a method which, when called upon, checks the currently active textbox. Here's an example of how you can use the **this** keyword:

```
<HTML>
<HEAD>
<TITLE>Java Function Example</TITLE>
<SCRIPT LANGUAGE="JavaScript">

<!-- Beginning of JavaScript code ------

function checkme(input)
{
   score=eval(input.value)
   if (score>5) {
     score=5
   }
   if(score<1) {
     score=1
   }
```

```
    input.value=score
}

// -- End of JavaScript code ------->
</SCRIPT>
</HEAD>

<FORM NAME="Myform">

On a Scale of 1-5  How Good Is this Page Overall?:<INPUT TYPE=text
NAME="Answer" SIZE=20 onChange=checkme(this)><P>

On a Scale of 1-5  How Are the Graphics on this Page?:<INPUT TYPE=text
NAME="Answer" SIZE=20 onChange=checkme(this)><P>

On a Scale of 1-5  How Are the Links on this Page?:<INPUT TYPE=text
NAME="Answer" SIZE=20 onChange=checkme(this)><P>

On a Scale of 1-5  How Good Is the Content on this Page?:<INPUT TYPE=text
NAME="Answer" SIZE=20 onChange=checkme(this)><P>

On a Scale of 1-5  How Neat Is the JavaScript on This Page?:<INPUT
TYPE=text NAME="Answer" SIZE=20 onChange=checkme(this)><P>

</FORM>
<BODY>
</BODY>

</HTML>
```

The Web page created by this code is shown in Figure A.3. The function **checkme**() is written to check all of the text boxes to see if each one contained a

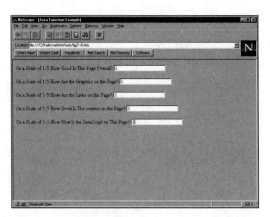

Figure A.3   A JavaScript example that uses the this keyword.

value in the range 1-5? What I did was substitute in the code the **this** keyword wherever I wanted to refer to a specific text box object. By using **this**, the code works on the current object that called upon it. So instead of writing 20 specific routines, each identical except for the object reference, I can use **this** and write one piece of code. Pretty neat, huh?

Defining Your Own Methods

Just as you can define your own objects, you can define your own methods. A method is simply a type of function that you attach to a specific object you've created. To do this, simply make a reference in your object definition to a specific function name which has been previously defined using the standard function definition syntax.

The general syntax for assigning a custom method to an object is:

```
object.methodname = function_name
```

where *function_name* is that actual name of a function that has been defined. The *function_name* and *method_name* can be the same. Once the function name is assigned to an object, you can call the new method in much the same way you call the built-in methods already present in JavaScript:

```
object.methodname(params)
```

Let's return to our earlier example where we created a custom object named **book**. We'll rewrite one of the functions used so that a custom method is assigned to the **book** object:

```
function book(name, series, topic)
{
   this.name = name
   this.series = series
   this.topic = topic
   this.showbook=showbook
}
```

Now **showbook()** is a method that can be accessed using a **book** object. Instead of calling the **showbook()** function directly, as we did in the previous example, we'll execute it as a method. To refresh your memory, we previously called the function using this HTML code:

```
<INPUT TYPE="button" VALUE="Object Print" onClick="showbook(this.form)"><P>
```

Now with the newly setup **showbook**() method, we can call it like this:

```
<INPUT TYPE="button" VALUE="Object Print"
  onClick="mybook.showbook(this.form)"><P>
```

Creating your own methods is perhaps one of the most challenging parts of mastering JavaScript. Coupled with what we learned about the creation of our own objects, we've actually learned the basics of an incredibly advanced method of programming!

JAVASCRIPT B VOCABULARY

This appendix lists all of the objects, properties, methods, events, functions, keywords, and identifiers used in JavaScript in alphabetical order. The type of word or phrase, its syntax, and notes about its use and effect are also supplied. For page references, see the index.

Word/ Phrase	Type	Syntax	Notes
%=	Assignment Operator	x%=y	Performs the assignment x = x%y.
*=	Assignment Operator	x*=y	Performs the assignment x = x * y.
/=	Assignment Operator	x/=y	Performs the assignment x = x / y.
+=	Assignment Operator	x+=y	Performs the assignment x = x + y.
-=	Assignment Operator	x-=y	Performs the assignment x = x - y.
=	Assignment Operator	x=y	Assigns the value on the right to the variable on the left.
&=	Bitwise Assignment	x&=y	Performs the assignment x = x & y.
^=	Bitwise Assignment	x^=y	Performs the assignment x = x ^ y.
|=	Bitwise Assignment	x|=y	Performs the assignment x = x | y.
<<=	Bitwise Assignment	x<<=y	Performs the assignment x = x << y.
>>=	Bitwise Assignment	x>>=y	Performs the assignment x = x >> y.
>>>=	Bitwise Assignment	x>>>==y	Performs the assignment x = x >>>y.
&	Bitwise Operator	x & y	Performs a bitwise AND. (Returns a 1 if both operands are 1s.)
^	Bitwise Operator	x ^ y	Performs a bitwise XOR. (Returns a 1 if one but not both operands are 1.)
|	Bitwise Operator	x & y	Performs a bitwise OR. (Returns a 1 if one of the operands is 1.)
<<	Bitwise Operator	x << y	Performs a bitwise left shift operation.
>>	Bitwise Operator	x >> y	Performs a bitwise right shift operation.
>>>	Bitwise Operator	x >>> y	Performs a bitwise zero-filled right shift operation.
/* */	Comment	/* comment */	Specifies a comment that can extend multiple lines.
//	Comment	// comment	Specifies a single line comment.
!=	Comparison Operator	x != y	Returns true if the operands are not equal.
<	Comparison Operator	x < y	Returns true if the first operand is less than the second operand.
<=	Comparison Operator	x <= y	Returns true if the first operand is less than or equal to the second operand.
==	Comparison Operator	x == y	Returns true if the operands are equal.

Word/ Phrase	Type	Syntax	Notes
>	Comparison Operator	x> y	Returns true if the first operand is greater than the second operator.
>=	Comparison Operator	x>= y	Returns true if the first operand is greater or equal to the second operand.
--	Decrement Operator	x--	Reduces the value of the operand by 1.
++	Increment Operator	x++	Increases the value of the operand by 1.
!	Logical Operator	!x	This logical unary operator negates its operand expression.
&&	Logical Operator	x && y	This logical AND operator returns true if both logical expressions are true.
||	Logical Operator	x || y	This logical OR operator returns true if one of the expressions are true.
-	Operator	x - y	Performs the subtraction operation.
-	Operator	-x	Performs a unary negation.
%	Operator	x % y	Returns the first operand modulo of the second operand.
*	Operator	x * y	Performs the multiplication operation.
/	Operator	x / y	Performs the division operation.
?:	Operator	x ?: y	Performs a conditional operation.
+	Operator	x + y	Performs the addition operation.
;	Statement Separator	i=10; x=20	Separates JavaScript statements.
+	String Operator	"aa" + "bb"	The concatenation operator combines two string values.
abs()	Math Method	Math.abs(-10)	Returns the absolute value of a number.
abstract	Reserved Keyword		A keyword reserved for the Java language.
acos()	Math Method	Math.acos(30)	Returns the arc cosine (in radians) of a number.
action	form Property	myform.action= "String"	You set the action.form property to a string that is the destination URL for data from that form when it is submitted.
alert()	window Method	window.alert ("string")	Creates an Alert dialog box with the string. sage.

Word/ Phrase	Type	Syntax	Notes
alinkColor	document Property	document.a linkcolor=""	You set the document.alinkcolor to a string that is a hexidecimal or color command that tells the browser what the color of an active link should look like in your document.
anchor	Object	document. anchors.length	Text that serves as the target of a hypertext link.
anchor()	string Method	document.write (mystring.anchor ("contents_ anchor"())	This is used to create an anchor. The text in mystring is the text you want highlighted (the user to see) in the document.
appCode Name	navigator Property	cName=navi- gator.appCode Name	By reading the navigator.appCodeName property you can see what the internal codename is for the current version of Navigator that the browser is using.
appName	navigator Property	appN=navigator .appName	By reading the navigator.appName property you can see what the official name is for the current version of Navigator that the browser is using.
appVersion	navigator Property	appVer=navigator .appVersion	By reading the navigator.appVersion property you get the exact version number of Navigator that the browser is using.
asin()	Math Method	Math.asin(60)	Returns the arc sine (in radians) of a number.
atan()	Math Method	Math.atan(90)	Returns the arc tangent (in radians) of a number.
back()	history Method	history.back()	Loads the previously visited URL in the history list. (This is the URL that is accessed when Netscape's Back button is pressed.
bgColor	document Property	document.bg Color=""	You set the document.bgColor property to a string specifying the color of the document background.
big()	string Method	document.write (mystring.big())	Causes string to appear as big text.

Word/ Phrase	Type	Syntax	Notes
blink()	string Method	document.write (ms.blink())	Causes string to appear as blinking text.
blur()	password, select, text, texterea Method	passwordName. blur(); textName.blur()	Removes the focus from a specified form element.
bold()	string Method	document.write (ms.bold())	Causes string to appear as bold text.
Boolean	Reserved Keyword		A keyword reserved for the Java language.
break	Control Statement	break	A statement that terminates the current while or for loop and transfers program control to the statement following the terminated loop.
button	Object	butt1.click()	Accesses a pushbutton on an HTML form.
byte	Reserved Keyword		A keyword reserved for the Java language.
case	Reserved Keyword		A keyword reserved for the Java language.
catch	Reserved Keyword		A keyword reserved for the Java language.
ceil()	Math Method	Math.ceil (200.546)	Returns the least integer greater than or equal to a number.
char	Reserved Keyword		A keyword reserved for the Java language.
charAt()	string Method	document.write (mystring.char At(3))	Retrieves the character at a specified position in a string.
checkbox	Object		Accesses a checkbox on an HTML form.
checked	checkbox, radio Property	cv=checkbox. checked	Reading this property will return a Boolean value (true or false) that indicates the current state of a specific checkbox or radio button object.
class	Reserved Keyword		A keyword reserved for the Java language.

Word/ Phrase	Type	Syntax	Notes
clear()	document Method	document.clear()	Clears the current document.
clearTimeout()	window Method	window.clear time(timeoutID)	This method will clear the current setTimeout command. TimeoutID is a variable that uniquely identifies the setTimeout command you want to stop.
clearTimeout()	frame Method	frameName.clear time(timeoutID)	This method will clear the current setTimeout command. TimeoutID is a variable that uniquely identifies the setTimeout command you want to stop.
click()	button, checkbox, radio, reset, and submit Method	buttonName. click();	Simulates a mouse click on the calling from element.
close()	window Method	window.close()	Closes the referred to window.
close()	document Method	document.close()	Closes the document.
confirm()	window Method	Window.con-firm("string")	Creates a Confirm dialog box with OK and Cancel buttons plus the current message.
const	Reserved Keyword		A keyword reserved for the Java language.
continue	Control Statement	continue	A statement that terminates execution of the block of statements in a while or for loop, and continues execution of the loop with the next iteration.
cookie	document Property	cookietext= document.cookie	Reading this property returns the string contents of the cookies.txt file.
cos()	Math Method	Math.cos(30)	Returns the cosine of a number.
Date	Object	Date.getdate()	A special purpose object for processing data and time information.
default	Reserved Keyword		A keyword reserved for the Java language.
defaultChecked	checkbox, radio Property	cv=checkbox. defaultChecked	Reading this property gives you a Boolean value which indicates the default selection state of a checkbox or radio button.

Word/ Phrase	Type	Syntax	Notes
default Selected	options array Property	Myform.options [i].default Selected = True	This property indicates the default election state of an option in a select object.
defaultStatus	window Property	window.default Status="My Document!"	This property controls the default message displayed in the status bar at the bottom of a window in Navigator.
DefaultValue	hidden, password, text, textarea Property	Text.defaultVal- ue="Coriolis"	This property controls a string value which is equal to the default value of a password, text, or textarea object.
do	Reserved Keyword		A keyword reserved for the Java language.
document	Object	document.writeln	Accesses the current document.
double	Reserved Keyword		A keyword reserved for the Java language.
E	Math Property	EulerConstant= Math.E	Reading this property returns Euler's constant, the base of natural loga- rithms, which approximately equals 2.718.
elements array	Object	formName.elem- ents[index]	An array of objects corresponding to form elements such as checkboxes, radio buttons, text object, and so on.
else	Control Statement	See if statement.	
encoding	form Property	enc=form.encoding	This property refers to a string that indicates the type of MIME encoding used on a specific form.
escape()	Function	escape("string")	Returns the ASCII encoding of a string in the ISO Latin-1 character set.
eval()	Function	eval(string)	Evaluates JavaScript expressions or statements.
exp()	Math Method	Math.exp(10)	Returns enumber, where number is the argument, and e is Euler's constant, the base of the natural logarithms.
extends	Reserved Keyword		A keyword reserved for the Java language.

Word/ Phrase	Type	Syntax	Notes
false	Reserved Keyword		A keyword reserved for the Java language.
fgColor	document Property	document.fg Color=""	This property controls the color of a document's text. It accepts a string value set to a hexidecimal indicator or a color command.
final	Reserved Keyword		A keyword reserved for the Java language.
finally	Reserved Keyword		A keyword reserved for the Java language.
fixed()	string Method	document.write (mystring.fixed())	Causes a string to be displayed in fixed-pitch font
float	Reserved Keyword		A keyword reserved for the Java language.
floor()	Math Method	Math.floor(199. 345)	Returns the greatest integer less than or equal to a number.
focus()	password, select, text, textarea Method	selectName.fo-cus(); textName. focus()	Assigns the focus to a specified form element.
fontcolor()	string Method	document.write (mystring.font color(color))	Causes string to appear in the color specified.
fontsize()	string Method	document.write (mystring.big())	Causes string to appear as bold text.
for	Control Statement	for ([initial-expression;] [condition;] [increment-expression]) { statements }	A looping statement. The loop will be repeated for a specified number of iterations.
for..in	Control Statement	for (variable in object) {statements }	A statement that iterates a specified variable over all the properties of an object.
form (forms array)	Object	formName. propertyName	Accesses forms and objects on forms.

Word/ Phrase	Type	Syntax	Notes
forward()	history method	history.forward()	Loads the next URL in the history list.
frame (frames array)	Object		The scrollable window used for array) navigating Web pages.
function	Control Statement	function name([param] [, param] [..., param]) {statements }	A statement that declares a JavaScript function name with the specified parameters param. Acceptable parameters include strings, numbers, and objects.
getDate()	Date Method	birthday=mybir thday.getDate()	Returns the day of the month for the specified date.
getDay()	Date Method	bweekday=mybir thday.getDay()	Returns the day of the week for the specified date.
getHours()	Date Method	bhour=mybir thday.getHours()	Returns the hour for the specified date.
getMinutes()	Date Method	bminutes=mybir thday.getMin utes()	Returns the minutes for the specified date.
getMonth()	Date Method	bmonth=mybirt hday.getMonth()	Returns the month for the specified date.
getSeconds()	Date Method	bseconds=mybir thday.getSeconds()	Returns the seconds for the current time.
getTime()	Date Method	birthtime=mybir thday.getTime()	Returns the numeric value corresponding to the time for the specified date.
getTime ZoneOffset()	Date Method	birthoffset=mybir thday.getTime ZoneOffset()	Returns the time zone offset in minutes for the current locale.
getYear()	Date Method	birthyear=mybir thday.getYear()	Returns the year in the specified date.
go()	history Method	history.go(delta | "location")	Loads a URL from the history list.
goto	Control Statement	goto label	
hash	link, location Property	Anchorname= link.hash	Reading this property of a link or a location returns a string which begins with a hash mark (#) that pulls out just the anchor name in the referred to URL.

Word/ Phrase	Type	Syntax	Notes
hidden	Object	hiddenName. propertyName	Accesses a hidden object on a form.
history	Object	history.go(-1)	Accesses information on the URLs the user has visited.
host	link, location Property	NameofHost= link.host	Reading this property of a link or a location returns a string that gives you the specific hostname:port part of the referred to URL.
hostname	link, location Property	Currenthostname =location.host name	Reading this property of a link or a location returns a string that gives you the specific host and domain name or IP address of the referred to URL's network host.
href	link, location Property	Hreference= link.href	Reading this property returns a string equal to the entire referred to URL.
if...else	Control Statement	if (condition) { statements1 } [else { statements2}]	A statement that executes a set of statements if a specified condition is true. If the condition is false, another set of statements can be executed.
implements	Reserved Keyword		A keyword reserved for the Java language.
import	Reserved Keyword		A keyword reserved for the Java language.
in	Control Statement	See for...in.	
index	options array Property	selectName. options[i].index	This property represents the index value of an option in a select object.
indexOf()	string Method	document.write (mystring.In dex Of(search Value, [from Index]())	Looks for the first instance of search Value (a string) in your current string. The string is searched forwards. FromIndex is a number that denotes where to start from and if omitted the search starts from the first character in the string.
instanceof	Reserved Keyword		A keyword reserved for the Java language.
int	Reserved Keyword		A keyword reserved for the Java language.

Word/ Phrase	Type	Syntax	Notes
interface	Reserved Keyword		A keyword reserved for the Java language.
isNaN()	Function	isNan(value)	Determines if a value passed is a valid number or not.
italics()	string Method	document.write (mystring.italics())	Causes string to appear as italic text.
lastIndexOf()	string Method	document.write (mystring. lastIndexOf (searchValue, [fromIndex]())	Looks for the last instance of search Value (a string) in your current string. The string is searched backwards. FromIndex is a number that denotes where to start from and if omitted the search starts from the last character in the string.
lastModified	document Property	document.write (document.last Modified)	This property consists of a string that represents the date that a document was last modified.
length	frame, history, radio, select, string, links window objects, elements, arrays, frames, options, Property	Lengthofstring= mystring.length	This property returns an integer reading equal to the length of the object or array specified.
link (links array)	Object		Text or image that is used as a hypertext link.
link()	string Method	document.write (mystring.link URL())	This is used to create a link to text you might write to the document. URL is a string denoting the specific URL and the text in mystring is the text you want the user to see in the document.
linkColor	document Property	Document.link Color=""	This property accepts a string value of either a hexidecimal color indicator or specific color command to control the color of a document's hyperlinks.
LN10	math Property	LogofTen= math.LN10	Reading this value returns the natural logarithm of ten, equal to about 2.302.
LN2	math Property	LogofTwo= math.LN2	Reading this value returns the natural logarithm of two, equal to about 0.693.

Word/ Phrase	Type	Syntax	Notes
location	Object	document. location	Accesses information on the current URL.
location	document Property	Currentlocation =document. location	This property returns a string equal to the complete URL of the currently viewed document.
log()	Math Method	Math.log(10)	Returns the natural logarithm (base e) of a number.
LOG10E	math Property	LogofTEN= math.LOG10E	Reading this property returns the base 10 logarithm of e equal to about 0.434
LOG2E	math Property	LogofE=math. LOG2E	Reading this property math.LOG2E returns the base 2 logarithm of e equal to about 1.442
long	Reserved Keyword		A keyword reserved for the Java language.
Math	Object	Math.sin(30)	A special purpose object designed for performing a variety of mathematical operations.
max()	Math Method	Math.max (100,220)	Returns the greater of two numbers.
method	form Property	form.method	Use this property to tell Navigator how to send field input from forms to the server.
min()	Math Method	Math.min (100,220)	Returns the lesser of two numbers.
name	button, frame, checkbox, hidden, radio, password, reset, select, submit text, textarea, window, options array, Property	Nameofbutton =button1.name	Reading this property returns a string specifying the name of the referenced object.
native	Reserved Keyword		A keyword reserved for the Java language.
navigator	Object	navigator.app name	Accesses information about the current version of Netscape that is running. Navigator is the top level object.
new	Operator	objectName = new objectType (param1 [,param2] ...[,paramN])	An operator that lets you create an instance of a user-defined object type.

Word/ Phrase	Type	Syntax	Notes
null	Reserved Keyword		A keyword reserved for the Java language.
onBlur	text fields, textareas, Event	<INPUT TYPE=INPUT NAME="TEXT 3" SIZE=20 onBlur="blurry (object)">	User removes input focus from form element.
onChange	text fields, textareas, Event	<INPUT TYPE= INPUT NAME= "TEXT2" SIZE=20 onChange= "changed(object)">	User changes text, textarea, or selects element.
onClick	buttons, radio buttons, checkboxes, submit buttons, reset buttons, links, Event	<INPUT TYPE= "button" VALUE= "Test Click Here" onClick="compute(object)">	User clicks on form element or link.
onFocus	text fields, textareas, Event	<INPUT TYPE= INPUT NAME= "TEXT3" SIZE= 20 onFocus="Focus On(object)">	User gives form element input focus.
onLoad	documents Event	<BODY onLoad= "JavaScript Code!">	User loads an HTML document in Netscape.
onMouse Over	links Event	<A HREF= "http://home.net scape.com/" onMouseOver= "JavaScript Code!">	User moves mouse pointer over a link or anchor.
onSelect	text fields, textareas Event	<INPUT TYPE= "text" VALUE=" " NAME=text1" onSelect="JavaScript Code!">	User selects form element's input field.
onSubmit	forms Event	form.onSubmit= "JavaScript Code!"	User submits a form.
onUnload	documents Event	<BODY onUnload ="JavaScript Code!">	User exits the page.

Word/ Phrase	Type	Syntax	Notes
open()	window Method	window.open ("URL", "window Name", ["window Features"])	Opens new window.
open()	document Method	document.open (["mimeType"])	Opens the referred to MIMEType in the document.
package	Reserved Keyword		A keyword reserved for the Java language.
parent	frame, window Property	Parentwindow= frame.parent	The parent property is a synonym for a window whose frameset contains the current frame.
parse()	date Method	timesince=parse (mybirthday)	Returns the number of milliseconds in a date string since January 1, 1970 00:00:00, local time.
parseFloat()	Function	parseFloat ("32.65")	Converts a floating point number represented as a string to a numeric value.
parseInt()	Function	parseInt ("intstring" [,radix])	Converts an integer represented as a string to a numeric value.
password	Object		Accesses a text field on an HTML form that is used to obtain a password. When a password is entered, the text is hidden using asterisks (*).
pathname	link, location Property	PathofURL= link.pathname	A string specifying the url-path portion of the URL.
PI	Math Property	Circumfrence= Diameter*math.PI	The property of this math object returns a value equal to PI or about 3.14159...
port	link, location Property	portoflink=link. port	This string specifies the communications port the server to the referred to link uses for communications
pow()	Math Method	Math.pow (base, exponent)	Returns base to the exponent power, that is, base exponent.
private	Reserved Keyword		A keyword reserved for the Java language.

Word/Phrase	Type	Syntax	Notes
prompt()	window Method	Window.prompt("string", [input Default])	Creates Prompt dialog box showing message. Gives user a box to reply. InputDefault may be used to give a suggested answer.
protected	Reserved Keyword		A keyword reserved for the Java language.p
protocol	link, location Property	Protocoloflink= link.protocol	This string specifies the protocol portion of a URL as specified by the referenced link or location. This is the part of a URL that takes place up to and including the first colon.
public	Reserved Keyword		A keyword reserved for the Java language.
radio	Object		Accesses a radio button on an HTML form.
random()	Math Method	Math.random()	Returns a pseudo-random number between zero and one. This method is available on Unix platforms only.
referrer	document Property	Callingdocument =document. referrer	This property controls the URL of the calling document when a link is chosen by the user.
reset	Object		Accesses a reset button on an HTML form.
return	Control Statement	return expression	Returns a value from a function.
round()	Math Method	Math.round(34.67)	Returns the value of a number rounded to the nearest integer.
search	link, location Property	SearchofURL= link.search	This property returns a string that begins with a question mark. The string equals the query information in a specified URL.
select (options array)	Object		Accesses a selection list or scrolling list on an HTML form.
select()	password, select, text, texterea Method	passwordName. select(); textName .select()	Selects the input area of the specified password, text, or textarea object.

Word/ Phrase	Type	Syntax	Notes
selected	options array Property	Currentlyselected= document.form. selectindex	This property controls a Boolean value (true or false) which specifies the current selection state of an option in a select object which is a select index as created by the <select>...</select> tags.
setDate()	date Method	mybirthday.set Date(25)	Sets the day of the month for a specified date.
setHours()	date Method	mybirthday.set Hours(13)	Sets the hours for a specified date.
setMinutes()	date Method	mybirthday.set Minutes(15)	Sets the minutes for a specified date.
setMonth()	date Method	mybirthday.set Month(6)	Sets the month for a specified date.
setSeconds()	date Method	mybirthday.set Second(00)	Sets the seconds for a specified date.
setTime()	date Method	mybirthday.set Time(msec)	Sets the value of a date object by giving it a number representing the milliseconds since January 1, 1970 00:00:00, local time.
setTimeout()	window Method	window.set Timeout("string", msec)	This method will execute the JavaScript code contained in the string in whatever number of milliseconds defined in msec.
setTimeout()	frame Method	frameName.set Timeout("String", msec)	This method will execute the JavaScript code contained in the string in whatever number of milliseconds defined in msec.
setYear()	date Method	mybirthday.set Year(1971)	Sets the year for a specified date.
short	Reserved Keyword		A keyword reserved for the Java language.
sin()	Math Method	Math.sin(30)	Returns the sine of a number.
small()	string Method	document.write (mystring.small())	Causes string to appear as small text.
sqrt()	Math Method	Math.sqrt(25)	Returns the square root of a number.
SQRT1_2	math Property	squarerootonehalf =math.SQRT1_2	This math object property returns the square root of one-half, roughly 0.707.

Word/ Phrase	Type	Syntax	Notes
sqrt2	math Property	squareroottwo= math.sqrt2	This math object property returns the square root of two, which is equal to about 1.414.
static	Reserved Keyword		A keyword reserved for the Java language.
status	window Property	window.status= "My Document!"	The status property of a window controls the message which is displayed on the status bar at the bottom of a window via a string.
strike()	string Method	document.write (mystring.strike())	Causes string to appear as striked text.
string	Object		A special purpose object designed for processing strings.
sub()	string Method	document.write (mystring.sub())	Causes string to appear as subscript text.
Submit	Object		Processes submit button on form.
submit()	form Method	formName.submit()	Submits the specified form.
subString()	string Method	Subsetstring= mystring.subString (indexA, indexB)	This method is used to refer to only a portion of a string. indexA and indexB are two numbers 0 to stringlength-1 which denote the specific section of the string to refer to.
sup()	string Method	document.write (mystring.sup())	Causes string to appear as superscript text.
super	Reserved Keyword		A keyword reserved for the Java language.
switch	Reserved Keyword		A keyword reserved for the Java language.
synchronized	Reserved Keyword		A keyword reserved for the Java language.
tan()	Math Method	Math.tan(60)	Returns the tangent of a number.
target	form, link, location Property	form.target= "TARGETFrame"	The target property works with forms, links, and locations. For a form it denotes the name of the window to send responses to when the form is submitted. For a link it tells Navigator which window to display the linked document in.

Word/ Phrase	Type	Syntax	Notes
text	Object		Accesses a text input field on a form.
text	options array Property	Selectedoption= document.my form.selectlist. options(X).text	This property controls via a string the text which follows an <OPTION> tag in a select object.
textarea	Object		Access a multiline input field on an HTML form.
this	Keyword	this[.property Name]	A keyword that you can use to refer to the current object. In general, in a method this refers to the calling object.
throw	Reserved Keyword		A keyword reserved for the Java language.
throws	Reserved Keyword		A keyword reserved for the Java language.
title	document Property	Document.title= "Title is My Document!"	This property controls the title of the document in the browser.
toGMT String()	date Method	birthGMT=my birthday.toGMT String	Converts a date to a string, using the Internet GMT conventions.
toLocale String()	date Method	birthLocale=my birthday.toLocale String	Converts a date to a string, using the current locale's conventions.
toLower Case()	string Method	document.write (mystring.toLow er Case())	Causes string to be converted to lowercase text.
top	window Property	Topwindownow =window.top	The top property is a synonym for the top-most Navigator window, which is a "document window" or "Web Browser window."
toUpper Case()	string Method	document.write (mystring.to UpperCase())	Causes string to be converted to uppercase text.
transient	Reserved Keyword		A keyword reserved for the Java language.
true	Reserved Keyword		A keyword reserved for the Java language.

Word/ Phrase	Type	Syntax	Notes
try	Reserved Keyword		A keyword reserved for the Java language.
unescape()	Function	unescape("string")	Returns the ASCII string for the specified value.
userAgent	navigator Property	userAgentHeader =navigator.user Agent	A string representing the value of the user-agent header sent in the HTTP protocol from client to server.
UTC()	date Method	birthmilliseconds from1970=my birthday.UTC()	Returns the number of milliseconds in a date object since January 1, 1970 00:00:00, Universal Coordinated Time (GMT).
value	button, radio, checkbox, hidden, checkbox, hidden, password, reset, submit, text, textarea objects, options array Property	Value=document. myform.text1.value	Reading this property returns a string equal to the value of the related object.
var	Declaration	var varname [= value] [..., varname [= value]]	A statement that declares a variable, optionally initializing it to a value. The scope of a variable is the current function or, for variables declared outside a function, the current application.
vlinkColor	document Property	document.vlink Color=""	This property controls the color of visited links. It accepts a hexidecimal string or color command string.
void	Reserved Keyword		A keyword reserved for the Java language.
while	Control Statement	while (condition) { statements }	A statement that creates a loop that evaluates an expression, and if it is true, executes a block of statements. The loop then repeats, as long as the specified condition is true.
window	Object	window.alert("hello")	The top-level object for each document object.

Word/ Phrase	Type	Syntax	Notes

with	Control Statement	with (object){
		statements
		}
			A statement that establishes the default object for a set of statements. Within the set of statements, any property references that do not specify an object are assumed to be for the default object.

write()	document Method	document.write ("string")	Writes a string or text to the document.
writeln()	document Method	document.writeln ("string")	Writes a string or text to the document.

whAT'S ON
The CD?

In the \BOOK directory on the CD-ROM, you will find directories that have names that correspond to chapters in the book. In these chapters you will find HTML files that hold the source code for the tutorials and figures in the book.

In addition to the source code, I have included several shareware tools that can be extremely useful in your JavaScript and Java programming. Shareware means that the author or authors of the software are allowing you to try out the software with the expectation that if you like it, you will pay them for it or upgrade to a commercial version. Freeware means that you can use the software as much as you want with no charge, but there is usually a more advanced version available for a price. Check for a README or LICENSE file with each of the applications you use to see what restrictions the author has placed on the software and its distribution ad use.

Now, let's go through and take a look at some of the more useful applications on the CD. Don't be afraid to experiment a little and play with all the different types of software. Most of the software is described below, but for those that aren't, just check in the applications directory for more information.

What: Clipart
Where on CD: \CLIPART
Where Online: http://www.lycos.com (Search for "CLIPART ARCHIVES")
                http://sunsite.nus.sg/ftpmultimedia.html
                http://seidel.ncsa.uiuc.edu/ClipArt/funet.html
Description: This collection of clipart was gathered from many different places. You can find images here that can really spice up your Web pages. Check out the collections in \CLIPART\ART\COHEN and \CLIPART\ART\FUNET to see some really impressive line art pieces. Some of the more useful images are in the

\BARS, \DOTS, and \SYMBOLS directories. These simple images don't take up much space, but they can really liven up a Web page and give it that custom look. There are also many images that can be used as separator bars and custom list bullets. Why stick to what Netscape has to offer you? Use custom images to give your page a unique style. But, be careful. Too many images can really slow things down! In the \CLIPART\AUDIO directory, there are many sound effects and samples that you can use to give feedback to the people visiting your pages. Once again though, you need to be careful that you don't use too many. Sound and video are also not supported on everyone's systems, so you may want to consider the people who will visit your site before you load up you pages with multimedia files.

What: Java Applets
Where on CD: \APPLETS
Where Online: http://www.gamelan.com/
Description: This directory contains over 50 Java applets in souce code form that you can look at and learn from. In order to run them, you will need to compile them with the Java compiler that comes in the Java Developer's Kit (JDK) from Sun. You can go to Sun's Web site (http://www.javasoft.com) and download the JDK for free. Please note that these applets are for your personal use only and can not be used for commercial gain, so contact the programmer when possible if you want to use the software in a product of your own.

What: Netscape Plug-ins
Where on CD: \PLUGINS
Where Online: http://home.netscape.com/comprod/products/navigator/version_2.0/plugins/index.html
Description: Here you will find a couple of the plug-ins that are currently available for Netscape Navigator. Make sure you go to Netscape's plug-in page listed above to see all of the plug-ins that are available. Here are a couple of the plug-ins on the CD:

- Real Audio   This plug-in is an incredible real-time sound player. It allows you to receive and listen to sound progressively instead of waiting for the entire file to be downloaded. They have also set up live broadcasts of radio shows and sporting events that you can listen to as you browse the Web. Very Cool!

- Amber   This plug-in from Adobe allows you to view Acrobat files right in your browser. Acrobat files might be likened to HTML files on steroids!

They allow very precise position of just about any type of static element. They are a great way to view and distribute documents that require a high level of accuracy.

Application: Paint Shop Pro
Where on CD: \TOOLS\PAINT SHOP PRO
Where Online: http://www.jasc.com/
Description: The complete windows graphics program for image creation, viewing, and manipulation. Features include: painting, photo retouching, image enhancement and editing, color enhancement, image browser, batch conversion, and TWAIN scanner support. Also included are 20 standard image processing filters and 12 deformations. It supports Adobe style image processing plug-in filters. Over 30 file formats are supported, including JPEG, Kodak Photo-CD, PBM, and GIF. This is one graphics package you won't want to be without. It has many of the features of much more expensive graphics programs at a fraction of the cost. If you have never bought a shareware package in your life, this may be the first!

Application: Programmer's File Editor
Where on CD: \TOOLS\ PROGRAMMERS FILE EDITOR
Where Online: http://www.lancs.ac.uk/people/cpaap/pfe/
Description: We can't say enough good things about this great program. You can use it for all your programming needs. And used as a text editor, it blows away Notepad! PFE is a large-capacity, multi-file editor that runs on Windows 95, Windows 3.1x and Windows NT 3.51 on Intel, and PowerPC platforms. Although it's primarily oriented towards program developers and contains features like the ability to run compilers and development applications, it also makes a very good general purpose editor.

What: Java & JavaScript Documentation
Where on CD: \DOCS
Where Online: http://www.javasoft.com/
http://www.netscape.com/
Description: The JavaScript documentation is all in HTML format, so just load the INDEX.HTML file into Netscape and browse away! The Java documentation comes in a few different formats. You can view it in either HTML format or Acrobat (PDF) format. Make sure you check out the JavaSoft Web site for the latest information.

Application: Stuff-It
Application: WinCode
Where on CD: \TOOLS\ENCODING\WINCODE
Where Online: http://www.netrover.com/ewincode.html
Description: WinCode is a nice little utility for encoding and decoding binary encoded files. Most often, that means UU encoded files. This encoding scheme is used most often for sending binary attachments to Internet newsgroups.

INDEX